DISCOVER THE MARSEILLE TAROT!

This book explores the fascinating history of this often misunderstood deck and provides practical insights into using it for readings on a variety of questions. Yoav Ben-Dov shares the meaning of the classic Marseille symbols and specific reading techniques that help you tap into your own intuition. *The Marseille Tarot Revealed* explains everything you need to know to start or deepen your Marseille Tarot practice, including:

- classic Marseille decks
- new Marseille decks
- the French school
- the English school
- tarot and the New Age
- handling the cards
- shuffling the deck
- how to read the cards
- the meaning of each card
- basic spreads
- reverse (inverse) cards
- tarot's symbolic language

ROY·DE·DENIERS

THE
MARSEILLE
TAROT
REVEALED

REYNE ·DEDENIERS

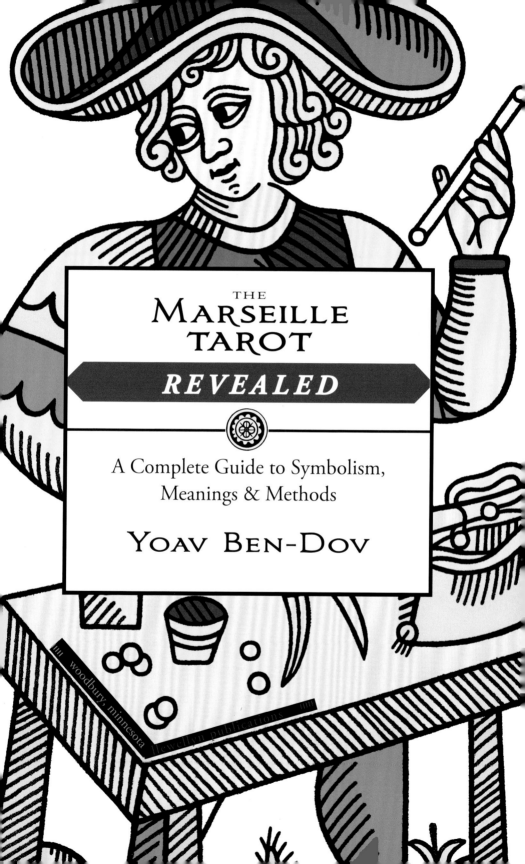

THE

THE MARSEILLE TAROT REVEALED

A Complete Guide to Symbolism, Meanings & Methods

YOAV BEN-DOV

woodbury, minnesota
llewellyn publications

FIRST EDITION
Fourth Printing, 2023

Book design by Rebecca Zins
Cover design by Ellen Lawson

Cards © 2011, 2015 by Yoav Ben-Dov
All the card illustrations in color, additional materials
to read and download, updates, and instructions
for ordering a deck of CBD Tarot de Marseille
are available at www.CBDTarot.com

Llewellyn Publications is a registered trademark
of Llewellyn Worldwide Ltd.

Library of Congress Cataloging-in-Publication Data
Names: Ben-Dov, Yoav, author.
Title: The Marseille tarot revealed : a complete guide to symbolism, meanings
    & methods / Yoav Ben-Dov.
Description: FIRST EDITION. | Woodbury : Llewellyn Worldwide, Ltd, 2017. |
Identifiers: LCCN 2017010657 (print) | LCCN 2016059617 (ebook) | ISBN
    9780738752280 | ISBN 9780738752853 (ebook)
Subjects: LCSH: Tarot. | Marseille (France)—Miscellanea.
Classification: LCC BF1879.T2 B395 2017 (ebook) | LCC BF1879.T2 (print) |
DDC
    133.3/2424—dc23
LC record available at https://lccn.loc.gov/2017010657

Llewellyn Worldwide Ltd. does not participate in, endorse, or have any authority or responsibility concerning private business transactions between our authors and the public.

All mail addressed to the author is forwarded, but the publisher cannot, unless specifically instructed by the author, give out an address or phone number.

Any Internet references contained in this work are current at publication time, but the publisher cannot guarantee that a specific location will continue to be maintained. Please refer to the publisher's website for links to authors' websites and other sources.

Llewellyn Publications
A Division of Llewellyn Worldwide Ltd.
2143 Wooddale Drive
Woodbury, MN 55125-2989
www.llewellyn.com
Printed in China

CONTENTS

6: The Major Cards . . . 111

1O: The Number Cards . . . 285

11: ADDITIONAL SPREADS . . . 339

12: QUICK INTERPRETATIONS . . . 345

LE · MAT

Preface

There is magic in the tarot.

Originally popularized as a humble means for playing games of chance, for several centuries this mysterious set of seventy-eight cards has captured the imagination of countless people. Some have used the cards as an instrument for divination and fortunetelling. Others have seen the tarot as a secret repository of ancient and powerful knowledge. Today many people use the tarot cards as a tool for consultation, guidance, and decision making. There are also those who employ them as a visual aid for guided imagination and meditation, or as magical amulets. And in the course of these centuries, countless human lives have been touched, and sometimes transformed, by the reading of tarot cards.

I have been with the tarot for thirty-four years: reading for people, teaching, writing, and experimenting. I am still learning the tarot. The subtle intricacies of the illustration details continue to present me with surprises. New and unexpected meanings never cease to emerge. And I am still amazed whenever people open up and share their most intimate feelings in a reading session, when just the right card appears for someone in need, or when an unexplained but meaningful coincidence (or synchronicity event) happens in the presence of the tarot cards.

And yet if asked what the tarot is, I would say that, first of all, it is a work of art—not like a painted picture, framed and hung as a finished product that cannot be changed. Rather, it is a capricious set of images to be handled and played with, evolving over many generations through the collective efforts of deck creators and visionaries. It is a wonderful work of art, rich and flexible enough to span the entire range of human experience, from our innermost feelings to the external events of everyday life. And it is through this art, in the details of the card illustrations, that the magic of the tarot is revealed.

The object of this book is threefold. First, it is a general introduction to the tarot cards and the reading process. As such, it can be relevant whether you want to read the cards yourself or if you are interested in tarot reading as a psychological device, as a cultural phenomenon, or as a way to find meanings in a work of art. Second, it is a guide for a method of tarot reading that I call "the open reading," based on looking at the card illustrations rather than learning fixed interpretations by heart. The open reading can be applied to different kinds of tarot cards, although it works with some more effectively than with others. Third, it is a handbook for reading the Tarot de Marseille, which is the classical version of the traditional tarot. In particular, it uses the CBD Tarot de Marseille, an edition of the cards that I restored from the most influential historical deck originally published by Nicolas Conver in 1760.

Welcome.

CHAPTER 1

THE TAROT DECK

A deck of tarot cards contains seventy-eight cards. These can be divided into two parts. The first part is called the major suit. It consists of twenty-two cards with elaborate illustrations, numbered consecutively and having a specific name for each one. The majors show images of people and animals along with many objects and symbols. Some of these are taken from social life. Others represent mythological, religious, or philosophical themes.

The remaining fifty-six cards are further divided into four suits. These are called the minor suits and have a simpler design than the majors. The four suits are named after four symbolic objects: coins, wands, cups, and swords. Each of the minor suits consists of fourteen cards of three types: one ace card, nine numbered cards (from two to ten), and four court cards identified by their rank: page, knight, queen, and king. The minor suits' structure is thus quite similar to normal playing cards, which also have four suits. The main difference is that playing cards have only three court cards: jack, queen, and king.

Tarot literature sometimes uses different names for the deck parts. The major and the minor suits are sometimes called major and minor arcana (from Latin *arcanum*, "mystery"). The major suit cards are also called trumps ("triumphs"), while the aces and numbers are sometimes referred to as pip cards.

Origin of the Tarot

Questions about the original creator of the tarot deck, the time and place of its creation, the significance of its complex symbols, and even the origin of the name "tarot" have long been debated, inspiring serious scholarship as well as wild speculation. Most historians today believe that tarot cards first appeared in northern Italy around the beginning of the fifteenth century. They also suggest that the tarot has undergone significant changes before stabilizing into the form we know today.

The two parts of the deck probably come from different sources. The minor suits are believed to have originated from playing cards first used in China. These were later propagated in India before reaching Italy through the Islamic countries in the late Middle Ages. Indeed, China and India have old games of cards with suits consisting of aces, numbered cards, and court cards. Muslim playing cards from the Mamluk period even show suit symbols that are visually very similar to the four tarot suit symbols.

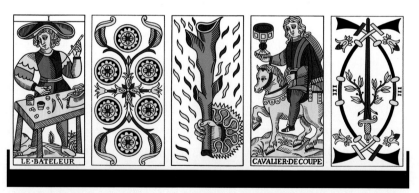

The Magician, 6 of Coins, Ace of Wands, Knight of Cups, 3 of Swords

The major suit, on the other hand, appears to be a European invention. There is nothing similar to it in Asian countries, and its imagery clearly points to late European medieval or early Renaissance influences. Historical records do not provide us with any hint as to why it was created or how it became united with the four-suit playing cards coming from the East. What we do know is that from the fifteenth century onward the combined tarot deck, consisting of both the major and the minor suits, was widely used for playing games of chance in both aristocratic and popular circles.

It is also unclear as to why the combined deck has become known as the tarot. Several hypotheses exist. My favorite one links the name *tarot* to the word *taroccho*, which in common sixteenth-century Italian meant "fool, a dumb person." This could, of course, be understood negatively as suggesting that only fools spend their time and money on card games such as tarot. But we can also think of other interpretations. In the major suit there is one card called "the Fool." It is often considered special and has a unique status in the suit, as we shall see later. The original meaning of the name "tarot cards" may thus have been "the Fool's cards," referring to this particular card or to the figure appearing on it.

Over the next few centuries the use of the tarot deck spread throughout different parts of Italy, followed by its migration to countries such as France, Germany, and Switzerland. There is some fragmentary evidence of the use of tarot cards in popular fortunetelling and possibly sorcery. However, these seem to be isolated cases rather than a widespread practice. During that time tarot cards were mostly used for gaming. But the combination of the two parts of the deck proved to be too complex for card games. Eventually, card players preferred the simpler pattern of only four suits with aces, numbers, and court cards. These became the ordinary playing cards that are used today all over the world.

The complete tarot deck continued to exist, but after the eighteenth century it was used mainly by fortunetellers and mystics. In various parts of Europe one can still find traditional card games with a seventy-eight-card deck resembling the tarot, but this is only a marginal practice today.

Academic historians who have studied the tarot tend to believe that this is the whole story. In their view, people at that time used the cards for the sole purpose of gaming, without paying much attention to the symbolism of the images. However, even without having solid proof that something is missing from this story, it is difficult to understand the role of the major suit in it. If people in Italy merely wanted to adopt an Oriental card game, why would they make it more complicated by adding twenty-two cards of such different character? Indeed, card players in Europe would later discover that it was more convenient to do without them.

The question seems even more puzzling when we consider the imagery of the major suit cards. Two cards bear images of the Emperor and the Pope. These were traditional figures of political and religious authority at that time. But other cards present strange themes and figures such as a female pope, a bisexual devil, a skeleton with a scythe, demons and angels, and a host of naked figures. All these appear to be on the same level as the figures of authority and social order. One card called the Wheel of Fortune even shows an image that traditionally represents revolutions and the casting down of rulers. At a time when any disrespect toward the king or the church was severely punishable, propagating this collection of unruly images seemed like asking for trouble.

Another point to remember is the fact that the images on the cards have no significance in gaming. The usual rules of card games refer only to the rank and value of each card, rather than the details of its illustration. The same cards could therefore be played in exactly the same way even if their

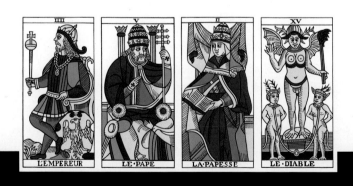

The Emperor, The Pope, The Popess, The Devil

images had been replaced, for example, by a simpler design consisting only of numbers and titles with some innocent decorations. Yet for nearly four centuries, tarot card makers preserved the original set of images. They did express their creativity by modifying certain details, but the general structure and the card themes have remained almost intact.

Why did they do it? Why did the tarot card makers insist on preserving a set of images loaded with such heavy and dangerous symbolism if it was irrelevant to the gaming needs of their clients? And how did it at all happen that a modest deck of playing cards picked up a set of symbols rich and potent enough to inspire centuries of varied interpretations, speculations, and activities, as the later history of the tarot shows?

Various answers have been offered for these questions. As we shall see later on, many authors who attributed mystical meanings to the cards believed that the tarot was created by ancient sages who wanted to express a secret spiritual message under the guise of seemingly innocuous playing cards. According to these authors, the secret of these playing cards was passed among tarot card makers for many generations. This unwritten tradition explained the true meaning of each card and instructed the card makers to preserve the original illustrations. In other words, the tarot makers were a sort of conspiratorial guild, manipulating European card players into spreading the ancient message without being aware of its real significance.

Card 13, The Star, The Lover, The Wheel of Fortune

Still, as a historical theory, this idea is very problematic. It is difficult to explain how such a secret could have been preserved through centuries of wars and social upheavals without ever being revealed. It is also unclear why, after four centuries of continuous transmission, the ancient tradition suddenly vanished without a trace, just as interest in the significance of tarot cards became widespread. At least, no traditional card maker has said anything about this since the beginning of the nineteenth century, when tarot cards first began to draw wide attention.

And what if there was no such secret tradition? If we accept this possibility, then it must have been something in the images themselves that influenced people's minds for centuries, motivating them to preserve this ancient set of symbols. Thinking further along these lines, we may note that many authors propagating the "secret society" theory give the impression of a highly disciplined group of initiated sages with a strong spiritual motivation. However, it is more reasonable to think that as a game of chance, the cards actually existed in borderline social areas such as in clubs of gambling, drinking, and cheap pleasures. The making of tarot cards itself seems to have been a shady occupation. In fact, many historical accounts are concerned with pirated, forged, and contraband card decks. Thus, it may be more reasonable to think of the tarot cards as a collective artwork evolving in marginal and half-legitimate popular circles, rather than as sublime teaching kept in secret temples of wisdom and spirituality.

What, then, was the role of these complex symbols, imbued with such strong spiritual and emotional meanings, in the questionable gambling venues? One possibility is to look for a psychological answer. Maybe the card images were somehow reflecting the subconscious conflicts and dilemmas of the card players. Maybe, in the very places where state authority (the Emperor) and the church (the Pope) lost their convincing power, people needed some reminder of the complex interplay between light and darkness in human life. We should remember, of course, that people at the time were very religious, so the thought of doing something forbidden must have evoked their deepest conflicts and fears. Maybe contemplating the complex symbols somehow helped them maintain a moral balance while also flirting with the dark and tempting world of sin. Such an idea might explain why they did not want the illustrations to be replaced by less charged images.

Yet something in the elusive and mysterious character of the tarot may inspire us to go beyond purely psychological explanations. We can at least play with the idea that there is something more to it. Maybe the magic of the cards represents some real magic in the world. Maybe there is a meaningful pattern originating in another level of reality, which the tarot cards channel and express at the human level.

The term *channeling* is usually associated with a message from a higher level of reality transmitted to our world through the mind of a single person. Yet the tarot cards may represent another kind of channeling—not a single message transmitted through a single person, but rather a web of small messages planted in the subconscious minds of many people at different times and places.

One can think of it as collective channeling, with each person experiencing the message as a tiny impulse or an intuitive urge. One person may feel a desire to print a set of cards preserving the old symbols. Another might have the urge to improve it by modifying this or that detail. Others may have an intuitive preference for a specific version of the cards, and so on. The impulse can be small and almost imperceptible on the level of a single individual. Sometimes it brings about real action, while in other cases it remains as an obscure and unfulfilled urge. It is the collective impact of all these little pushes that finally gives rise to the large-scale evolution of tarot cards in human history.

THE FRENCH SCHOOL

In the first few centuries following the appearance of the tarot cards, their symbolic significance did not receive much attention. There are two treatises from sixteenth-century Italy giving a moralistic interpretation to the tarot, but their impact appears to have been marginal and short-lived.

Besides these two documents, written records about the tarot from this period refer only to gaming or card production.

A significant turning point in the history of tarot interpretation occurred in 1781. A French scholar and mystic named Antoine Court de Gébelin published the eighth volume in a huge treatise, mostly fictional, titled *The Primeval World, Analyzed and Compared to the Modern World*. Among a range of other things, de Gébelin's treatise contained a detailed discussion of the tarot. This volume was the first written record of tarot cards being used for popular fortunetelling as well as for gaming. But in de Gébelin's view, people using the tarot just for gaming or fortunetelling were missing its full potential. In fact, he claimed, they were unknowingly holding in their hands the secret key to an ancient repository of knowledge that, once deciphered, could give them mysterious powers and a deeper understanding of the universe.

In de Gébelin's view, tarot cards were a sophisticated device created by the ancient Egyptian sages, experts in magic and the occult. In order to preserve their secret knowledge for later generations, they translated it into a language of symbolic illustrations. To hide the powerful knowledge from unworthy eyes in the most effective way, they decided to put it in plain sight but under the guise of a seemingly innocuous game of chance. This way, people would propagate the illustrations from one generation to another without being aware of their deep significance.

De Gébelin's speculations about ancient Egypt are not taken seriously today, but at the time his ideas were very influential. Fortunetelling with cards became fashionable in Parisian salons and even reached the imperial court of Napoleon. There were numerous fortunetellers using ordinary playing cards, but some of the more sophisticated among them, inspired by the supposed connection with sublime Egyptian mysteries, adopted the tarot.

The use of tarot cards for fortunetelling continued to gain popularity in the first half of the nineteenth century, but de Gébelin's ideas about the deeper significance of the card symbols were mostly ignored. Too many people were interested just in having their fortunes told. New tarot decks were printed for this purpose, with simple and straightforward illustrations replacing the traditional design. Gradually, the whole matter came to be regarded as something between supposedly supernatural divination and an amusing social pastime.

Toward the middle of the nineteenth century, a group of French mystics started to develop de Gébelin's ideas in a more serious direction. Although they had no direct connection to Judaism, these mystics were interested in the Jewish mystical tradition called the Cabbala. They believed that the tarot and Cabbala had both originated in ancient Egypt as two different but parallel representations of the same secret knowledge.

The most influential among the French tarot mystics was Alphonse Louis Constant, who, inspired by his interest in Cabbala, adopted the pseudo-Hebrew name Eliphas Lévi. Lévi believed that behind the methods of practical mysticism, such as fortunetelling, magic, and sorcery, there were hidden laws and forces comparable to those of modern science. He also believed that these laws were known to the ancient Egyptian sages, and that the Cabbala and the tarot were two representations of them. Thus, in his view, it should be possible to create a sort of dictionary in which each tarot card would correspond to a Cabbalistic symbol. By using such a dictionary, one could reach a better understanding of the laws of magic, relying both on the Cabbalistic texts and on the tarot.

In the system Lévi outlined, the twenty-two cards of the major suit corresponded to the twenty-two letters of the Hebrew alphabet, to which ancient Cabbalistic texts ascribed mystical meanings and magical powers. The four minor suits corresponded to the four letters of the tetragrammaton, God's name in Hebrew, which is so magically powerful that it is never to be pronounced. Lévi further linked ten cards of each minor suit (the aces and the numbers) to a famous Cabbalistic scheme called "the Sefirot Tree," or Tree of Life, which describes ten different aspects of the divine essence. Using these correspondences as cornerstones, he outlined a whole theory of mysticism and magical forces in which the tarot cards played a central role.

Eliphas Lévi's ideas initiated what we can call the French school of tarot. His writings gained popularity in France during the second half of the nineteenth century and eventually gave rise to a whole tradition of interpreting the tarot in mystical and Cabbalistic terms. Many tarot readers, especially in France, are still inspired by it today. In the French school of tarot, the card illustrations are usually traditional (with a few exceptions of newly designed decks), and the use of correspondences is according to Lévi's scheme. On the other hand, in English-speaking countries tarot became popular through the influence of another school, which changed both the correspondences and the card illustrations.

THE ENGLISH SCHOOL

Toward the end of the nineteenth century Lévi's ideas reached England, where they were adopted by a mystical association known as the Order of the Golden Dawn. The leaders of the Golden Dawn valued Lévi's work highly but also introduced significant modifications in his teachings, eventually creating a new tradition: the English school of tarot.

Like Lévi, the Golden Dawn people believed that the ancient sages had access to an arcane wisdom of magical forces. They also believed that in the wrong hands this powerful knowledge could be used for evil purposes. Therefore, it was put in the custody of a small circle of well-chosen spiritual masters solemnly sworn to keep it secret. For many generations these hidden masters distributed parts of the knowledge to the rest of humanity. However, to avoid abuse, they did it in gradual and fragmentary ways. Myths, religious traditions, and magic rituals in different cultures, as well as symbolic systems such as the Cabbala and the tarot, are all expressions of the same secret knowledge. But each of them contains many errors, distortions, and misleading hints, some intentional and others that accumulated through inaccurate transmission over the years. Only in our times has humankind reached a new stage of development where it can deal with the full knowledge, and the hidden masters chose the Order of the Golden Dawn leaders to reconstruct and teach it.

With this in mind, the Golden Dawn leaders expanded Lévi's idea of a dictionary. To overcome the mistakes and omissions of each particular tradition, they created a huge table of correspondences, putting together symbols, mythologies, and mystical systems from all over the world. As a basis for the table, they took the two sets of symbols that they regarded as the most accurate expressions of the ancient knowledge: the Cabbala and the tarot. In a way essentially similar to Lévi's (but different in the details, as we shall see in chapter 5), each major tarot card was matched with a Hebrew letter. But in the Golden Dawn table there were many other columns, correlating the card and its letter with a host of mystical symbols and deities from different cultures. These included, for example, ancient Egypt, India, China, Islam, Greek mythology, astrology, alchemy, various traditions of magic and sorcery, and so on.

The leaders of the Golden Dawn order also created a tarot deck of their own, with a new design based on the table of correspondences. On some cards they kept the original images but added hints and references to other traditions, while other cards were completely redesigned with new themes. To keep it secret, students of the order received a copy of the deck only for a short time, during which they were allowed to copy it by hand for their own use. In the end, however, neither the original deck nor the copies survived. Today we have only some reconstructions of the Golden Dawn tarot deck, based on personal recollections and a few written descriptions by the initiates.

Tarot and the New Age

One of the most influential members of the Golden Dawn order was Aleister Crowley. Crowley, who did not suffer from excessive modesty, saw himself as a prophet announcing a new age for humanity. According to him, the course of history could be divided into three ages. First, there was the "age of the mother," in which religion was focused on nature rites and feminine deities. About two thousand years ago began the "age of the father," as expressed by religions of the single male god. Today we are witnessing the birth of a third age: the "age of the child," characterized by playfulness, creativity, and a pluralism of gods.

Writing at the beginning of the twentieth century, Crowley predicted that methods of magic and practical mysticism that were kept secret in previous eras would become widely known and find a new harmony with science and technology. Mystical experience would once again become a vital part of human existence, and in order to attain it people would practice various methods—from yoga and meditation to pagan cults, magic rituals, sexuality, dance, and drugs.

Crowley's personality was problematic and gave rise to many scandals, but his creative work was thorough and extensive. He reworked the symbolic system of the Order of the Golden Dawn and popularized it in his books. In the 1940s he also published a new deck of tarot cards expressing his ideas. For several decades his vision was shared only by small marginal groups, but during the 1960s Crowley's "new age" concept resonated well with the alternative counterculture. Indeed, Crowley's face appears on the famous sleeve of the Beatles' 1967 LP *Sgt. Pepper's Lonely Hearts Club Band*, and symbols from his teachings often can be found in rock music culture.

The combination of a renewed interest in mysticism and the 1960s counterculture of love and freedom gave rise to the New Age movement, the nondenominational and pluralistic movement of postmodern spirituality that gradually became a worldwide phenomenon. The New Age movement adopted many of Crowley's ideas, although usually in a softer version that avoided dark and violent aspects. Under the influence of Crowley and of other Golden Dawn teachers, tarot reading became a popular and widely accepted activity.

The New Age movement gave the tarot cards a significant push forward. This new surge in interest originated mainly in the United States and then spread to tarot readers all over the world. New tarot decks with various designs started to appear in increasing numbers—first a few dozen, then hundreds of new decks every year. Over the last few years the Internet has accelerated this process, with small publishers and individual artists distributing their own decks globally. Today one can find a huge selection of available tarot decks in many stores and websites selling items of mysticism and alternative products. As a result, there are more people reading the tarot today than ever before.

The New Age not only popularized the use of tarot cards as practiced by the English school, it also transformed it. The Golden Dawn leaders took their methods and rituals, their table of correspondences, and their hierarchy of magical grades very seriously. In contrast, the New Age movement is marked by a free and playful approach that is not fixed to well-ordered tables. It also shuns the idea of grades and authority. With regards to the Golden Dawn reading methods and correspondences, many New Age tarot books recognize their value. However, they present them as an invitation to expand and enrich the reading of the cards, rather than an absolute truth.

Another key difference between the New Age movement and the Golden Dawn order is that the Golden Dawn leaders had no psychological dimension in their teaching. They spoke of occult forces existing "out there" and saw tarot reading as a means of communicating with these forces. But following the ideas of Carl Gustav Jung, who gave psychological interpretations to mystical symbols, the New Age movement began to regard tarot reading as a way to connect with our own subconscious mind. As a result, authors and teachers in the New Age movement started to distance themselves from old-style divination and future prediction and instead saw tarot reading mainly as a means of consultation, therapy, and guidance in personal processes.

The Tarot de Marseille

Apart from a few fancy decks commissioned by noble houses and painted by hand, the earliest tarot cards that have survived to our days are printed decks from the sixteenth century. Until the middle of the nineteenth century the method of production remained the same. Black lines were printed on large paper sheets from ink-smeared woodcut plates that were designed by master artisans. To add the colors, thin boards with cut-out shapes (one for each color) were put on the printed sheets and smeared over with paint, a technique known as "stencil coloring." Finally, the colored sheets were glued on stiff cardstock and cut into single cards. This method made possible a mass production of affordable cards for the use of players and gamblers all over Europe.

Initially, card makers from different regions of Italy, France, and other countries printed different versions of the tarot. But in the seventeenth and eighteenth centuries, the city of Marseille in southern France became a leading center of card production. Its printers adopted a standard model for the tarot cards. The decks that they created over the years varied in the elaboration of details and the richness of the coloring, but the main themes and elements of each card remained the same.

The Marseille model was not a purely local invention. In the sixteenth century similar decks were already being produced in southern France and northern Italy, and many of the basic elements can be traced back to the earliest popular decks that have survived to the present. For all we know, it may be quite close to the original version of the tarot as it was first created, but the Marseille card makers gave this model its mature form. Their role was important in propagating the tarot as their products became increasingly popular all over the country. When the French Cabbalists in Paris began to study the tarot, they used card decks that were produced in Marseille. Under their influence, the traditional model of the tarot, which later became the standard tool for divination and mysticism, came to be known as the Tarot of Marseille.

The writings of de Gébelin, Lévi, and their followers were not only central in the French school of tarot, but they also served as the starting point for the English school. As a result, both the French and English schools have accepted the Tarot de Marseille as the genuine model of the traditional cards. During the twentieth century, however, these schools have diverged in their attitudes toward the original illustrations.

New English Decks

The English school of tarot did not attach too much importance to the detailed illustrations of the traditional cards. The Golden Dawn leaders were much more interested in mystical and philosophical principles that, in their view, stood behind the tarot. They also believed that one could express the same principles in other symbolic languages. In fact, they thought that such new representations could even be better than the original, as they would rely on the well-ordered table of correspondences rather than on the chaotic history of the traditional tarot images.

Consequently, followers of the English school in the twentieth century started to create a growing number of tarot decks. The new decks generally had the same structure as the old cards, but each of them had its own imagery and illustration style. Gradually, these became more and more distant from the original.

The primary inspiration for the new English-school decks was the Golden Dawn tarot deck mentioned previously. Following the disintegration of the short-lived order, several of its former members created tarot decks of their own. Among them was Arthur Edward Waite, whose deck was well received by the New Age movement and thus became the most popular twentieth-century tarot deck outside France.

The deck that carries Waite's name was actually created under his supervision by a commissioned artist named Pamela Colman Smith, who was also a Golden Dawn initiate. It was originally published in 1909 by the London-based Rider company and so is sometimes called the Rider-Waite Tarot. Today it is more fashionable to call it the Rider-Waite-Smith (or RWS) deck. The Waite deck combines elements from different sources, such as the Tarot de Marseille, the Golden Dawn Tarot, and other decks. In addition, many of its details are now believed to be the product of Smith's creative imagination.

An important innovation in the RWS deck was the design of the minor suits' number cards, which Waite regarded mainly as a tool for divination. The simple and abstract design of the Marseille number cards shows only the suit symbols surrounded by floral decorations. But number cards in the Waite deck show realistically drawn landscapes with human figures in specific situations. These explicit scenes have made the Waite deck more accessible for beginning readers and have thus contributed much to its popularity.

Most of the new English-school decks that appeared in the twentieth century adopted this innovation. Typically, their number cards show scenes that are basically taken from the Waite cards, redrawn and adapted to the specific theme of each deck. The variety of the themes reflects the wide range of interests of the New Age movement. Some decks present motifs taken from various religious and artistic traditions. These include, for example, decks inspired by Japanese, African, Basque, and Native American traditional art, New Orleans voodoo deities, and many more. Other decks show a feminist orientation, a hippie-like or childish character, inspiration of New Age spiritual teachers and gurus, motifs taken from various scientific fields, animal characters instead of human figures, and so on. Most of the new decks preserve the basic five-suit structure of the traditional tarot. However, the details of their illustrations usually have very little, if any, in common with the original Tarot de Marseille cards.

NEW MARSEILLE DECKS

In contrast to the English school, authors and readers from the French school generally attached more importance to the details of the traditional illustrations. Accepting the Tarot de Marseille as the genuine tarot, they preferred to keep on using it instead of looking for new and modified versions. Some newly designed decks did originate in the French school—the best known among them named after its creator, Oswald Wirth—but their use remained limited.

The French school's interest in the precise details of the traditional cards became especially significant during the twentieth century. Ironically, this came a little too late. The shift to industrial card-printing at the later part of the nineteenth century brought about a simplification of the image details and an impoverishment of the variety of colors. As mechanical card production became dominant, the continuous line of master card makers who passed their expertise from one generation to another was broken, and the old secrets of the trade were lost.

In response to these losses of the nineteenth century, several attempts were made during the twentieth century to restore the original depth and richness of the traditional Marseille cards. But what exactly is the traditional model? Many tarot decks have been printed in Marseille, and although they all follow the same basic model, there is great variation in the fine details. Those aiming to restore the original model have had to face the obvious question: among all the Marseille decks that have survived to the present day, which one is the closest to "the real thing"?

Over the years, a general consensus has emerged among followers of the French school that the most authentic version of the traditional tarot is a deck printed in 1760 by a Marseille card maker named Nicolas Conver. Not much is known about Conver himself. But many influential tarot books from the later part of the nineteenth century onward declare his deck, time and again, to be the most faithful and accurate representation of the ancient tarot symbols. No other traditional deck has been held in such high esteem.

Several new Marseille-type decks appeared in the twentieth century that were based mostly on the Conver cards. The most popular of these is the Ancient Tarot de Marseille created in 1930 by Paul Marteau. It was published by the Grimeau Company and dominated the French tarot scene for much of the twentieth century.

Another popular type is the restored Tarot de Marseille created in the 1990s by Alejandro Jodorowsky, who was my own tarot teacher in the 1980s, and Philippe Camoin, who comes from the family that inherited Conver's printing house. There are also some other, less popular ones. The CBD Tarot of Marseille, whose images accompany this book, is also a restoration of the Conver deck.

CBD Tarot de Marseille

When I started working on this book I did not plan to publish my own tarot deck. My initial idea was to use illustrations from one of the Marseille versions that were already in print. There were some available options, but the process of copyright negotiation made me think again. I saw this as an opportunity to create the deck that I always wanted for myself: an edition of the Tarot de Marseille that captures its magic in the most effective way, with the smallest amount of distortions and omissions, and which can be used for actual reading.

The question of where to look for this magic seemed simple enough. Among the different versions of the Tarot de Marseille, Conver's 1760 deck clearly holds a special position. One could say that it stands exactly at the point of transition between the two great eras in the history of the tarot. On one hand, the Conver deck is the product of four centuries of tarot evolution and development. It appears just a short time before the great changes of the nineteenth century, while still continuing the old tradition of the earliest popular decks. On the other hand, among all the Marseille decks, this is the one that has made the strongest impression on later generations of tarot readers and has become commonly regarded as the closest to "the real thing." It has also served as the main source for the new twentieth-century Tarot de Marseille restorations.

We can think of this in the following way. Clearly, tarot cards have some mysterious qualities that have a strong effect on people's minds. The concrete expression of this "magical" quality is the fact that the tarot cards inspire and awaken strong emotions in so many people over so many generations. From such a viewpoint, we might agree that the Conver deck, which became the most influential and appreciated among all the traditional versions, is the one that expresses the magic of the tarot cards in its strongest form. But until now, it couldn't be found in a version both practically usable and faithful to the original.

There are decks available today that are facsimile copies of original Conver cards preserved in libraries and private collections. But these cards have undergone centuries of use and wear. Their colors are faded, and many line details are missing or have become unclear. People buy these decks for research and study or as collector's items, but they are not suitable for actual reading.

On the other hand, there are several new Marseille decks that are based on the Conver cards, such as the previously mentioned decks by Marteau and Jodorowsky-Camoin. These new decks are designed for use in reading, and they are printed in clear lines and fresh colors, but they are not really faithful to Conver's original. Their creators have changed many of the card details, adding elements from other decks or just giving them new forms according to their own personal ideas.

The reason for this lies in the basic vision of the tarot shared by these creators. In one way or another, they were influenced by the idea that the original tarot was conceived by a group of secret initiates and then transmitted through the centuries, with occasional mistakes creeping in. In this vision later decks such as Conver's are just degraded copies of the original and should therefore be rectified in order to restore "the real tarot."

My vision is different. First, as I have already explained in this chapter, the secret tradition theory seems to me very dubious historically. Second, even if we want to restore "the real tarot" that supposedly existed in the late Middle Ages, we have no available original from that period. Therefore, in practice the method used by the new decks' creators was to take the Conver deck and modify it according to their own ideas of "what the real tarot should have been." And third—and, for me, most important—the tarot is not a representation of some message that existed in the remote past and has since been lost. Instead, it stands in its own right as a mysterious and magical work of art, evolving through the centuries and achieving its most potent form in the Conver deck. Therefore, instead of trying to improve on Conver, I wanted to remain faithful to his original designs while minimizing the effects of my own interpretation.

For this purpose I have used copies from several decks of the original Conver cards. These decks were made at different dates, but their lines were all printed from the same original woodblocks. I have had to rely on several decks as in each one different details were blurred or missing. As for the colors, the decks that I used differed from each other because the coloring templates were worn out after some years of use, and in later printings they were replaced by inexact copies. As a rule I followed the earliest printing that I had available, which I assumed to be the closest to, if not the same as, Conver's original design.

A special challenge in all this was the fact that in the Marseille cards, and particularly in Conver's deck, there are many anomalies in the image details. There are, for example, objects that merge into other ones, ambiguous shapes that can be interpreted as parts of different objects, irregular anatomical features or impossible perspectives, coloring that breaks the shapes of objects or continues outside their borders, irregularities and inconsistencies in the spelling of card titles, and so on. Creators of other restored decks have often tended to "correct" such anomalies, but whenever possible I have preferred to keep them. This is not only because I wanted to remain faithful to the original, but also because they enhance the feeling of magic and mystery of the cards, opening them up for new and interesting interpretations.

Still, what I have tried to create was not an exact copy of a 250-year-old deck, but a deck intended to be used by people reading the tarot today. This meant that however faithful to the original I wanted to be, I still had to make some adjustments and modifications. It is impossible to reproduce exactly the techniques, the coloring materials, the quality of the paper, and the human expertise of the eighteenth-century card industry. And even if we succeeded in imitating them with artificial means, the visual impression on the observer would be completely different. Our eyes and brains today are accustomed to a different world of images and graphic material. This is especially relevant in tarot card reading, where the "feel" that the reader gets from the card is the most important factor.

These considerations influenced my work on the cards at several points. For example, sometimes I had to soften an abnormal detail that modern printing techniques would make too eye-catching. I made especially significant changes in the facial expressions, since an exact copy would have made them too gloomy and depressive to a present-day reader. Still, I tried to preserve the general physical traits. In addition, since there is no way of replicating the original shades of color pigments and the impressions that they made at that time, I have had to define for myself the scale of shades of the various colors. This means that a red surface in Conver's cards is still a red surface in mine, but I had to decide which shade of red to use. In order to adapt the cards to the visual sensitivity of present-day readers, I tested early versions of the deck with various people, some of whom had previous knowledge of tarot while others did not. I made necessary changes according to the reactions that I received.

Most of these considerations I did not decide in advance. Instead, they emerged as part of the process, as if the cards and not myself were making the key decisions. Initially the idea was to undertake a short and simple project that would take a few months, just in order to illustrate a book. Yet a series of seemingly accidental circumstances, along with the feeling I had that the cards demanded more effort, eventually led to a three-phase process, with each phase taking about a year or more.

At first a commissioned illustrator (Leela Ganin) copied the lines of the old woodcuts on paper using an ink nib, working "by the eye" in real size. Then a digital graphic designer (Nir Matarasso) did corrections on the line details, adding the card titles in letters copied from the originals, as well as adding color to the high-resolution scans of Leela's drawings. Finally, after learning the necessary digital graphics techniques myself, I reshaped all the lines and colored areas, comparing them with scans of the original cards, until the final result seemed to have the right feeling and a satisfactory degree of exactness.

The outcome of this effort was published in 2011 as CBD Tarot de Marseille (CBD standing for Conver–Ben-Dov), and its illustrations appear in this book. Additional details about the CBD Tarot deck and where it can be purchased are available on the website www.cbdtarot.com. The website also includes pictures of the cards in home printing resolution for personal use. The illustrations are distributed under a Creative Commons license, which means that they can be freely reproduced and distributed for any noncommercial purpose. For further details, please consult the website.

CHAPTER 2

THE READING SESSION

Although tarot cards can be read by an individual or in a group situation, the classic reading session is where one person performs a reading for another. In this book we refer to these two participants as the querent and the reader. The querent is the one who seeks advice about an issue in his or her life. The reader is the person who conducts the process and interprets the cards for the querent.

The basic structure of the reading encounter is inspired by its origins as a fortunetelling session, even though most tarot readers today use the cards as a tool for guidance and advice and not for future prediction. Usually, the querent sits in front of the reader with a low table between them. The relationship between both is important. With two people who are already in a close relationship it is possible to sit on adjacent sides or sit together at one side of the table facing the same direction. But when the reader and querent are relative strangers, sitting together may be too intimate, and it is better to sit face to face with the table between them as a reassuring space of separation.

The general structure of the session, on which we shall elaborate, is as follows. The reader takes the deck of cards out of its box, and then both reader and querent take turns shuffling it. The reader lays a number of cards out on the table in a layout—called a spread—and then studies the cards and interprets them for the querent. In this chapter we shall discuss the dynamics of the encounter between the querent and the reader, while in chapter 3 we will focus on the actual reading of the cards.

Everything Is a Sign

The reading of tarot cards involves a particular perception of reality. In the normal everyday perception, which is sometimes called consensus reality, the cards are pieces of printed cardboard and shuffling them is a random process. Yet when we read the cards, we shift to another framework of reality perception in which there is one basic rule: everything is a sign.

This rule is first and foremost expressed in the fact that we interpret the cards not as a random collection of cardboard pieces, but as a meaningful sign with a message for the querent. However, the signs to be interpreted are not limited to the specific cards in the spread. Everything that takes place in and around the reading session may also be seen as a sign. In other words, during the reading session our perception of reality is that nothing happens by mere chance. Everything is a sign.

We may start to apply this rule by observing the querent's behavior. The way they present themselves and their question, the choice of words and the tone of voice, the degree of openness and initial exposure—these are all signs expressing their emotional attitude toward the issue in question, toward the cards, and toward the reader. The way the querent shuffles the cards—whether in a self-confident or hesitant manner—is a sign. If the querent apologizes for not knowing how to shuffle properly, it is a sign. If the querent touches and rearranges the cards once they are laid on the table, then the quality of their hand movement and the change in the cards' layout are signs. The body language and the sitting position of the querent are signs. Also, the design and colors of their clothes and accessories, especially if they resemble details in the cards, are signs. Everything is a sign.

Unusual occurrences that happen during the reading are also signs. If at the initial shuffle in the reader's hands a certain card pops up time and again, it's a sign. If during the shuffle a few cards fall from the querent's hands, we can look at them and try to understand what they signify. Maybe it is something that does not fit with the way the question was formulated or maybe it is a message that the querent rejects as being too much for them to hold. If the same cards appear time and again in consecutive spreads, it is a sign. If they appear in different spreads for the same querent, they might hold a special message; if the same cards appear in sessions with consecutive querents, it may be a message for the reader. If there is a candle in the room and its flame suddenly moves or emits sparks, or if a loud noise is heard from outside, it is a sign emphasizing what is being said at that precise moment. *Everything is a sign.*

We might not understand and interpret all the signs as they appear. Some signs we understand only in retrospect, at a later stage of the reading. Signs also may have different levels of meaning, which we may discover one after the other. We can at first give a certain interpretation to the sign and then realize that we can understand it on a deeper level. So we should not try to grasp all the signs at once. Instead, we should strive to open ourselves to the signs, take note of them when they appear, and search our imagination for their possible meaning. This is more an intuitive than a rational process. The meaning should appear as a moment of realization, in which we suddenly see a connection between the sign—a certain detail in the card illustration or something that happened in the reading space—and the querent's life.

THE READING SPACE

Traditions of magic and sorcery often prescribe elaborate rituals to invoke supernatural forces or entities. However we interpret these claims—whether from a magical viewpoint or from a psychological one—the time-tested rules of these rituals can teach us something about the proper way to go beyond ordinary reality.

One essential feature of such rituals is a separation between the space and time of the ritual on one hand, and that of normal everyday life on the other. For example, in many traditions magical rituals are performed within a well-marked circle. Often, in order to strengthen its effect, magical words are written around the circle. In a similar manner, the time of the ritual is marked with symbolic actions such as consecration or self-cleansing, the lighting of candles or incense, and so on. These actions signify a moment of transition between the ordinary time of everyday reality and the consecrated time of the ritual.

Reading the tarot cards also involves going beyond the ordinary perception of reality. In the realm of the ordinary, the cards are cardboard pieces shuffled at random. But during the reading nothing happens by chance and everything is a sign. In accordance with the time-tested principles of the magical tradition, we may perform some symbolic actions marking the limits of the reading session in space and time. In this way we can clearly feel the transition between the two domains as we switch from one perception of reality to the other.

According to the type of reading, we can adjust the level of care and effort that we invest in marking the limits of the reading space. When reading the tarot in an informal and noncommitted spirit—for example, at a party or in a pub—it may be enough to clean up a table corner and lay the cards on it. But for a consultation that touches sensitive issues in the querent's life and which can affect them on a deep emotional level, we should prepare a quiet, neatly arranged space with a serene and comfortable atmosphere.

It is a good idea to remove everyday objects from the reading space. Instead, at least for the time of the reading, we can put pictures or objects that have a symbolic and spiritual effect—religious or New Age pictures, crystals, plant arrangements, water vessels or fountains, and so on. The colors in the room should be calm and pleasant, and the general design simple and harmonious.

In doing this, we can follow the aesthetic principles of mystical traditions—for example, feng shui or Japanese Zen—or simply act by our own feeling and intuition. In many magical and mystical traditions it is customary to mark the four cardinal directions—north, south, east, and west. We can translate this into the symbolic language of the tarot itself and put copies of the ace cards in the four directions according to the correspondence table in chapter 7.

Just as the reading space needs to have a special quality, much like a temple or sacred space, so the time of the reading should also be clearly marked to separate it from the mundane time of ordinary reality. A simple way to do this is by lighting a candle at the beginning of the reading and putting it out at the end. In certain traditions of fortunetelling it is also customary to put a receptacle full of water in front of the candle, symbolizing the two complementary elements of water and fire.

After lighting the candle—note that a wooden perishable match is better than a lighter—we can "collect the light" by passing one or both hands over the flame and drawing them in as if washing our head and body with its symbolic energy. A similar gesture is done by Jewish women lighting the Shabbat candles and by Hindus in their temples.

It is also a good idea to stop at this point for a moment of self-concentration, meditation, or even a quiet prayer before beginning the actual reading. Some tarot readers prefer to light the candle before the querent enters the room, so that the querent's presence should not distract them. Yet there is an advantage to doing this in the querent's presence, so that they also may feel the special quality of the moment and enter into a state of calm concentration. We can also mark the entrance to the reading space by removing our shoes. Of course, such actions should correspond to the sensibilities of the reader and the querent. For example, some people may appreciate the smell of incense, while for others it may be annoying.

HANDLING THE CARDS

Developing a close relationship with our cards is a gradual process. A new tarot deck usually arrives in a cellophane wrapping inside a cardboard box. At this stage the cards are still an anonymous industrial product, identical to thousands of others that came out of the same machine. But from the moment we open the package and touch the cards, they become "our" cards. From then on, they are a part of our reading history, accumulating our own and our querents' emotional energies and fingerprints, and sometimes their tears. Thus, the first opening of the card package is a special moment in our relationship with the cards.

It is a good idea to open the cards for the first time as part of a little ceremony in a quiet, isolated place. We can prepare the place and the time in much the same way as we would prepare the reading space, sitting for a while in a state of calmness and concentration, and maybe lighting a candle or an incense stick. We may then open the package, take out the cards, and touch them one by one in order to feel them in our hands.

We may now look at the cards, starting to get used to their feel. But it's better not to spread them right away on a specific question. Instead, we may look at the images without haste, taking the time to notice our feelings as we observe each card. Some readers like to perform a purification ritual to initiate their relationship with the cards; for example, to pass them through the smoke of burning incense or dry sage leaves, and perhaps to create bodily contact with the cards one by one.

Instead of the industrial cardboard box, we may prefer to keep the cards in a more personalized container. A common practice is to keep the deck inside a bag or wrap it with a piece of cloth, and then put the wrapped cards in a box of our own choosing. It's a good idea that the bag and the box be made of organic material (such as wood, felt, or natural fiber), rather than an artificial material such as plastic or animal skin, which may carry negative associations. The box may carry mystical symbols or just nice decorations, preferably not something dissonant with the intimate spirit of tarot reading such as a commercial logo. We should also be sensitive to the color and texture of the bag and the box. For example, dark blue or soft purple induce a feeling of calmness and opening to the spiritual level, while bright red may be energetic but perhaps too aggressive.

Besides the bag and the box, it's a good idea to have a reading mat made of thick cloth on which the cards are laid out. As with all other tarot accessories, it is advisable to use the reading mat only for this purpose. The material, color, and feeling of the reading mat can be chosen with similar considerations as the bag and the box. Instead of a separate bag, some readers use the same piece of cloth both to wrap the cards and to lay them out for reading. In mystic shops and on tarot websites it is possible to find many bags, boxes, and reading mats especially made for this purpose, but perhaps we may want to choose something more unique and personal for our cards instead of a ready-made solution.

Shuffling the Deck

Shuffling the cards at the beginning of the reading may seem like a simple technical action, but actually it has subtle aspects that deserve our attention. Shuffling the cards has two main functions. We can say that these functions are in some sense contrary to each other. One of them expresses our control of the shuffling outcome, and the other expresses our lack of control.

The first function of the shuffle is to establish a bond between our actions and the cards in the spread. We do this by shuffling the cards in our hands, deciding how to shuffle and for how long. In this way, the shuffling outcome—which cards are physically laid out on the table—is determined by our actions and choices. The second function of the shuffle is to introduce an open and uncontrolled factor into the reading. This is due to the fact that we shuffle the cards facedown, not seeing their illustrations. Therefore we cannot have any conscious or deliberate control over the choice of cards for the spread.

The two functions of the shuffling express two key principles that can guide us regardless of the precise way in which we choose to shuffle. The first principle is that our actions and decisions (that is, the querent's, the reader's, or both) should determine the choice of cards. The second principle is that the choice should be free of our deliberate control. In other words, in our conscious experience it should appear as effectively random.

To understand the logic behind the first principle, we can draw on two conceptual frameworks: magical and psychological. In magical terms, the shuffling creates an energetic link between the querent and the cards. In psychological terms, the querent can feel an emotional bond with the cards because the cards came out of their hands: in a sense, they are the querent's cards and the querent is the one responsible for their appearance in the spread.

This understanding can also guide us on the matter of the desired order of shuffling. The exact ordering of the shuffled cards depends on the querent's and the reader's actions, as well as on the previous shuffling of the deck in earlier readings. The role of the reader and of the previous reading is not problematic by itself. Within the reading space we can accept it as a sign: it is significant that the querent chose to have a reading with us and with our deck at this precise moment, in which the cards are thus ordered and not otherwise. Notwithstanding this, the reading is focused on the querent and the issues in their life. In order to strengthen their bond with the spread, it is better that the querent should have the last word in the choice of cards. For example, if both the reader and the querent take turns in shuffling the cards, let the querent be the last one to shuffle.

The second principle is common to all methods of divination, as they always involve an uncontrollable and apparently random element. In this sense, shuffling the cards is not different from tossing coins, throwing seashells, observing a formation of tea leaves, or any other of the countless methods of divination used throughout human history. All of them are based on mechanisms that are regarded as random in the normal vision of reality. Therefore, even if we don't understand the logic of this principle, in practice we should best observe it since it is an essential ingredient of the time-tested experience of divination.

Still, if we do try to figure out the reason behind the second principle, we would find that our two conceptual frameworks diverge from each other. The magical language applies within the reading space in which everything is a sign. In order to let the sign manifest "from the universe," we have to relinquish control and have the cards appear without depending on our deliberate intention. The psychological viewpoint is relevant outside the reading space. It can interpret the random factor as a trigger to disturb the existing thought processes and drive them in a new and unexpected direction. Once this happens, the final message emerges not from the cards by themselves but as a product of the dynamic process of reading, which involves both the reader's interpretation and the querent's reaction and presence.

As these two sets of considerations apply in two different practical domains, one inside the reading space and one outside it, they don't really contradict each other. Instead, they complement each other to give a more complete vision of the reading process. Those who are acquainted with the physical theory known as quantum mechanics can compare it to the question "What is an electron?" In quantum mechanics there are two disparate answers: "The electron is a particle" and "The electron is a wave." Each one is valid in a different practical context of measurement, so that they complement each other to give the most complete possible answer to the question. In a similar way, the magical and the psychological visions can complement each other to give us a fuller understanding of the reading process.

Each reader has their own favorite way of shuffling, and no single way fits all. But however we choose to shuffle the cards, it advisable to do this in accordance with the two principles. My way of doing it is to take the cards out of their box and to shuffle them gently facedown while I listen to the querent's story. In this way I renew my bond with the cards, reshuffle the arrangement that remained from the last reading, and also put in something of the querent's presence as I feel it. Then I hand the cards to the querent, still facedown, and ask them to shuffle the cards. Once this is done, the querent returns the cards to me, still facedown. One by one

I then take the first cards from the back of the deck (that is, from the top side of the facedown pack) and arrange them on the table in the spread layout.

When putting the cards on the table, I prefer to turn them faceup all at once, so that I can see immediately the complete picture. But there are readers who prefer to lay them facedown at first and reveal each card one by one during the session. It is also possible for the reader to shuffle the cards faceup, noting cards that attract the reader's special attention, and then let the querent shuffle them facedown. Another common practice is to ask the querent to "cut" the deck—that is, to split it into two or three parts, put the parts side by side on the table, and then join them together again in an inverse order.

Readers of the Tarot de Marseille often use only the twenty-two cards of the major suit. In such cases it is also possible to use the following method. Instead of letting the querent shuffle the deck, we can spread it in front of the querent facedown, creating a fan-like form, and ask them to pick up cards by the intuitive feel of their hand. In this way, we conform with the two principles: the querent picks up the cards, but the cards are facedown so that they can't choose any card intentionally.

When the circumstances do not allow us to use our usual shuffling method, we can improvise by using other solutions while keeping in mind the two principles. For example, sometimes I have to do a reading over the telephone. I prefer an actual meeting face-to-face, but it may happen that a querent needs immediate advice and can't come over. So I shuffle the cards in my hands with the querent on the telephone line and ask them to tell me when to stop according to their feeling. At this moment I take out the first card from the top of the deck. I repeat the process for the next card, and so on. In this way, the querent's choice of when to stop each time determines the cards that will come up, but this happens without them having deliberate control over the outcome.

Another method popular today is to do a computer reading. As far as shuffling is concerned, we can accept it as a legitimate method that conforms to the two shuffling principles. The card choice by the computer is not really random. It is dependent on the state of the computer's memory at the exact moment when the querent activates the shuffling algorithm (that is, when the "choose the cards" button is pressed). Thus, the outcome depends on the querent's action, as the first principle demands. On the other hand, the choice of cards in the computerized reading cannot be deliberately controlled. These considerations obviously apply only for the electronic "shuffling" of the cards and not for their interpretation. This still remains a human process, whether it is done directly from the card images or by figuring out the meaning of the written texts that the software brings up on the screen.

THE SESSION DYNAMICS

People usually turn to tarot reading when they feel they need help with their personal problems. In this, the tarot reading presents itself as one option in a vast field of alternatives, ranging from divination methods to more conventional forms of personal guidance, consultation, and therapy. To be sure, the rules and procedures of divination are different from those of psychological therapy. Unlike psychology, they are not motivated by the need to conform to a scientific worldview. Instead, they trust the accumulated wisdom of age-old traditions, which have evolved by adapting themselves to human needs over many generations. But the aim is the same: to give new insights and to help the querent undergo internal processes that will lead him to a better situation.

For tarot readers, what this means is that we should not only pay attention to what we see in the cards. First and foremost, we should be aware of the emotional process that the querent is going through. To guide this process in a helpful and productive way, it is useful to have some knowledge and experience in other forms of therapy. We can achieve this in a variety of ways, from participating in New Age and self-awareness workshops to taking courses in conventional psychology. It is a good idea to spend some time undergoing therapy oneself, whether personal treatment or by participating in a therapy group. Books by professional therapists and psychologists can also provide us with useful insights for the reading session. For example, I often advise students in my tarot courses to read Irvin Yalom's book *The Gift of Therapy*. Many of the tips that he gives to apprentice psychologists are also relevant for tarot readers.

Still, we should remember that unlike conventional psychology, which often involves long-term treatment, in tarot reading we usually have to open the process and close it within one session. The session itself may last for up to an hour, more or less. To trigger an effective change in such a short time, it is useful to have some idea about the stages that we are going to pass through.

The first moments of the session are the most important in creating the atmosphere that will prevail throughout. During these moments the querent and the reader test each other and try to assess the amount of trust and exposure that they can allow themselves to express. My way of handling it is to light a candle and strike softly a resonating metal bowl. While the sound is fading I sit down calmly in front of the querent and have a moment of silent welcome. I take out the cards and ask the querent an open question that does not require a specific answer. A typical question may be, for example, "What brings you here?" or "What can I do for you?" It is also a good idea to mention the querent's first name in order to strengthen their sense of being here and now.

While the querent speaks in reply, I shuffle the cards, trying to be attentive not only to the explicit content, but also to the tone of voice, the choice of words, and the degree of openness and self-awareness that is expressed. These impressions will serve me later in assessing the emotional attitude of the querent toward the problem, as well as guide me in formulating my messages in words that they can understand and accept. For the moment, of course, I keep my observations to myself.

Now I hand over the cards to the querent and instruct them to shuffle as if they were putting themselves and their question into the cards. Sometimes the querent continues to talk while shuffling, and in such cases

I ask them to be quiet and concentrate on the cards. The way they shuffle and the length of time that they devote to the shuffling depend on their personal feeling, but if it's necessary I show them how to do it without wrinkling or folding the cards. If I feel that the querent is prolonging the shuffling, as if they're trying to avoid the moment of truth in which the cards will be spread, I make a gentle remark like "Hand me the cards when you're ready."

With the cards laid out on the table, a new phase of the reading session starts. At this stage it is advisable not to be hasty and look for the answer right away. Instead, we may look at the cards in silence for some time. We can begin with our eyes wandering over them without focusing, letting the impressions flow in freely. Now we can note to ourselves the general character of the spread, the visual patterns that the cards form together, common objects or features in different cards, and perhaps some image details that specifically draw our attention. Still, we should remember that during those moments the querent is in a state of tense expectation, looking at the cards and at our facial expressions and trying to guess what we are going to say. It is important not to lose contact with the querent's presence.

Now we can begin the conversation and start interpreting the spread. At first we may describe the general impression we got from the cards without making statements that are too strong. Even if the message of the cards is already clear to us, we still do not know to what extent the querent is ready to accept it. We can talk for a few minutes, suggest possible directions and interpretations, and then ask the querent to express their feelings about what we have just said.

During the session it is important to pay constant attention to the querent's reaction and to adapt what we say to what they can hear and accept. Challenging and difficult contents should first be presented with caution, and we should gradually prepare the querent to receive them. Even if a message is correct by itself, if the querent is not ready for it, their reaction will be to shut off and reject it, and then we would lose contact with them. On the other hand, if we initially soften the messages and put them in a form acceptable for the querent, their trust and openness will grow so that finally we may be able to say things in a more explicit way. If we feel that the querent refuses to accept a specific message, we shouldn't insist on it. When this happens there is no point in asking who is right. Rather, we should drop the issue, go back to the cards, and try another direction.

Of course, throughout the session our attitude should be open and reassuring, accepting and not judging, positive and emphatic. It is important to remember that the reading is not something that happens between us and the cards, with the querent just sitting there hearing our words. Instead, it is a process that the querent goes through, and our task is to guide them in this process according to the hints that we get from the cards. The important thing is not that we give a message that is objectively right, but that the querent leaves the session with a new insight or advice that they can assimilate and apply in a way that will lead to a positive outcome.

As a rule, we should not present things in an absolute and rigid form: "this is the way things are," "such-and-such will happen." This is especially true when we express difficult content. It is important to remember, and to remind the querent when necessary, that what we say is only our personal perception of the cards. They can get useful insights from it, but still it comes from us and reflects our limits, weaknesses, and blind spots. Sometimes it is useful to open a sentence by saying "I think that..." or even "I ask myself whether it's not..." This way we take responsibility for our point of view instead of trying to force it on the querent.

People often come to tarot readings in a situation of difficulty or distress. Sometimes it happens that they express strong feelings during the session; for example, they may start to cry. We should not be afraid of such moments. They show that the querent feels confident enough to open up and that something in the reading has really touched them. Of course, in such a situation we should remain calm, delicate, and supportive, remembering that the querent is in a very vulnerable state. But even if we do have difficult moments during the session, we should remember to finish it in an uplifting tone, empowering the querent and giving them the feeling that they can do something to improve their situation. For this reason, it is better if such emotionally charged moments happen before the last quarter of the meeting, so that we have enough time to finish the session in a positive emotional tone.

Toward the end of the session, it's a good idea to check with the querent whether there are other issues or questions they want to bring out. In principle, one can open new cards for additional questions, but usually I prefer to look again at the cards that are already on the table and interpret them in a new way for the other question. In many cases, I find that the second question, while supposedly dealing with a completely different issue, nevertheless reflects a similar pattern in the querent's life and is therefore connected to the first question.

During the last minutes of the session, we should recap and summarize the main points and insights. It's a good idea to ask the querent for some feedback—how they feel, what they understand from the session, and what they take out with them. If we feel that we're leaving matters in an unfinished state, we should devote a few additional minutes in order to wrap them up properly. For this, we should plan ahead and leave some spare time after the scheduled ending so that we can prolong the meeting if necessary. It's also a good idea to suggest that the querent doesn't return right away to everyday reality. Instead, they may take some time to sit in a quiet, calm place or in a neutral environment such as a café, and work out their emotions about the content and experience of the reading.

WHAT IS THE QUESTION?

Many tarot books attach much importance to the explicit formulation of the question, as if the cards were somehow obliged to answer the exact wording of the query. But as I see it, even if the querent comes to the reading with a clear and precise question, we should regard it only as a starting point. People are not always self-aware enough to know what exactly it is that troubles them. And even if they are, they don't always feel free to reveal it right away during the first minutes of a meeting with a total stranger. In other words, the question that the querent presents at the beginning of the reading is not always the real question that we are supposed to answer in order to help them.

That is why at the beginning of the session I prefer to let the querent present their story as they choose, listen to them, and maybe ask some questions of my own when something seems strange or unclear to me. Eventually we may arrive at a focused question and lay out the cards in order to answer it, but we may also just describe the situation, open the cards, and see where they lead us. While the querent is speaking, I pay attention to the way they present things and interpret it by the rule that everything is a sign. If the querent starts out with a long and detailed story, perhaps the first thing that they need is just someone to listen to them. If the story is complicated and winding, they might be avoiding the real problem and trying to hide it behind a cloud of details. On the other hand, if the querent declines to give us information or challenges us to find out by ourselves what is the matter with them, we should note their closed and defensive attitude and understand it as a need for protection. We will probably have to work hard to gain their confidence, so that they may allow their defenses to be brought down.

We should be suspicious of an all-too-clear and explicit question, as it might be just a cover, hiding the really essential point. For example, a man may ask how he can improve his situation at work or with his life partner. During the reading the question may come up as to whether he wants to remain in his present job or relationship at all. Of course, in such a case we are not supposed to give him a definite yes or no answer, only to open him to new insights on the subject that he can later process with himself. In another instance, a woman may tell us about a business problem, but the reading may show that a family complication is bothering her and not letting her devote her energies to her business. In such a case, the real question is what to do about the family complication.

Many people come for a tarot reading expecting a fortunetelling session, as if the cards are to say what will happen to them. So they may ask a question about future events: When will I get married? Will the business succeed? Will the quarrel end? Taking such a question at face value and giving them a definite answer is usually not productive. Right or wrong, an optimistic prediction may lower the motivation of the querent to make an effort, as they may believe that success is guaranteed. A pessimistic one could also lower their motivation, this time because they may think all is lost anyway. The point is that such questions are formulated in terms of the future only on the surface of things. It is a language in which the querent expresses their present fears and concerns about the future. It is important to calm fears when they arise. But the real question—which has practical consequences—is not about the past or the future but always about the present: what can the querent do now in order to improve their situation?

The querent's reactions at the end of the meeting should also not always be taken at face value. Sometimes it happens that people tell me things like "You didn't tell me much that was new" or "I didn't relate to the message you conveyed." But a few months or years later I meet them by chance, and then it turns out that the reading was meaningful and occupied their thoughts for a long time. In such cases one can hear things like "I didn't understand at the time what came up in the reading, and only a few months later did it dawn on me." It is important to remember that the prospect of real change always arouses real resistance at first. The significant test is over time, after the querent has digested and worked out what came up in the session. Thus, the criterion for a successful and productive reading is not whether the querent comes away from it with an immediate feeling of satisfaction. Rather, it is whether in retrospect they consider it as having been a positive and helpful experience.

CHAPTER 3

READING THE CARDS

In this book I present the open reading, which is my way of reading the tarot cards. The original inspiration for the open reading came from the teachings of Alejandro Jodorowsky, whose lectures and workshops I attended for three years in Paris during the 1980s. Later I developed and added to it from my own ideas and experiences. The open reading approach can be applied to different kinds of cards. But its full potential emerges through the Tarot de Marseille, the product of many centuries of trial and error, adaptation and evolution.

The following three points can summarize the open reading approach and the way in which it differs from more conventional methods. First, a tarot card does not have a fixed meaning that can be learned in advance; rather, the meaning emerges from what we can see in the card during the reading. Second, the function of each position in a spread is also not fixed; rather, it depends on the combination of cards that actually appear. Third, we don't start by interpreting each card separately; instead, we first try to see the whole picture that the cards form together. We shall discuss these points in detail throughout the rest of this chapter.

THE MEANING OF THE CARDS

In the open reading approach, the meaning of a tarot card is what we see in its illustration when we do the actual reading. This means that there is no point in memorizing "the meaning of each card" beforehand. In other words, a tarot card is not a symbol with some fixed meaning that we should retrieve from our memory when we see it in the reading. Instead, it is a visual tool that stimulates our perception and brings up messages from the unconscious part of our mind when we look at it.

Of course, previous knowledge about the cards is useful. The card illustrations are complex and tricky. There are many things in them that we don't notice on first sight, and a good acquaintance with the card details can guide our attention toward them. Also, the symbols in the cards are charged with cultural, philosophical, and mythological meanings. Knowledge about these symbols and their significance, whether in general culture or in different schools of tarot reading, can suggest a wide range of associations when we look at a card. But all this prior knowledge should not limit our ability to see the cards in a fresh perspective each time and to let them lead us in new and unexpected directions.

The important point here is that the cards are a visual tool that works directly on the unconscious layers of our mind. In looking at the cards, what we see reflects what we feel deep inside, but the visual impression that the card makes on us will be different each time. Therefore, the meaning of the card cannot be fixed once and for all. Rather, the visual appearance of a card depends on the whole context of the reading.

Several factors contribute to this difference in visual impression. First, the card looks different when other cards are placed beside it. Second, the querent's presence and query have an emotional effect on us, which influences our ability to see certain things in the card and ignore others. Third, we are also not the same. We come to each reading with a different life experience and in a different emotional state.

To be sure, the fact that the card meaning changes each time does not mean that we shouldn't trust the message that we see in it. As discussed in chapter 2, in each card reading everything is a sign. This includes not only the choice of cards in the spread, but also the fact that this querent chose to come to us at this particular moment. In other words, it is possible that the querent would get a similar answer from a different reader working with different methods. But in such a case, the shuffling would also be different and the answer would come from looking at different cards. The cards tune themselves to the general context of the reading, so to speak, including the previous knowledge and the emotional state that we bring into it.

Even in the course of the same reading, then, our vision of a card can develop. We may give a certain interpretation to a card at the beginning of the reading, and later on in the same session arrive at another deeper and more focused one. We can also see in the same cards a number of parallel stories or parallel layers of a story. In other words, even at a single moment in the reading, a card can have more than one valid meaning.

Jodorowsky helped me understand this important lesson a few years ago when I visited him in Paris. I asked him about the symbolic meaning of various details in the deck he had published with Philippe Camoin. "No problem, Yoav," he said. "Anything that you ask me, I will tell you. But if you ask me again next week, maybe I will tell you something different."

It is important to understand this in the context of this book as well. This is why in the following chapters there may appear to be different interpretations for each card or image detail. The interpretations in the book are possible hints and suggestions that you can follow. But they should serve only as a starting point and not block you from finding your own way. Looking at a card, it can also happen that you have an unexpected insight that is completely original, different from anything you have learned before. Such a spontaneous interpretation, which emerges in the middle of a reading, often turns out to be the most emotionally charged element in the session.

Here are two examples of such spontaneous interpretations that particularly impressed me. A young man had difficulties in his relationship with his girlfriend and wanted to know where it would lead. The main card that drew my attention was the Lover.

The Lover

The common interpretations of the card speak of love or choice. But when I looked at the figure of the man between the two women, one younger and the other older, I felt that the card presented an image of the relationship itself. Often we can see in the card a man who is in a complex relationship, with his female partner on the one hand and with his mother on the other hand. But something in the querent's presence made me approach the image from a slightly different direction. Instead of concentrating on the relationship between the querent and his own mother, I asked him what was happening between him and the girl's mother. His answer was that indeed there was some flirting going on between them, and this caused tensions and quarrels in his relationship with her daughter.

In another instance, a woman told me about the difficulties she was experiencing in different aspects of her life, including her relationships with men. Two cards that appeared side by side attracted my attention: the Star, followed by the Emperor to its right.

Usually the Star is regarded as an expression of sincerity, purity, and innocence, while the Emperor represents a strong and protective figure. But at that particular moment I felt something sinister in the picture of an overpowering man waving his masculine-looking club over a naked and cramped woman. In such matters one should be delicate enough not to pose a direct question, but I threw a hint in the air. The querent caught it and told me that she had been sexually assaulted by a relative at a young age and had never spoken about it.

The Star, The Emperor

Once such a spontaneous interpretation appears, it becomes a part of our collection of tools for future readings. But we should also be careful not to become too attached to it. We should not think of a sexual assault every time we see this card combination. One can see completely different stories in the combination of the same cards. For example, it can represent a woman who allows herself to be exposed and vulnerable because of the protective and confidence-inspiring presence of her partner. But, as we shall see in the next chapter, the gender roles can also be reversed—that is, the masculine figures in the cards may also represent women in real life, and vice versa.

THE BASIC SPREAD

Before we start reading the cards, we must arrange them on the table. For this we have to choose a spread layout. In tarot books and on websites, one can find a huge collection of spreads, some simple and others very complicated. From this collection each reader chooses a small set of several spreads that can be used for different types of questions. Many readers also invent spreads of their own.

In the open reading approach there is no need for large, complicated spreads. The cards' illustrations themselves are rich enough. They offer different aspects and possibilities, especially if one uses the powerful illustrations of the Tarot de Marseille. Too many cards on the table can also distract our attention from a difficult or challenging card, increasing the chances that we will be tempted to ignore it.

As I learned from Jodorowsky, for almost all types of queries we can use a basic spread of three cards out of the twenty-two of the major suit. This is a recommended option, especially for beginning readers who don't yet know the minor suit cards well enough. But many French tarot readers use it throughout their career, feeling that three major cards from the Tarot de Marseille are enough to produce a deep and productive reading. The three cards are laid down in a row from left to right and then read as a story, which normally advances in this direction.

The path Jodorowsky followed in order to reach this minimal spread is interesting. He used to tell how, during his first years with the cards, he started laying out the spreads with more and more cards. Since the cards of one deck were not enough, he would shuffle together three decks. The table soon wasn't large enough anymore, so he started spreading on the floor. He would lay down the cards like a large maze and physically lead the querent through the spread while reading it. But then he realized that there was no end to this process; one could always add more and more cards and still feel that it wasn't enough. Jodorowsky stopped his quest for ever bigger spreads, and afterwards he almost always used the basic spread of three cards from the Marseille major suit.

There are also cases in which a single card is read. For example, in a workshop we can have each participant pick up a card and discuss it with the whole group or with another participant. Also, sometimes in a reading session I ask the querent to draw a single card (usually from the twenty-two majors) in order to clarify a specific point. But in a normal reading session, a single card is usually not enough to describe the various and usually complex aspects of a personal issue.

In many tarot books, a spread layout usually appears as a geometric arrangement of empty frames, each one with a description of what it represents in the reading. For example, in a typical spread layout there may be one position representing the past, another representing the future, other representing the querent's hopes or fears, strengths or weaknesses, the influence of their environment, and so on. As the cards are put down on the table, each one of them is interpreted according to its position. The important point is that in this conventional approach, the function of each position is fixed in advance before the cards are laid out.

In the open reading approach, though, the spread layout is treated differently. It only tells us how many cards to draw and how to arrange them on the table; it does not tell us in advance the function of each position in the spread. Before we see the cards on the table, we can't say what each of them represents: the querent's past or future, weaknesses or strengths, or anything else. Instead of using predefined functions, in the open reading we look at the cards and try to understand the role of each one in relation to the full spread.

For example, when we use the basic three-card spread and read it from left to right, it may happen that the left card would represent the past, the middle card represent the present, and the right card represent the future. Yet in many cases the roles of the cards may be different. Sometimes the figure in the middle is the querent, and the two cards on both sides are two paths, two tendencies, or two possibilities open before them. We can see such a thing in the following spread:

The Devil, Temperance, Justice

Even without knowing the common interpretations of the cards, we can feel the contrast between the Justice card, expressing rigidity and firm structures, and the wild, unruly passions of the Devil card. The figure of Temperance in the middle mixes liquids from two jars. She may be expressing a compromise or a combination of the two elements represented by the two sides: normative and orderly behavior on the one hand, impulsive passions and breaking of rules on the other.

Sometimes one of the cards has a visual presence that stands out among the others. For example, it can be especially colorful and dramatic, or the figures on the other cards may all be looking at its direction. When this happens, it's possible to see the outstanding card as expressing the main issue of the reading, regardless of its position on the right, on the left, or in the middle. We can see something like this in the following spread:

The Tower, The Hermit, The Fool

The Tower card is full of action, color, and drama. Maybe it represents a crisis or some sort of drastic change in the querent's life. In the middle card we see the serene hermit figure looking at the event with a concentrated look, as if trying to figure out its meaning. On the right the fool turns his back to the event and goes away in a new direction.

We can interpret this arrangement from left to right as a timeline: a crisis, then trying to figure out the implications of what happened, and finally embarking on a new path. Yet it may be that all the phases of the process have already occurred, so that the three cards represent the past, or maybe all three speak of a possibility that can happen in the future. Alternatively, we can read the whole sequence not as a time sequence but as a question of choice. In this interpretation what has happened is already there. Now the querent should decide whether to stay fixed on the past, as in the middle card, or to let go of it, put on his shoulder whatever assets that he can take with him, and walk away to find something new.

There are many more ways of reading the basic three-card spread. One can see the middle card as the heart of some issue and the two side cards as two aspects of it. One can follow a traditional language of symbols and see the right card as an active and outgoing factor, the left card as a passive and receiving factor, and the middle card as a combination or compromise between the other two. One can also see the middle card as the querent, the right card as what helps them, and the left card as what obstructs them.

THE FULL PICTURE

Conventional tarot textbooks often present the reading as going from the details to the whole—that is, from the single cards to their combination in the spread. According to this approach, we first interpret each card separately, taking into account its customary interpretation and the predefined role of its position in the spread. Only then do we combine the interpretations of the different cards into a complete answer. In contrast, the open reading advances from the whole to the details. First we try to grasp the full picture formed by the combination of cards. Only then do we proceed to analyze the role of each figure or image detail and its contribution to the whole picture.

This difference is significant, especially in the first minutes of the reading. Sometimes when the cards are laid down we may have a feeling that one of them already gives a definite answer, but it's not a good idea to become fixed on this. When we examine the full picture, things might look different. Instead of searching for the final answer right away, it is better to free our mind, look at the combination of cards in front of us, and try to understand what characterizes the spread as a whole.

The first things that may attract our attention are the human figures. We can start by checking where each figure is looking—in what direction and at what object or figure, whether in its own card or in its neighbor. We note whether the figures are making eye contact or avoiding each other's gaze. We try to figure out what their posture and body language express. They may be moving toward each other or away from each other, or maybe one is trying to get closer but the other is blocking him. We try to feel their emotional attitude toward each other. At this stage we don't need to understand right away how what we see is linked to the querent's story. This may come later.

Another thing to notice is the general composition—that is, lines or surfaces that connect neighboring cards or lead from one card to another. Sometimes an oblong object in one card will continue the line marked by objects in other cards, and sometimes it will block or divert it. The flow lines of objects or surfaces in neighboring cards may approach each other or move away from each other. They may also meet at some point in yet another card. It's a good idea to identify flow lines that cross all the cards in the spread. Such lines may indicate a direction for the whole layout.

Often we can see shapes or surfaces that continue from one card to another. Same-color surfaces in neighboring cards may join to form one shape. Parallel lines of earth or water in one card may meet with similar areas in the next card. The horizon and the ground shapes may continue from one card to another. In other cases we can see cards that are disconnected from each other, such as a card with long vertical lines blocking the flow of lines and surfaces from the neighboring card. This way we can get a feeling about the continuity or the break between the cards.

Apart from such continuing lines and shapes, there are other kinds of links that can connect different cards. Sometimes we can see the same arrangements of figures in different cards; for example, two small figures side by side or one figure above and two figures below it. If such a structure repeats itself in several cards, it may represent different phases or different aspects of the same situation or relationship.

We also can notice repeating numbers of objects; for example, a group of three objects appearing in each card. The objects themselves may be different, but their number and perhaps also their arrangement (for example, in a triangle) will be the same. In such a case we can see the number as indicating something about the spread as a whole. The meaning of this number can be literal if the question involves a quantity, a date, and so on. For example, three objects can represent three children or three months. But it can also be symbolic, in which case we may interpret it using the symbolic language in the next chapter. For example, four objects arranged in a square can indicate a stable structure.

In other cases we may notice connections between the card numbers; for example, a spread with three consecutive numbers, such as 3, 4, and 5. These cards may indicate sequential phases of a process, and it is interesting to compare the order of the card numbers with their ordering in the spread. For example, if the card numbers read from left to right follow each other in an increasing order (3, 4, 5), it signifies an ascent and development; if they form a decreasing series (5, 4, 3), it may mean retreat or decline.

Sometimes we may notice a resemblance between figures in different cards. This may indicate that they represent a single person or maybe different people acting in a similar way. We may also see a similar object appearing, with slight differences, in two or more cards. For example, it can be a wand or a stick that each figure holds, a crown on each figure's head, or common clothing items between the figures. In such a case we can think about the symbolic meaning of the common object. For example, a crown may represent a dominating position (the king of the situation) or perhaps wisdom (stressing the upper head). A wand or a stick may remind us of the suit of wands, which represents activity, desire, and creation, as we shall see in chapter 7. It may also happen that we find similarities in landscape details between the cards, such as a stone structure, a pool of water, or an opening in the ground.

More general characteristics of the figures can also appear in different cards. In one spread we might notice that all the figures are male, and in another spread they may all be female. It may be that in most of the cards the figures are naked, or maybe they are heavily clothed. Maybe most of them are shown in an open space, or maybe they are surrounded by closed and blocking constructions. All the figures may express power and authority or maybe weakness or delicateness. Sometimes all the figures in a spread will be holding some objects in their hands, and sometimes some of them will have their hands empty or hidden.

If the same characteristic appears in all the cards in the spread, it may reflect an important feature of the situation or some essential quality that accompanies the querent in different stages of the process. To give it a meaning, we can rely on the symbolic language outlined in the next chapter, on suggested interpretations appearing elsewhere in this book, or on our own intuition and general knowledge. It's also possible to point it out to the querent and ask them how they feel about it or what it brings to their mind.

Some Examples

Here are some examples of the basic three-card spread and its interpretation in the open reading approach. Of course, the story given here is not the only possible way of reading each card combination. It may be a good exercise to look at the spreads yourself and to give them your own alternative interpretations.

The Sun, The Empress, The Magician

The Empress figure at the center may be a married woman, whose children appear in the left-hand card. The sun above them can represent the father of the family: leading and providing but also "in the sky"—that is, remote and not really accessible. Maybe he is too busy with his career or other occupations and doesn't find the time and energy to invest in close emotional contact with his wife and children.

A young man now appears in her life, represented by the Magician on the right. He is light-spirited and avoids commitment, as the fancy clothing and the legs spread to both sides indicate. But as an illusion-weaving showman he may also have personal charm and courting tricks. His stare at her body indicates that he is interested in a sexual relationship with her.

The sitting position in the well-protected chair shows that, at this stage, she remains loyal to the family framework. She embraces the eagle coat-of-arms, which is a symbol of the royal family, and holds her scepter as a barrier in front of the new man's face. But her eyes directed toward him indicate that the attraction is mutual, and the white scepter handle based on her pelvis can suggest an open way in which her desire can move forward. We can conclude that if the woman's husband doesn't wake up to give her more attention, it is likely that, sooner or later, she will succumb to the young man's advances.

The Pope, The Moon, The Sun

The Pope in the left-hand card can represent a teacher or a father, and the two small figures seen from behind may be two students or children. His attention isn't divided equally between them, and it seems as if it is more oriented toward the one on the right. Perhaps one of the brothers feels rejected, not getting as much of their father's attention as his brother.

In the upper part of the middle card we see the moon replacing the Pope. Maybe the father figure has died and now he is "in heaven." In his absence, strong animal-like emotions of jealousy and mutual resentment arise between the brothers, represented by the two dogs barking at each other. The crustacean at the bottom of the card can indicate deep and dark feelings rising to the surface. The moon face looking toward the first card can indicate that the present relationship is still motivated by past emotions.

The card on the right can be seen as a reparation of the fraternal relationship. The two figures are once again human. Their mutual touch expresses warmth and trust, and the mythological father figure in the sky is shining light equally on both of them. It is as though they have overcome their jealousy and the old competition for the deceased father's attention, understanding that both did, in fact, benefit from it.

The following story appeared some years ago on an Internet tarot forum. A woman who described herself as a devoted employee in a big organization found herself the object of her immediate boss's attentions. He was a married man, and she had no romantic interest in him. She felt confused, blamed herself for the situation, and wondered whether she should give in to his advances or look for another job. In her distress she drew three cards from a full deck (including the major and the minor suits) and asked the forum members for advice. She didn't say which deck she was using, and probably it was not the Tarot de Marseille. Still, I felt that a significant answer could emerge from the Marseille counterparts of her cards. These were:

Judgment, The World, 8 of Coins

Looking at the World card in the center, and in spite of her own subjective feeling of helplessness, I could see her as the active figure in the spread. The dancing posture indicated that even within the limited space available to her, she can still find freedom to maneuver. As to the two objects in her hands, these may represent two options that she can put in front of her boss.

The Judgment card on the left, with a trumpet whose sound is heard far and wide, represents one option. The central figure seen from the back is rising from a hole in the ground, possibly indicating hidden things being revealed in broad daylight. The dramatic character of the card shows what will happen if she chooses this option: to blow the whistle and make a public scandal. It would surely hurt him and possibly ruin his career.

The other option is represented by the card on the right with a solid and regular pattern of coins, possibly representing the ongoing routine of a workplace. The pairs of coins layered on top of each other may also symbolize an office building or simply the orderly structure of management and subordination in a big organization. In this option everything returns to normal: no more harassment, no ruining of career and personal life, everyone goes back to work as if nothing ever happened.

My advice was that she let him realize this perspective, not by making an explicit menace but by giving a clear hint that now it is she who has power over him. His own fears would do the rest and make him go for the second option. As the querent later wrote in the same forum, this is exactly what happened.

When I do consultations at home, I usually put enlarged copies of the cards on a board behind me so that the querent can see them and understand what I am talking about. Often I leave the cards on the board after the reading, and later when I look at them I can see meanings for myself. It is in this way that I got the following combination of cards. It appeared when I was mourning the loss of an old friend who died while I was preparing this book. My feelings and my thoughts were occupied with heavy questions about the meaning that we may find in our life and about the role of choice and giving.

Temperance, The World, The Lover

The dancing figure appears again in the center of the spread, but now all the other elements in the cards surround it in what looks like layers over layers. This image may represent the innermost part of our being, from which we make the meaningful choices in life. On the left we see a self-centered figure who lives only by and for herself, keeping others at a distance and guarding her personal space with her elbows. The two pots she is holding can symbolize the pot of resources and the pot of needs. The figure pours from the first pot into the second, fulfilling her own desires and needs while leading a comfortable life of self-gratification. But as she becomes older the pot of resources diminishes and the pot of needs becomes heavier. Eventually a moment comes when the resources are insufficient to fill up the needs, and then there is no real reason to prefer life over death.

On the right we can see a man standing between two women. His head is turned toward one of them, but the rest of his body leans toward the other one. He may be hesitating over which one to choose, and Cupid's arrow from above indicates that he really loves the one on his right. She has her hand on her belly, which may indicate a future pregnancy and the formation of a family. But for this to happen he must forgo the other woman—that is, to make a choice, to commit himself, and to pay a price. This is the kind of commitment that we can take for the sake of a life partner, a child, or maybe another person or cause that we really care about. It requires us to give up the fulfillment of some of our needs and desires. But in such a situation, if we die, this will cause sorrow and pain to people that we are committed to. This feeling can provide us with a good enough motivation to go on living.

Finally, during the restoration work on the CBD Tarot de Marseille, I printed a draft copy of the final version of the cards. The first spread I did to inaugurate the cards was about the CBD deck itself. I was wondering what the cards could tell me about themselves and about the process of making them.

Judgment, The Magician, The Popess

The Magician, who brings his tools in a bag and spreads them on the table, looks like an artisan, but not an accomplished one: the young face and the number 1 indicate a beginning stage. This reflects how I felt. I had brought my previous knowledge and tools to the process, but now I was trying to apply them in a domain of graphic design and printing that was new to me.

The Judgment card on the left, receiving the gaze and attention of the figures in the other cards, could represent the restoration process. The figure in light blue rising from the earth, hinting at the Christian resurrection of the dead, may be Conver's deck again coming to life in a new body of paper and color. The man and the woman on each side may be the female illustrator and the male graphic designer who worked for me, while the angel above may represent the feeling that accompanied me, as if the project was not really directed by my own decisions and preferences. At key moments things would happen beyond my control, compelling me to change direction—and, in retrospect, I could see that these changes were always productive and necessary. So, in my feeling, the angel could represent the "spirit of the cards" guiding things and making choices that proved better than those I could make on my own.

The Popess appears in the right-hand position, which normally represents the future. But her coverings and the veil behind her hint at mystery and things unknown. Maybe it's simply the uncertainties about outcomes—how the deck of cards will look in the final print, what feelings it will awaken in people, and what they will do with it. But maybe it is also about the mystery of the cards themselves, whose magical power still continues to enchant me after this experience of plunging into them as they break up into a myriad of surfaces, lines, and pixels. And finally, the book in the Popess's hands could be just the tarot deck itself, which is put in front of anyone who wishes to read it and to get hints about what is hidden behind the veil.

INVERSE CARDS

Except for some of the number cards in the minor suits, most of the Tarot de Marseille cards are not vertically symmetrical. This means that there is a clear difference between a card that is straight (with the earth below and the sky above) and an inverse card (the other way around). There are several approaches to inverse cards. Some tarot readers ignore the matter altogether and read all the cards as straight. For beginners, this is often a recommended way. However, more advanced readers may prefer the broader range of possibilities and nuances that inverse cards may offer.

Fortunetelling methods sometimes adopt the opposite approach and regard the inversion of a card as an inversion of its meaning. For example, if it's a card whose straight meaning is deprivation or failure, then inverse it will signify abundance or success. This approach is problematic if we consider the visual aspect of the card. For example, a card with heavy atmosphere and dark colors does not become happy and bright when inverted.

In the open reading approach, the inversion of cards can be interpreted at several levels of meaning. The first level is similar to the way many tarot books treat the subject. When a card appears inverse we shall read it as the same factor working in the opposite direction, which is contrary to the querent's wishes or interests. This means that the inversion stresses the less positive aspects of the card.

In the lists of card meanings offered later in this book, I include a number of possible interpretations for each card, some of which are favorable or positive, while others are challenging or negative. When the card is inverse we can put more weight on the challenging and negative aspects. For example, if the figure on the Star card spills her water to the ground, it may indicate overflowing generosity and abundance. In an inverse card we may interpret it as wastefulness and squandering.

While this approach may be useful, we may feel that it is still too formal and doesn't relate to the most basic fact about inverse cards: when a card is inverse, it looks different. Therefore, to go deeper into the meaning of an inverse card, we need to consider the visual effect of its inversion.

An important visual change in the inverse card is in the relation between the sky and the ground. The white sky in the Tarot de Marseille gives an impression of openness and lightness, which is made weaker when the ground is on top. In addition, the reversal changes the visual flow lines of the card image, and this can also create a different impression. For example, the Moon card in a straight position generally has a heavy and closed character, but the image still suggests an upward movement. When the card is inverse, the earth and the pool above intensify the feeling of heaviness and closeness, and now the movement is downward. This may strengthen the association of the card with hard and depressive feelings.

The Moon (inverse), Force (inverse)

A card inversion also changes the symbolic relation between the top and the bottom. For example, in the Force card we see a woman's head above and a lion's head touching the woman's pelvis below. We can interpret this image as the intellect (head) controlling the animal desires and impulses (pelvis, lion). When the card is inverted the animal is on top, and this may indicate that the querent's desires are more dominant than their rational self-control.

An inverse card also plays a different role in the full picture. A figure facing right in a straight card will face left when the card is inverse, so that its gaze and posture will relate differently to figures in other cards. The flow of lines and shapes between neighboring cards will also be affected by the inversion. To appreciate these changes it is useful to turn the card around to the straight position and compare the two situations.

An important point to remember is that straight and inverse are only a matter of perspective. When we look at an inverse card from the opposite side, it looks straight. For example, if I see a spread with all or most of the cards inverted, I often interpret it as a need for the querent to change their attitude or point of view so as to see the cards from the other side. Looking at things in a new perspective, the same factors can now be going with them and not against them.

An interesting situation is the appearance of cards with figures that are originally drawn upside down. These are the major cards of the Hanged Man, the Tower, and one of the figures in the Wheel of Fortune. If we identify such a figure with the querent and one of the other cards is inverse, then from the querent's unique point of view that card is straight. In other words, what others see as a disadvantage, the querent can see as an advantage.

When inverse cards appear in the reading, it is not necessarily a negative thing. The card is already there on the table, and we can simply stretch our hand and straighten it. In other words, the factor or influence represented by the card is already present in the querent's life. There is no need to bring in new elements. Instead, the querent can try to turn around the existing elements so that they work in the querent's favor.

An inverse card can thus indicate a point where the querent can improve their situation with resources that they already have available. This makes inverse cards especially meaningful. During the reading I usually straighten up inverse cards one by one in order to understand what changes the querent can make in their life and how things will look if they do so. We can see such a thing in the following example:

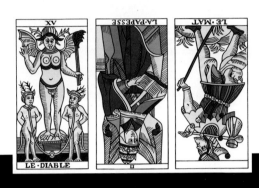

The Devil, The Popess (inverse), The Fool (inverse)

The Devil card on the left may symbolize a particular kind of romantic relationship. It is full of passions and desires, but at the bottom lies a dark underground level. The two little imps tied at their necks can symbolize the partners in the relationship, who cannot break their mutual bond even if they feel it is unhealthy. The Popess can be a woman with high abilities and intelligence, but inverse she lowers herself and sees herself as weak. The many covers around the figure may express disconnection and enclosure in an inner, secret world of her own. The inverse Fool card describes the confusion and the loss of direction she feels, her gaze fixed on the relationship from which she can't detach herself.

LE·DIABLE   LA·PAPESSE   LE·MAT

When we straighten the Popess card, though, she becomes aware of her strengths. Now she looks at the relationship from a position of comprehension and some detachment. The closed character of the card may now express that she is able to keep up her boundaries. The Fool card, when straightened, shows the possibility of leaving the problematic relationship behind and embarking on a new path. We can understand that for this to be possible, the querent should first straighten the middle card and try to improve her own self-esteem.

A technical matter, yet an important one, is how to get inverse cards from the shuffle. There are different ways of doing this, and here is mine. After I take the cards out of their box, I shuffle them in my hands. Every now and then I stop, split the deck into two parts, and rotate one of them so as to invert the orientation of the cards. Having done that, I recombine the two parts into one pack again. I continue to shuffle, stopping once again to split and rotate one part. I repeat this several times. Now I hand the deck to the querent and ask them to do the same: to shuffle, invert one part, shuffle again, and so on, until they feel they have had enough.

If the querent is sitting in front of me, as is usually the case, then when they hand back the cards I consider them as straight or inverse from their point of view. However, as I take the cards from them, I see the cards from the opposite side. In order to see the cards from the querent's perspective, I invert the whole deck once again, and only then do I draw the cards. I take care to draw the querent's attention to this action. The reason for this is not to let them be confused seeing the cards from the other side while I speak of the cards as straight or inverse.

CHAPTER 4

THE SYMBOLIC LANGUAGE

Each card in the tarot deck is unique, but there are common elements that reappear in different cards. To be consistent in our interpretation we need a symbolic language that gives meaning to these elements. For example, what is the significance of the color red? How do we interpret the number three (as a card number or as the number of objects)? What do the right and left sides of the card represent? What is the meaning of animal figures?

New decks from the twentieth century are often based on a symbolic language that can be learned from books or other written sources. For example, when Waite or Crowley designed their tarot decks, they also published books explaining the significance of various symbols in the cards. But the Tarot de Marseille evolved for many centuries in the hands of many people who left no written records about its meaning. Therefore, we don't have direct access to its original symbolic language. We have to figure it out for ourselves.

To construct a consistent symbolic language for the Tarot de Marseille we can rely on several sources. First, many symbols in the tarot also appear in other works of art from the medieval and Renaissance periods. It is likely that they kept much of their original significance when transferred to the tarot cards. Second, there are various spiritual and cultural traditions that give meanings to symbolic elements that appear in the cards (for example, colors, numbers, or animal figures). Third, we can profit from the experience and insights gained through more than two centuries of tarot interpretation by many authors. And last but not least, we can each rely on our own intuition and feelings, taking the cards themselves as our guide.

In the following sections I present the main elements of a symbolic language that can be applied to the Tarot de Marseille: directions, colors and shades, numbers, figures and body parts. Since the Tarot de Marseille is the original basis for almost all other tarot decks in use today, many elements in this symbolic language can fit other decks as well.

Before we continue, a word about cultural and ethnic biases. The Tarot de Marseille deck is a product of the Renaissance and early modern Europe. As such, its illustrations reflect the biases and limitations typical of this particular culture. For example, religious symbols are Catholic, couple relationships are heterosexual, "flesh color" is a reddish tone of beige, warrior figures are male, and so on. To understand the card symbols as originally intended, we have to consider them from a point of view that takes these biases for granted. However, when using the cards, we should look for the broader meaning behind them and adapt it to the particular circumstances of the querent. For example, we may interpret the Catholic symbols as representing the religious or spiritual aspirations of the querent, whatever their religious affiliation might be. We shall elaborate more on this point later on, when we discuss male and female figures in the cards.

Directions

LEFT AND RIGHT

The horizontal axis that goes from left to right is marked in the card illustrations by the ground surface, and so it brings to mind the earthly reality of everyday life. Movement along this axis can represent the sequence of events in our lives, from childhood to old age. This raises the question of time and its direction along the horizontal axis: is the past on the left and the future on the right or vice versa?

To answer this question we can turn to the cards themselves. Among the major suit cards there are two that are exceptional: the Fool and the card numbered 13. All the other major cards have both a name and a number written on them, but the Fool has no number and card 13 has no name. Note that although the illustrations are quite different, the two figures have a similar posture.

The Fool, Card 13

As we shall see in the detailed card descriptions of chapter 6, these two cards can represent two aspects of the concept of time: the moment of the present and the timeline of events. The Fool appears to be living only in the here and now. Thus, he can symbolize the present moment: always between the past and the future, always on the move. In contrast, card 13 expresses the timeline of history; that is, the sequence of events in which everything is born, lives, and dies in order to clear the ground for new things. In both cards the figures walk to the right. If they represent our movement in time, from the past to the future, it means that the past is on the left and the future is on the right. We can notice that the French script on the cards also goes from left to right, and consider that for people used to reading in European languages, movement in this direction appears natural.

This idea of movement from left to right can be applied both to the image of a single card and to the ordering of several cards in a spread. In a single card a figure walking, looking, or pointing to the right is oriented toward the future, while a figure looking to the left of the card is referring to the past. We can also think of the right direction as expansion and moving out, while the left represents retraction and drawing in. In a spread we read the cards as a story that goes from left to right. The cards on the left speak of what came before, and the cards on the right speak of what comes after.

In speaking of the arrangement of objects and figures relative to the card frame, this interpretation of left and right is clear. But when we consider a human figure in the card illustration, another question arises: which side of the figure is the right one and which is the left? For example, if the figure is shown facing us, should we consider it like a real person (so that her right hand is on our left side) or rather like a reflection of ourselves in the mirror (so that his right hand is on our right side)?

This question is significant if we want to interpret the sides of the body according to the traditional symbolism of right and left. The right side of the body is taken to represent hardness, action, and initiative. The left side represents softness, reception, and containment. So, which side of the figure represents action and which one represents reception?

We can get hints about this question from three major cards that show traditional symbols connected with body sides. As we shall see in chapter 6, the lower part of the Lover card probably refers to a mythological story about Hercules standing between a younger woman and an older woman. According to the legend, the older woman stood to his right. But in the card illustration the older woman is on the left side. This is like a person standing in front of us, not like a mirror.

A similar conclusion can be drawn from the Justice and the Pope cards. In sculptures and paintings of the Justice figure, such as can be seen in courts today, it is holding a sword in its right hand and a balance in its left hand. In the illustration of the Justice card, the sword appears on the left side and the balance on the right side. The Pope figure makes the Latin gesture of benediction with two straight fingers, which is done in the Catholic tradition using the right hand, yet the hand making the gesture is on the left side of the card. Thus, in all three cards we see the left and the right sides of the body as if it was a real person in front of us. We can assume that the same holds true for other cards as well.

The Lover, Justice, The Pope

UP AND DOWN

The traditional shape of the tarot cards is a narrow rectangle. In the Conver and the CBD decks, the proportion between the sides is almost exactly two to one, like two squares standing on top of each other. This shape suggests the idea of dividing the card area into a top and a bottom part, giving each one of them a specific meaning. In the actual card illustrations we can see such a division, not exactly into two equal parts but still present. But as we go over the suit cards, we can see this division taking two distinct forms.

Most of the cards at the beginning of the major suit show a large figure filling the card. Around the middle of its height there usually appears a clear horizontal line or stripe dividing it into a top and bottom part. As we shall see later when we discuss the significance of body parts, the top part can represent the higher functions of reason and emotion, while the bottom part can represent the basic or lower functions of body and desire. Thus, the way in which the two parts of the figure relate to each other can represent the relation between the higher and lower functions in the querent's life.

Most of the cards in the last part of the suit show a different division of the vertical axis. At the bottom of the card there is some happening taking place on the ground, while the top shows some object in the air or in the sky. The relationship between these parts can be interpreted as an encounter or a link between the earthly reality at the bottom and a celestial or higher reality at the top. We can understand this as some connection with superior levels of being; for example, getting messages or protection from above. It can also be a representation of heaven and what it stands for: superior good, happiness, charity, spirituality, enlightenment.

In some cards of the major suit there is also a third level: an abyss that appears as an opening in the ground or as a black surface at the bottom of the card. The abyss may represent deep forces acting in the unconscious mind, hidden dark passions, or something secret buried under the ground. When the abyss is black we can interpret it as pain, fears, or traumatic memories of past experiences in the querent's life or family history. It can also be interpreted as difficult or unresolved issues from past incarnations.

The vertical axis is therefore manifest in the arrangement of three layers, one on top of the other: the abyss, or hell; the earth; and the sky, or heaven. We can take this to be its basic significance, even though in most of the cards only one or two of the three layers appear. Thus, in contrast with the "external" horizontal axis, the vertical axis can represent inner experience—how the querent feels emotionally and spiritually. For example, a card illustration that suggests a movement going down can indicate difficult and heavy feelings, while going up represents lightness, optimism, and happiness. A possible exception is the vertical axis in the number cards, as we shall discuss in chapter 10.

The combination of the two axes is also meaningful. Sometimes we can notice a diagonal flow line going through a single card or perhaps passing between several cards in a spread. Such a line can be perceived in the arrangement of eye-catching image details, in the orientation of colored shapes or lined areas, in oblong objects directed along it, and so on. If such a diagonal line goes from the bottom left to the top right, it is ascending: as time advances in the right direction, the line is rising. Thus, it may indicate a positive direction of improvement and advancement. In contrast, a diagonal line leading from the top left to the bottom right marks a descent with time, thereby indicating recession and decline.

COLORS

The colors of the cards have a great impact on the emotional effect that they produce in us. Bright colors give the card a light and happy character, while dark colors make it heavy and grim. Warm colors create an atmosphere of action and movement or, when restrained, of human contact and feeling. Cold colors suggest calmness, withdrawal, and emotional distance. Colors also have a great impact on the visual connections between cards. Areas with the same color in neighboring cards may continue each other and thus bring together the separate cards into one image. This effect is especially strong in the Tarot de Marseille, where the cards are painted with a restricted scale of uniform, basic colors that easily join across different cards.

To compensate for the limited color scale, which was made necessary by the stencil coloring technique, traditional tarot card makers introduced a distinction between clear areas, which are plain colored, and shaded areas covered with parallel black lines in addition to their coloring. There are several lining patterns for the shaded areas, and each can be given its own meaning.

Sometimes the lines are short and cover only one side of a colored shape, which is thus divided into a shaded part and a clear part. The shaded side may represent a dark or hidden aspect of an issue, while the clear side may represent a lit and visible aspect. Other areas, such as ground formations, bodies of water, and also some objects, are filled with long parallel lines. When the lines are wavy they may express flow, movement, and instability. When they are straight they may indicate something solid and stable. Straight lines can also suggest an artificial object or tilled land, that is, something on which work has been done.

In various versions of the Tarot de Marseille there are usually between seven and ten colors (including the white background and the black printed lines). In the Conver and the CBD tarot decks there are eight basic colors: white, black, red, blue, yellow, green, light blue, and flesh color. The black and white naturally appear in all the cards, but some of the painted colors are used only in part of the deck. With few exceptions, the major suit and the court cards show all the eight colors. The number cards are painted only in yellow, red, and light blue. The aces in the coins and cups suits have yellow, red, light blue, and green, to which the aces of wands and swords add the flesh color.

In the CBD deck there are additional color effects that I have introduced for various reasons. In some of the original Conver cards two colors are painted one on top of the other. For example, yellow is painted over black at the bottom part of card 13, and light blue over yellow (which creates a greenish tone) in the Ace of Coins and the Ace of Cups. To reproduce a similar effect with the modern printing techniques, I used a computer-colored texture.

I also added a lighter shade of flesh color. In the original Conver deck many of the faces and some hands were left white—that is, without coloring. However, the contrast between flesh color and the white paper is much stronger in modern printing techniques. Leaving these faces white would have made them weird and lifeless. On the other hand, I didn't want to lose Conver's distinction between the white faces on some of the cards and the flesh-colored faces on other cards. My solution was to do the originally white faces in a lighter shade of flesh color, which may express a more detached and less emotional attitude.

It is interesting to note that in the complete deck, the painted colors (that is, except black or white) are present in different amounts. The total area of shapes colored in yellow is by far the greatest. This is followed by red, light blue, flesh color, green, and blue. We can see that the warm and active colors, yellow and red, are the most common, while the cold and calm colors, green and blue, are the rarest. If this choice was motivated by artistic and not by practical considerations (for example, an excessively high price of the blue pigment at that time), we can understand that Conver wanted to give his cards a warm and dynamic character, rather than cool and absorbing.

In the symbolic language framework, each color in the cards can be given a specific meaning. The following list of meanings for the eight colors of the Conver and CBD decks is derived from various sources, including traditional and modern art, mystical theories, and tarot writings. I have also added a correspondence of the eight colors to a model of eight elements. This extends the classic model of four elements in Greek and medieval cosmology. The eight elements are light, darkness, earth, fire, water, air, vegetable, and animal.

WHITE: The source and the unification of all colors, suggesting light from a superior source and pure spirituality. As the background color of the cards, it represents an open space of possibilities, the undefined and the limitless. In the card illustrations it appears as the color of the sky, symbolizing high and benevolent levels of existence beyond the material world. Details in white appearing in an image represent purity and innocence, an idealistic action, or remoteness from practical reality. It can also express feelings of superiority, emotional frigidity, or a lack of life energy.

black: Appears on all the cards as the illustration lines, which define the concrete and limited aspect of the image details. In some cards there are also surfaces painted in full black. They can express shaded aspects of reality or dark layers of the soul, such as the depths of the subconscious, past traumas, or feelings of pain and distress. In the symbolic language of alchemy black is the color of the basic matter, which is refined in order to become the philosopher's stone. In this respect, black surfaces can represent the starting point for a process of development leading from darkness to the light.

yellow: A bright color that gives the cards a warm, illuminated, and optimistic feeling. In the tarot tradition it usually symbolizes intelligence applied to practical needs. Yellow coloring of objects such as crowns, cups, and coins may suggest that they are made of gold. As such, it can symbolize material success and plenty or an active and beneficial force, as in the alchemical symbolism of metals. In many cards the ground appears in yellow, as if it is illuminated by sunlight. This may represent a blessing coming from above or favorable conditions for growth and advancement. Yellow signifies the element of earth.

red: A strong and dynamic color, full of passion and energy, red expresses activity and movement, the power of instincts and desires, outward-oriented action, or anger and aggression. Red is connected with the planet Mars in astrology, with iron in alchemy, and with war gods in various cultures. It can represent combativeness, assertiveness, or courage in front of challenges. Red signifies the element of fire.

BLUE: A deep and calm color, blue appears in the cards as the opposite of red. It symbolizes attraction and inbound movement, the ability to contain and to accept, submission to circumstances, self-reflection, intuitive understanding, or empathy and compassion. The color blue in a card can also symbolize deep feelings and sentiments that are difficult to express in clear words. Blue signifies the element of water.

light blue: The color of the sky, a lighter degree of blue indicates a combination of matter and spirituality. It can also express clarity and transparency, truth and honesty, but also coldness and detachment. One can see in it a symbol of a wider, more comprehensive perspective or an action that rises above petty and selfish considerations. Light blue symbolizes the element of air.

green: The color of plants, the vegetable element representing growth and change, green hints at nature and natural things. Green may represent an impulse of growth and development, a potential for fertility, a new beginning, or a simple, unsophisticated vision of reality.

flesh color: A reddish tone of beige expresses what is alive and human. It may represent the body, sensuality, animal drives, or the fulfillment of physical needs. Also, as the animal element, it can represent motion and sources of movement. As the color of the naked body, it may also represent openness, exposure, or vulnerability. A flesh-colored object may represent something that is part of the querent's identity or personality.

NUMBERS

A number can appear in a tarot card in several ways. It can be the serial number of a card in the major suit (for example, card 4, the Emperor) or in a minor suit (for example, the 6 of Wands). It can be the number of a group of objects or the details in a card illustration, such as three windows in the Tower card, two cups in the Temperance card, or seven little stars in the Star card. A card may also show a geometric shape expressing a number, such as a triangle representing the number three or a square representing the number four.

There are various methods of attaching meanings to numbers, a practice known as numerology. Most of the Western systems of numerology derive from the ideas of the ancient Greek mathematician Pythagoras. In the Pythagorean system the even numbers are considered feminine, stable, and containing, while the odd numbers (except for number one) are masculine, forward-moving, and active. The number one is considered the root of all numbers, so it represents a unity beyond the opposition of male and female.

Mathematical relations between numbers are also related to their meaning in numerology. For example, four is two times two, which stresses the stable character of the even numbers. Thus, four can symbolize the stability of matter. The number six is the multiplication product of the first feminine number (two) and the first masculine number (three). In Pythagoras's system this is a symbol of marriage, so six may represent harmony and integration of opposites.

There are other numerological systems, and some of them have been applied to the tarot. For example, several tarot decks of the English school are based on the Golden Dawn system, which gave the numbers additional meanings connected with Cabbalistic symbolism and the Hebrew alphabet. The major suit of the tarot can also serve as a numerological source because for each number we can attach the meaning of the corresponding major card. For example, if we ask ourselves about the meaning of the number three, we may think about the Empress, which is number three in the major suit.

The numbers between one and ten are considered most significant, and higher numbers are often regarded as a repetition of the basic ten. Several tarot authors accept this vision and regard, for example, the Devil card (number 15) as a more complex aspect of the Pope card (number 5). Yet sometimes numbers larger than ten can have their own distinct identity. For example, twelve is the number of zodiac signs—that is, a full cycle that goes through all possibilities. The number thirteen adds another unit, so it represents a disruption of the cycle and an opening to a new and uncertain domain.

Combining elements from various systems of numerology, here is a list of meanings for the first ten numbers that can be used in tarot readings. Some numbers also have typical geometric forms associated with them.

ONE: The basic unit, root of all numbers. As the beginning of the number series, one opens every process, thereby containing its whole course as a potential. It can also represent wholeness and the union of opposites. The geometric shape associated with it is a point, which represents concentration and focus, especially when it appears at the center of a circle. In the major suit the number one is the Magician, which opens the suit and also expresses the individuality of the single person. In a minor suit it is the ace card, which represents a beginning, a drive, or an action in the suit's domain.

Two: Opposition, duality, polarity. It can represent a partnership or a romantic relationship, a conflict between two elements, or a quandary between two options. The tension between the poles has a potential of generating movement, but due to the static nature of the even number it does not happen yet. In the Chinese tradition the number two represents the complementary elements yin and yang, the feminine/passive and the masculine/active. In the major suit it is the Popess with a screen dividing the world into two parts, revealed and hidden. Two points, two objects, or two parallel lines in a card express a pair of opposites. These may be active and passive when side by side or heavenly and earthly when one is above the other.

Three: The third unit breaks the stalemate of the number two and adds movement and creation. The number three represents dynamism, flow, fertility, and the forces of nature. In many cultures it is a number associated with sorcery, such as a conjuration formula repeated three times. Its corresponding shape is the equilateral triangle, but it can also be represented by three parallel horizontal lines, symbolizing the abyss, the earth, and the sky. Three objects or three points may represent a movement toward realization. In the major suit it is the Empress, often associated with fertility and growth. In the Christian tradition it also hints at the Holy Trinity, thus representing a divine presence in the material world.

Four: Solid, stable, secure, and conservative. It represents material, earthly, and tangible things, practical considerations, and the structure of established systems or institutions. It also symbolizes matter (the four elements of earth, water, air, and fire) and physical space (the four cardinal directions). Its typical shape is a square, with a stable base securely resting on the ground. In the major suit the number four is the Emperor, expressing domination in the physical world. Four objects in a card can represent a practical realization or the act of reaching a tangible goal. One can also see them as symbolizing the four minor suits, representing balanced achievements in different life domains.

Five: The odd unit breaks the stable structure of the number four and adds to it something from another plane. This can represent a disruption of a stable and secure structure, but also the opening up of a new dimension. The corresponding shape is a five-pointed star with two possible positions. When the tip points upward, it represents the figure of a human being (head, two arms, two legs) and serves as a magical symbol with a benign influence. When the tip points downward, it can represent negative forces and black magic. Five is also represented by a square-based pyramid, with four corners on the ground and one apex in a higher plane. In the major suit it is the Pope, acting within an earthly establishment but pointing to a higher spiritual level. The number five also symbolizes the structure of the tarot deck itself, with one major and four minor suits.

Six: The number six expresses harmony, as a union of opposite factors (2 x 3) or as a combination of two complementary processes (3 + 3). The Pythagoreans called it a perfect number because it is equal to the sum of all its divisors (1 + 2 + 3). In the Cabbala it is identified with Tiferet, the center of the Sefirot Tree, representing the ten aspects of the Divine. The shape representing it is the Star of David, which is a fusion of two complementary triangles. In the major suit it is the Lover, expressing a romantic relationship and also a harmony between human choices on earth and the decree of heaven.

Seven: As 6 + 1, the number seven creates a new movement out of the harmony of six, yet as 4 + 3 it expresses a combination of material stability and the energy of motion. Thus, it has a mysterious and sometimes confusing character, with an unsolved inner opposition between abundance and success, on the one hand, and disruptive instability on the other hand. Such an opposition is expressed by the Chariot card, with a square structure enclosing the triangular shape of the rider's head and arms. The inner tension of the number seven can also have a productive aspect, opening up a whole spectrum of possibilities, such as the seven colors of the rainbow, the seven days of the week, the seven metals in alchemy, or the seven planets in ancient astrology.

Eight: The different combinations of two and four (2 x 2 x 2, 2 + 2 + 2 + 2, 4 x 2, 4 + 4) bring together the dividing aspect of the number two, with the ability to distinguish between opposites, and the solid framework of the number four. Thus, eight can represent rational constructions, well-defined systems of rules and laws, discerning and going into detail, or long and patient work needed to build a stable structure. In the major suit it is the Justice card, whose upper part suggests a logical and stern framework with straight lines and right angles.

Nine: A combination of dynamic processes (3 x 3 and also 3 + 3 + 3) that express complexity, a variety of possibilities, and movement that does not proceed in one clear direction. The number nine is also almost ten, so it expresses a strive to perfection but also an inability to reach this goal completely. In the major suit it is the Hermit card, which expresses a spiritual quest and self-examination. It can also hint at a reality beyond the senses and is related to intuition and mysticism.

Ten: As the basis for the number system, ten stands for a totality or culmination. In the Cabbala it symbolizes the Tree of Sefirot, which are the ten aspects of the Divine. Ten represents the final outcome of the evolution, which starts with the number one, and the opening of a new cycle of numbers. As 5 + 5 it can represent a combination of both good and bad, like a cyclical process that involves both ascent and decline. In the major suit it is the Wheel of Fortune, which expresses the completion of a cycle and a return to the starting point.

FIGURES

Human figures appear in the major suit cards and in the court cards of the minor suits. It is interesting to note the difference in gender representation between these two parts of the deck. In the court cards of each suit there are three men and one woman. This can reflect the fact that the minor suits have developed separately, and their court cards are modeled after the traditional power structures of society.

In contrast, the major suit shows no clear preference of men over women. There is even some balance between masculine and feminine roles, such as the Emperor and the Empress or the Popess and the Pope. The equal status of the two genders can look surprising if we remember that the major suit cards were designed in a very conservative era. Still, the opposition of male and female is a basic feature of most traditional symbolic systems. We can assume that although the creators of the major suit cards didn't show a basic preference to either side, they did have such an idea and sought to express what each of the two genders symbolized.

In many of the traditional systems the masculine side, or the yang element as it is called in Chinese culture, is regarded as active, firm, moving forward, and outgoing. The feminine side, or the yin element, is regarded as passive, gentle, containing, and inward oriented. This opposition, which may be inspired by the shape and function of the sex organs, is reflected in traditional symbolic systems by other pairs of opposites: right and left, the sky and the earth, the sun and the moon, the rational and the emotional, the lighted and the shaded. With some exceptions (for example, a male moon god and a female sun goddess in Japan), the first element in each of the pairs is generally regarded as masculine, while the second element is regarded as feminine.

We can also note that three cards of the major suit show a pair of human (or semihuman) figures that look like male and female. These are the severed heads in card 13, the little imps in the Devil card, and the two parental figures in the Judgment card. In all three the figure on the right is masculine, while the figure on the left is feminine. This may suggest that tarot symbolism also accepts the identification of the right side as male and of the left side as female.

Card 13, The Devil, Judgment

Still, there may be some deeper structure of male-female interplay in the cards. If we look at animal figures we can see some pairs that vaguely look male and female. But if we identify them as such, their arrangement is the opposite compared to the human figures. Jodorowsky notes that in the Chariot card, the horse on the right looks feminine while the horse on the left looks masculine. The same may also be said about the two fantasy fish heads in the 2 of Cups, or even the two dogs in the Moon card when we look at their muzzles.

The Chariot, 2 of Cups, The Moon

Relying on traditional associations of male and female may seem out-dated in our day. But an important point to remember is that a figure of a woman in the cards does not necessarily represent a woman in reality. Today we are aware that in each of us, regardless of our biological gender, there is both a masculine and a feminine side. Therefore, a woman figure in the card can represent a feminine aspect, or a behavior traditionally considered as feminine, in a man. And, of course, a man in the card can represent a woman in reality who acts in a way traditionally associated with masculinity. We can thus rely on the traditional symbolism of male and female without assuming anything about the actual status that men and women should have in society.

Similar considerations apply to the age of figures in the cards. A young figure can symbolize the beginning of a process or the first steps taken in a new domain of action. It can also represent stamina, naive self-confidence, or rashness. An older figure can symbolize maturity, experience, and moderation. These qualities may describe the personality, the behavior, or the position of the querent, regardless of their biological age.

Children and animals, too, can symbolize aspects of personality and behavior. The figure of a child in a card may express childlike qualities such as spontaneity, imagination, playfulness, and short-sightedness. Animals can represent a primordial and undeveloped state or animal instincts and impulses. Specific animal figures can represent personality traits and behaviors traditionally associated with this kind of animal. For example, a lion can symbolize bravery, power, and danger. An eagle can symbolize sharp perception or the ability to soar high above common ground. A dog can symbolize loyalty. A more formal way to interpret the lion or the eagle, which appear in the World and in other cards, is to identify them with the minor suit domains described in chapter 7. In such a scheme, the lion corresponds to the suit of wands and represents desire and creativity, while the eagle corresponds to the swords and represents the intellect.

BODY PARTS

Body parts of the tarot figures can be interpreted in several ways. One way is to interpret the body parts metaphorically according to their function and use. For example, a hand symbolizes what the querent is doing. An eye symbolizes what they can or want to see. The shoulders can represent the burden they are carrying. A belly is what they contain and keep inside. A woman figure with a round belly can express pregnancy with something, not necessarily a real child. The legs represent the stability of the querent's position or their ability to move. Whatever is under them can be the basis on which they stand.

I have also learned another way to interpret the body parts from Jodorowsky. It is based on the symbolic language of the minor suits. As we shall see in chapter 7, the four suits represent four domains of human activity: body, desire, emotion, and intellect. These four domains correspond, from bottom to top, to four parts in the human body: legs, pelvis, chest, and head. When we see a figure in the cards, we can check the position and appearance of each part and the relation and coordination between them. This can teach us about the corresponding domains in the person's life.

THE LEGS represent the suit of coins and the material and physical domain, or "what we stand on." Strong and stable legs represent a secure position, a solid material base, and good health. A walking figure means that the querent is advancing in some direction. Standing with the feet pointing in one direction expresses a desire or an intention to move there, without an actual movement yet. Standing with the feet spread in both directions can express confusion, contradicting plans, and hesitation and quandary between different courses of action.

THE PELVIS, which includes the sexual organs, represents the suit of wands and the domain of desire and creativity. A prominent pelvis indicates strong passions. A hidden or covered pelvis can express repression, blocked sexual desires, or a lack of sexual self-awareness. The pelvis can also symbolize creative expression, as it represents giving birth to something coming from within ourselves: children, ideas, or projects.

the chest, seat of the heart, represents the suit of cups and the domain of emotion. A wide and open chest represents emotional receptivity and sensitivity, or the capacity to express and to react to others' feelings. A contracted or blocked chest—for example, in tight clothes or behind armor—can symbolize closeness, emotional protectiveness, and a difficulty to express intimacy. Touching the area of the heart indicates a relationship based on warmth and trust. If the chest leans toward another figure, it may indicate affection and positive feelings or a desire to have a romantic relationship with that person.

the head represents the suit of swords and the domain of the intellect. A head turned to one side means that this is the direction of the querent's thoughts. A covered head or gathered hair symbolizes controlled and orderly thoughts, while loose and flowing hair represents fresh and open thinking. A line separating the head from the rest of the body can express an inner detachment, with the querent's thoughts disconnected from other parts of their personality.

CHAPTER 5

THE MAJOR SUIT

When people consider the magic and the symbolic power of the tarot, which is responsible for its huge impact on many generations, they usually think about the twenty-two cards of the major suit. Without the major suit we would have a deck similar to the normal playing cards: a convenient means for games of chance and popular fortune-telling, but not something that could motivate centuries of preservation, development, interpretation, and creativity, as the tarot cards have done.

THE SUIT AT THE CENTER

The relationship between the major suit and the four minor suits can be seen symbolically in the World card, which is the last one of the major suit. In its corners there are four living creatures taken from biblical tradition: bull, lion, human, and eagle. These can symbolize the four minor suits and the four domains of life, which we shall review in chapter 7: body, desire, emotion, and intellect. The four figures define a solid rectangular frame, which also brings to mind the regular structure of the four suits. The dynamic element appears in the middle, in the form of a naked figure dancing within an oblong wreath. In the tarot deck it can represent the major suit. In the human sphere it can symbolize consciousness, which unites the different functions into a single entity.

Many tarot readers see the minor suits as representing only external and practical dimensions of life events. In the cards of the major suit they see a fuller and deeper representation of human life: both the external events and the inner life of self-consciousness, psychological processes, and spiritual intuitions. This may be the reason why popular fortunetellers, who are not interested in going into deep levels of analysis, usually use only the normal playing cards, which are equivalent to the four minor suits. In contrast, tarot readers attach much more importance to the twenty-two major cards.

Order and Chaos

The major suit differs from the minor suits not only in the richness and complexity of its card illustrations but also in its less orderly and more chaotic structure. The four minor suits follow a fully predictable pattern. After the 4 of Cups comes the 5 of Cups, and just as there is a Knight of Swords, there is a Knight of Coins. In contrast, the cards in the major suit display a complex and unpredictable sequence. To demonstrate this point, let us consider a situation where people see all the cards from the beginning of the major suit up to a certain card. From this information, they would still have no way of guessing the title or the subject of the card that follows.

This characteristic sets the major suit apart from other systems of symbolic illustrations that were common during the Renaissance. An interesting example is a collection of card-like prints from the later fifteenth century. They are known as Tarocchi del Mantegna (the Tarot of Mantegna), although they are not really tarot cards and the attribution to the famous painter Mantegna is unfounded.

The Mantegna prints are divided into five suits of ten images each, with symbolic subjects taken from the conceptual world of the Renaissance. The five suits represent themes like professions and social positions, liberal arts and sciences, the nine muses, moral virtues, and celestial objects. Some of the subjects are similar to tarot cards. For example, there is an Emperor, a Pope, and images representing Force, Justice, the Sun, and the Moon.

Still, the Mantegna prints are very different from the tarot. First of all, it is not even clear that they were meant to be used as a deck of cards. In the surviving originals the images are printed on thin paper and bound together as a book, perhaps for educational purposes. This gives them a well-defined and single standard ordering. In contrast, tarot cards can be arranged and read in any order. This means that there is an element of chaos inherent to the tarot cards by the fact that they exist as a set of separate images that can be freely arranged.

The more orderly character of the Mantegna prints is further expressed in the regular structure of the five suits, none of which are exceptional in size or structure. All the illustrations are consecutively numbered, and each one of them has a title written at the bottom. Moreover, when sets of symbols are used they are presented in their completeness. For example, all the nine muses appear consecutively, without any one missing, and the same is true of the seven traditional planets, the four cardinal virtues, and so on.

In contrast, the tarot major suit presents a complex interplay between order and chaos. Time and again orderly patterns appear, and time and again they are broken. Each rule seems to have its exceptions, and the exceptions again differ from each other.

Most cards in the major suit carry titles and ordinal numbers, but the two cards that we have already discussed as representing time in the previous chapter, the Fool and card 13, are exceptional. Card 13 has no name, and the Fool has no number. In addition, there is an empty band on top of the Fool card where the number should be, but there is no similar band for the missing name in card 13. This means that each one of them is exceptional in its own way.

Trying to go over the major suit cards by sequential numbers as a way of establishing a standard ordering proves to be quite confusing. Already the Fool is problematic because without a number, we can't know for sure where it should be. Putting it aside and looking at the sequence of the other cards, we quickly find that it is very difficult, if not impossible, to find any clear logic.

Just after the beginning of the suit, there are four cards with figures of authority and government in an order that is surprising by itself: the Popess, the Empress, the Emperor, and the Pope. But both before and after them there is something completely different. The Magician that precedes these respectable figures looks like a dubious street person. And after the Pope with its Christian symbols there is something even stranger: the Lover with a pagan Cupid and three human figures touching each other. It's not clear exactly what we see here and why it appears right after the four representative figures of the established social order.

The Magician, The Popess, The Empress,
The Emperor, The Pope, The Lover

More patterns appear further along the line, only to break down once again. Three major cards present, at equal intervals, three of the four cardinal virtues in Christian tradition: Justice (eight), Force (eleven), and Temperance (fourteen). But the fourth virtue, Prudence, is missing. The Temperance card presents another exception. It is the only card in the major suit whose French name is written without the definite article, as "Temperance" and not "La Temperance."

Justice, Force, Temperance

Further along in the suit there are three cards with astronomical and alchemy-inspired symbols: the Star, the Moon, and the Sun. Yet before them we find the Tower, with a different symbolic language whose origin is unclear. And after these cards comes the Judgment card, which is again linked to Christian symbolism.

The Tower, The Star, The Moon, The Sun, Judgment

Many tarot books over the last two centuries have tried to find a uniform and logical order in the major suit. Some of their authors have based their attempts on the ordering of the cards, for example by dividing the suit without the Fool into three sets of seven cards, or into seven sets of three cards. More complex patterns were also tried. None of them have proved convincing enough to gain general acceptance.

Other authors have tried to find order in the cards by imposing a system of symbols taken from other sources. For example, many have tried to establish a correspondence between the major suit cards and the astrological symbols of planets and zodiac signs, but notably each have done so in a different way. The Golden Dawn leaders tried to integrate the cards into their huge table of worldwide correspondences. But again, a disagreement soon appeared as to how exactly to do it. Apparently, in each of these schemes some cards naturally find their place. But then there are others that do not fit so easily, and finally there are some that really have to be forced into their corresponding slots.

Some of the correspondences created over the years are interesting and may enrich our understanding of the cards. One such example is the correspondence between the cards and Hebrew letters, outlined later in this chapter. But perhaps we should not attach too much importance to any orderly table or any scheme for the definite arrangement of the cards. The breaking of patterns in the major suit could itself carry an important message for us.

Scientists today speak of the phenomenon of life as emerging "on the edge of chaos," a sort of intermediate region between chaos and order. The perfect order is expressed by a solid crystal, where everything is well-ordered and fixed. It has no potential for movement, and thus no place for life. The total chaos is expressed by smoke, which has no stable shape. Here, too, there can be no life because every structure would quickly dissipate. Biological and social life processes take place somewhere in between the crystal and the smoke. They are characterized by a certain degree of order and stability, but also by creative unpredictability and an occasional collapse of ordered structures.

The cards in the major suit, which express and reflect the infinite complexity of life, also can be thought of as a system on the edge of chaos. They show some degree of order and structure, but also chaotic irregularities and pattern-breaking. Therefore, it might be pointless to look for an ultimate structure behind them. The only pattern in the cards is the cards themselves.

Titles and Numbers

In the Tarot de Marseille the number of each card appears in roman numerals. The notation is a long one in which, for example, nine is written as VIIII and not as IX. Perhaps this was done to prevent confusion when the cards were held upside down. In new decks of the English school the numbers are sometimes written in roman numerals in short notation (i.e., nine is IX) and sometimes in modern numerals.

The numbers and titles of the major suit cards are basically the same in both schools, but there are two differences. The Golden Dawn leaders wanted to have more order in the cards. For this reason they made the two exceptional cards in the Tarot de Marseille conform with the others. They gave the title Death to card 13, and this title appears in many decks of the English school. They also put the number zero on the Fool card, thus placing it at the beginning of the suit. There are also some decks in which the Fool is given the number twenty-two and placed at the end of the suit.

Another difference between the two schools is in the numbering of the Justice and Force cards. In the Tarot de Marseille and other traditional decks, Justice is number eight and Force is number eleven. But in new decks from the English school, Force is eight and Justice is eleven. The reason for this lies in the complex system of Golden Dawn correspondences. Putting tarot cards, Cabbalistic texts, and astrological signs together, the leaders came up with a correspondence of the twelve signs to twelve cards arranged by their numbers. Writing it down, the Justice card was correlated with the sign of Leo (lion) and the Force card with the sign of Libra (scales). This, however, looks strange because scales appear in the Justice card, and a lion appears in the Force card.

The Golden Dawn leaders believed that the original tarot possessed a perfect order and that this anomaly reflects some mistake that crept in during the ages. To set it right, they switched the two cards. In their system Justice became eleven with a correspondence to Libra, and the Force, which they renamed Strength, became eight with a correspondence to Leo. This modified numbering became the standard for all new decks in the English school.

LADDER OF CREATION

Why is it at all important to know the true ordering of the cards if we can place them anyway in the order we wish? The answer is that both schools believed that the ordering of the cards was not arbitrary. Rather, there was some message or story that the suit sequence was meant to express.

Many tarot interpreters, in their quest to figure out this message, were influenced by Neoplatonist philosophy. Neoplatonism is a set of beliefs that appeared in the first centuries BCE, was later revived in the Renaissance, and also influenced the Jewish Cabbala. According to the Neoplatonist view, the world was created in a series of "emanations," a ladder of consecutive steps in which the divine plenitude, or light, descends. The highest level is pure spirituality, and coming down from it the light gradually becomes tangible and concrete. Finally it reaches the earthly level, which is the everyday reality of matter and action.

Some of the first French tarot Cabbalists interpreted the card sequence of the major suit as an image of Neoplatonic emanation. They considered the Magician (number one) and the following cards as a representation of the highest spiritual level. Further on, they claimed, the sequence of cards descends in the scale of emanation, finally reaching the last card of the suit, the World (number twenty-one), which represents material reality.

The leaders of the Golden Dawn further developed this idea. They arranged the cards in the form of a traditional Cabbalistic diagram, the Sefirot Tree, which describes ten aspects of the divine essence and the twenty-two paths connecting them. They saw the highest spiritual degree in the Fool card, which they put at the beginning of the deck as number zero. Therefore, in their system it appears at the top of the tree. Then, going down the tree paths, they arranged all the other cards by their consecutive numbers, finally reaching the World at the bottom.

This vision also influenced the design of new decks in the English school. For example, in the Tarot de Marseille and other traditional decks, card number one, the Magician, shows a young street illusionist in a somewhat hesitant posture. But in the Golden Dawn vision, card one should represent a high spiritual degree, and the figure was modified accordingly. In Waite's 1909 deck the same card displays a powerful magic master who looks self-confident in his commanding authority, with the symbol of infinity hovering over his head.

Still, this reading of the suit sequence as descending from high above to earth seems problematic if we examine the card themes more closely. The first cards of the suit (with low numbers) show figures whose social role and status is clear. For example, they show a street magician, an empress, a warrior, and a wandering hermit. In contrast, the last cards show celestial bodies and nude human figures in mysterious and imaginary situations. These include, for example, a girl pouring water under the stars, an angel blowing his trumpet over three figures rising from the ground, and a dancing woman surrounded by four divine living creatures. Looking at these images, we may think that perhaps it's the *first* cards that are earthly and mundane, while the last cards hint at a more lofty and mysterious level of reality.

Another clue in this direction comes from the traditional use of the cards for gaming. In old tarot games, as in most ordinary card games today, a card with a high number wins over a card with a low number. The last cards in the suit have the greatest value, beating all the cards that precede them. It is reasonable, then, to suppose that their themes are meant to represent the higher levels of reality, not the lower ones.

Such considerations motivated other authors from the French school to adopt an opposite reading. In their view, the suit described a ladder of reality levels that extends from the material to the purely spiritual. But contrary to the previous reading, the suit sequence advances from bottom to top. The first cards are earthly and the last cards heavenly, not the other way around.

Parts of the Suit

For a better understanding of the major suit sequence and its evolution, let us examine its different parts in more detail. Most of the cards at the beginning of the suit show figures with a well-defined social status or professional activity. The street magician, the empress, the pope, the warrior in a chariot, and the wandering hermit are all figures that have their place in the social world of the Middle Ages. Most of the figures in these cards are large enough to fill the whole card, and they are all dressed in a way that fits their status and occupation. Thus, at the beginning of the suit we can see people living in normal human society.

Later on in the suit we see allegorical figures of virtues cherished by medieval Christian society: Justice, Force, and Temperance. The figures are still large and fully dressed, but now they represent general ideas and not concrete people. Their actions, such as holding a lion by the mouth or the act of pouring liquid between two pots, also seem more like symbolic representations rather than things that real people actually do.

To these we can add another allegory: the Wheel of Fortune, which is differently designed and shows a traditional symbol of ups and downs in social position. Together these cards can represent the two basic concepts of virtue and fortune, which are very typical in Renaissance thinking. Renaissance scholars debated the question of whether virtue, which is a person's moral quality, or fortune, which is capricious luck, is more important in human life. Thus, although these four cards show abstract concepts rather than particular people or social roles, they still operate in the earthly sphere of human life.

The next part of the suit does not refer to social positions or accepted norms. Instead, we see disruptive and challenging cards that are detached from the common social order. The figures in these cards have no status marks, their actions seem mysterious or supernatural, and some of them are nude. The Hanged Man shows a man in an unusual situation, and it is unclear whether it expresses suffering or a choice to mortify himself. Card 13 shows a skeleton with a sickle in a field of amputated limbs. The Devil card, with an insolent bisexual body and two tied imps, mocks the conventional norms. Even the Tower card, which at first sight might seem to be a realistic image of lightning hitting a tall structure, rather hints at "fire from heaven" with the mysterious reference to God's house in its title.

Toward the end of the suit we see another kind of change, not only in the themes but also in the structure of the cards. Now they are vertically divided between some action on the ground and some object or figure in the sky. The human figures are smaller, and many of them are partially or fully nude. In contrast to the concrete activities or the simple allegories at the beginning of the suit, it is now unclear what exactly the figures are doing and why they are doing it. Who is the nude girl in the Star card, and why is she pouring water into the river? What is the relation between her and the star that gives the card its name? And what about the two semi-nude children under the sun or the two dogs and the crustacean under the moon? All of these are far removed from the common world of practical life and simple allegories. Instead, they look mysterious, mythological, and dreamlike.

As in any pattern in the cards, here too there is no uniform and orderly development. Rather it is a complex story with twists, jumps, and exceptions. The different parts of the suit interpenetrate each other, with no clear separation between them. The Lover card appears at the beginning of the suit, although its structure resembles the last part: a division between ground and sky, several small figures, and even a nude angel or Cupid. Temperance appears at the middle of the suit as a large fully dressed figure in a relaxed attitude, in contrast with the dramatic character and nude figures of its surrounding cards. And at the end of the suit, the World has a symmetric and formal structure of its own that does not resemble any other card.

Closeness and Exposure

In the first half of the major suit, almost all of the figures are dressed. Some of them are also heavily covered—for example, by shawls and coverings in the Popess card, or by armor in the Chariot card. In contrast, many figures in the second half of the suit are nude to some degree: partly nude in the Sun and the World cards, fully nude in the Devil, the Star, and Judgment cards, and naked "to the bones" in card 13. The appearance of so many nude figures in tarot is surprising, especially if we remember that the cards were designed in a conservative era.

In our society nudity is usually associated with sexuality. But the only card where nudity seems to appear in a sexual context is the Devil, whose semihuman figures are lewd and shameless rather than sexually attractive. It seems that the appearance of nudity in the cards is not about sex. Instead, it could be linked to the idea of social status. At the beginning of the major suit, the clothing not only covers the body but also tells us something about the position and the profession of the person. All the figures are dressed in a way that expresses their social occupation: armor for the combatant, a royal gown for the emperor, a simple robe for the hermit. The same is true in real life. In a traditional society there are clear rules as to who may wear what clothes, and in our society too one can usually guess people's occupations and status by the way they dress.

Toward the end of the suit, the signs of social status disappear along with the clothing. Neither the names of the cards nor any details in their illustrations tell us who these people are and what is their social position. This removes the figures from the context of earthly life. Interestingly, along with the removal of social signifiers, a new structure appears in the card illustrations. Now they show things happening on two levels: one on the ground (earthly) and the other in the sky (heavenly).

The appearance of the sky may also signify an opening to a higher level of reality and consciousness. It is like entering the reading space or the circle of the magical ritual. We establish contact with higher spheres by letting go of our mundane social identity and our defenses, so that we stand exposed in our mysterious existence as human beings. This may be the reason why in many cultures it is common to perform rituals of magic in the nude or in a uniform and simple dress that avoids all distinctions of social status.

When people enter a reading they become exposed, revealing intimate details of what goes on in their life and mind. This is one of the most impressive features of tarot reading: how quickly and intensively people open up and share contents that they usually keep sealed and hidden from others and sometimes also from themselves. But doing so, they expose themselves as human beings who share the same worries and concerns regardless of social status, wealth, or level of education. In front of the mysterious forces that we can feel through the cards, we are all just plain humans. The nudity of the figures may be just the cards' way of reminding us of this.

In a reading nudity can also be part of the symbolic language of the cards. It can symbolize exposure, openness, and the removal of defenses and barriers. The association of nudity with a heavenly level in the cards can also signify openness to messages from higher spheres. In a negative sense it can be interpreted as dangerous exposure, vulnerability, and defenselessness. On the other hand, tight and heavy clothing can signify suspicion, closure, difficulty to let go, necessity to keep up defenses, and self-preservation.

The landscape in the card illustrations can also reflect the opposition of open and closed. An open field expresses exposure and removal of barriers. Walls and other obstructing constructions signify defenses and blocking. We can interpret the clothing or the nudity of a figure in terms of attempts to keep oneself protected or to become exposed, while the nature of the surrounding landscape can signify the amount of openness or closure that the environment provides.

As with any pattern in the cards, the interplay between closed or dressed and open or nude is not linear and uniform. Starting around the middle of the suit, after every open or nude card there is a card with blocking struc-tures or dressed figures, and vice versa. In the Hanged Man (12) the figure is dressed and blocked from all sides by a wooden frame. Card 13 presents extreme nudity to the bones, and card 14 shows the figure of Temperance dressed to its neck. Card 15 presents the Devil and his imps brazenly nude, while card 16 shows a brick construction and clothed figures.

The Star (17) again presents free and flowing nudity in an open field, while the Moon (18) shows a blocked landscape with sealed towers. But now a third option appears, a sort of fusion between open and closed, with the low wall and the partial nudity of the Sun card (19). Judgment (20) again shows nude figures, and here even the earth and the sky open up to each other. The suit ends in the World card (21) with a new combination of open and closed: a nude figure partially covered by a light scarf and dancing inside a soft protective garland.

THE FOOL'S JOURNEY

We can't know for sure the intentions of the original creators of the tarot. But if they did have some Neoplatonic ideas in mind, it seems more likely that they meant to indicate a progression from the mundane to the heavenly and not the other way around. Examined in this way, we can interpret the sequence as a dynamic story of personal evolution or as an initiation quest. The story begins with a person's awakening from being enclosed in the earthly world of social status and material possessions. The journey passes through self-trials and the endurance of hardships, which leads to a full realization of human existence with spiritual awakening, openness, and self-exposure.

In the New Age movement this reading became popularly known as "the Fool's journey." The idea is that the numbered cards of the suit represent consecutive stages of a spiritual quest. Only the exceptional Fool card does not seem to represent any particular stage. Instead he is the traveler himself, the person who is going through the journey. Step by step he advances through the stages signaled by all the other cards, finally reaching his full realization with the image of the World.

This idea is best exemplified with the Tarot de Marseille, in which the Fool card is exceptional because it has no number. This is different from the Golden Dawn vision that saw the Fool (0) as the final goal of the journey, not as the person going through it. We may also see a hint of this idea in the derivation of the name "tarot" from "the Fool's cards." In the cards' language, maybe the Fool carries in his bag all the other cards, taking out each one as he reaches corresponding stations along the way.

Following the first introduction of this idea by the New Age tarot writer Eden Gray, there were many versions of the Fool's journey. Here is a version inspired by the Conver-CBD images of the Tarot de Marseille. It is not meant to be "the true story" behind the suit sequence, nor is it the universal model to be followed by any spiritual seeker. The cards can be rearranged in many possible combinations, and anyone can find their own way through them. Instead, the narrative of the Fool's journey is a way to put in our mind the idea of the major suit sequence as a coherent story, with a direction, sense, and purpose, before going into the details of each separate card.

The Fool, The Wheel of Fortune

The Wheel of Fortune, with the number ten (which is significant in numerology), can be regarded as a turning point of the story. The rotating wheel can symbolize the cycles of normal life with their ups and downs. For example, it can represent the repeating cycle of working days from waking to sleep. It can symbolize a week or a year, with their regular cycles of holidays and communal gatherings. It can also stand for the cycle of generations in a family. And in Buddhist terms we can see it as samsara, the repeating cycle of birth and rebirth.

The cards with numbers lower than ten can represent stages of growing up in normal society. The Magician, as the number one, represents the first awakening of our own individuality. His tools spread upon the table can stand for capacities and potentials that may or may not be realized. The four following cards are significant figures of authority that influence our early years: parents in the Empress (3) and the Emperor (4), teachers in the Popess (2) and the Pope (5).

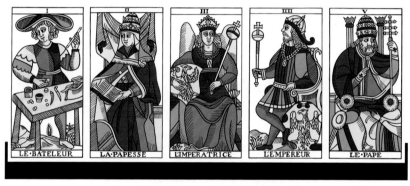

The Magician, The Popess, The Empress, The Emperor, The Pope

The Lover card (6), with its unusual design for this part of the suit, turns our attention back to the individual now coming out of his child-hood years. The figure standing between two women possibly indicates the choices that we make as young adults, with consequences that accompany us for the rest of our lives. And the appearance of the heavenly Cupid in the card may symbolize the uplifting and near-mystical quality of our first encounters with love.

The Lover

We can see the next three cards as a single unit. The Chariot (7) and the Hermit (9) can represent two opposites. The Justice card (8), with its scales and sword, can be weighing them one against the other, as well as cutting and choosing between them in a particular moment. For example, we can see the serene adult figure in the middle as striking a balance between the young and old figures on its two sides. The Chariot may symbolize youthful vanity and the desire to go out and conquer the world, while the Hermit stands for maturity and a cautious outlook based on experience. Alternatively, the Chariot can symbolize an occupation with external achievements, while the Hermit indicates an inner quest for wisdom and self-awareness. The Justice card can also represent the laws and norms of society, which govern both our external actions and the shaping of our inner values.

The Chariot, Justice, The Hermit

All this is part of human life in normal society. The quest for awakening to a higher level of existence starts only after the Wheel of Fortune card. The Force (11), with a woman taming a lion whose head comes out of her own pelvis, can signify a moral battle with oneself in order to control one's animal desires. The mysterious Hanged Man (12) carries his own self-examination to the extreme. By hanging himself upside down, he is putting in question all his previous assumptions about what is above and what is below. He also takes a risk by giving up the solid base of accepted reality as he hovers above an abyss with his hands held behind his back.

Force, The Hanged Man

The next group of cards shows dramatic challenges and trials with a transformative effect. The dark appearance of card 13 makes it stand out among all the other cards. Even its missing title may hint at things too scary to be named. The sturdy skeleton figure, the sharp edge of the scythe, and the severed heads and limbs indicate disintegration and irrevocable change. The crowned head on the right can symbolize past authority figures and guiding values that are now thrown down and trampled over.

Card 13, Temperance, The Devil, The Tower

The Temperance card (14) appears as a temporary relief with gentle reconciliation and appeasing of tensions. It may signify taking some time to patiently work out the outcome of the extreme trial in the previous card. It may also be needed before facing the lascivious paradoxes and the bawdy anarchism of desires stemming from the dark lower levels of the Devil (15). In the Tower (16) we can see the collapse of old established structures and values, but also an opening to higher forces coming from above. Also, it can represent giving up high-rise, vain illusions and coming down to the humble but fertile ground of actual existence.

The three following cards can signify together an awakened state that comes after those trying experiences. Now life on earth is infused with an awareness of higher levels, symbolized by the appearance of heavenly bodies above. But we can also see it as another evolution: from the naive full exposure in the Star (17) through the confrontation with deep and obscure layers of the mind in the Moon (18) and finally the arrival at the balanced and restrained acceptance of heavenly bliss in the Sun (19).

The Star, The Moon, The Sun

The last two cards, whose imagery is taken from the traditional Christian vision of final redemption, may indicate the desired state of spiritual consciousness at the end of the quest. In the Judgment card (20) we see the heaven, the earth, and the abyss opening toward each other. The spiritual vertical axis meets the earthly horizontal axis, and the three figures can bring to mind a psychological reparation of the initial relations with the parent figures. The balanced and symmetric World card (21) is the final station of the journey, with all the elements finding their place in perfect harmony.

Judgment, The World

Still, this sublime vision can also be a trap. From a perfect situation there is nowhere to go, no place for further improvement. Perhaps it is better to think of the Fool's journey not as a straight line but as a circle repeating itself on a higher level each time. With this vision we can interpret the strange oblong shape between the Magician's table legs both as an opening from which he is born and as an emptied form of the World's wreath, now perceived as a womb. As the World gives birth to the Magician, it is time to start the journey once again.

We may also think that the very image of the cards as fixed stations on a linear track is too restricted. Maybe it is better to see it as just one possible story among many. A richer image appears in a 1932 fantasy novel by Charles Williams called *The Greater Trumps* (an old-fashioned name for the major suit cards). Williams imagines the tarot cards as three-dimensional golden figures who move incessantly in a complex dance that reflects the great dance of life. Looking at the dance of the tarot figures, one can understand and predict the corresponding movements of real life events.

Amid all the dancing figures, only the Fool appears to be standing motionless. It is said that whoever understands the meaning of this fact will decipher the great secret of the tarot. The secret as such isn't revealed in the book, but we can find a hint of it in one of the female characters, who is an enlightened person with all-encompassing love. Only she sees the Fool constantly jumping to and fro, disappearing and reappearing once again, each time filling the empty gaps between the other cards.

HEBREW LETTERS

Many writers in both the French and the English schools believed that the twenty-two cards of the major suit corresponded to the twenty-two letters of the Hebrew alphabet. This correspondence was significant for them because traditional Cabbalistic texts attach spiritual meanings and magical powers to the Hebrew letters. But each of the two schools had their own method for establishing the exact correspondences.

The founder of the French tradition, Eliphas Lévi, matched the first letter, *alef*, to the Magician, which is the first card in the suit. Lévi also saw the shape of the Magician's body, with one arm raised above and the other below, as hinting to the shape of the Hebrew letter *alef*. He matched the second letter, *bet*, with the Popess card (number two), and so on, proceeding by the standard ordering of the Hebrew alphabet.

This correspondence creates other interesting links between the cards and the letters, some of which Lévi may have been aware of. The letter *kaf* was matched to the Force card. In Hebrew *kaf* means "palm," like the palms holding the lion in the card. The Hanged Man in card 12 with his bent leg resembles the shape of the letter *lamed*. The letter *mem* was matched to card 13, which is sometimes called Death (*mavet* in Hebrew). The Devil got *samekh*, the initial letter of Samael, which is the devil's name in Hebrew. The body and the legs of the falling figure on the left of the Tower card are similar to the shape of the letter *ayin*. Lévi also put the Fool at the place before the last, matching it with the letter *shin*. This is the initial letter of *shoteh*, which in Hebrew means "fool." *Tav* is the initial of *tevel*, which in Hebrew means "the world."

The English school of tarot adopted a different system. As the Fool card was moved to the top of the suit, it was matched to the first letter, *alef*. The rest of the cards were matched according to the sequence order, which made *bet* correspond to the Magician, *gimel* (the third letter) to the Popess, and so on. This correspondence may seem strange to those who know gematria, the traditional notation of numbers by Hebrew letters, which is very important in the Cabbala. For example, *bet* in gematria is two, but in the Golden Dawn method it corresponds to card number one. Nevertheless, the Golden Dawn leaders adopted it. Later, Crowley further modified their correspondence by switching between the letters of the Emperor and the Star.

The result is that there are different ways of matching the Hebrew letters with the tarot cards. This is a bit confusing because in several new decks the Hebrew letters are explicitly written on the cards. As some of these do it by the English system and others by the French system, different decks show different letters on the same card.

For an open reading on personal issues with the Tarot de Marseille, the question is not so important, as the Hebrew letters don't actually appear on the cards. Therefore, the whole issue can just be ignored. Still, readers who speak Hebrew or know the Cabbala can use the correspondences as an additional layer of meaning for the cards. For example, there are many who believe that a person's name has an influence on their life. To understand the influence of a specific name, we can write it down in Hebrew, lay down the corresponding cards in a row, and read them. A similar method can be used with Cabbalistic letter combinations, which are supposed to have positive effects. Doing this, we can create a luck-bearing talisman made from tarot cards. Alternatively, a card appearing in a spread can be given a specific meaning by looking for a person or a place whose first initial is the corresponding Hebrew letter.

If we wish to use a Hebrew letter correspondence, which system should we adopt? A reasonable choice would be to go by the deck we are using. With the Tarot de Marseille and other French-school decks, we may use Eliphas Lévi's system of correspondences. With decks from the English school, such as Waite's, we may use the Golden Dawn system. If you don't know to which school your deck belongs, it's a good idea to check the numbers of Justice and Force. In the French school Justice is 8 and Force is 11, and in the English school it's the other way around.

The following table lists all the major suit cards with their titles, numbers, and the corresponding Hebrew letters in both schools. The first items for each card are as in the French school: card number (in modern numerals), card name (as in this book), card number as a roman numeral, title (as in Conver's Tarot de Marseille), and Hebrew letter and glyph (by Lévi). The English school items follow, including the number and the Hebrew letter (standard Golden Dawn). Note that in the Tarot de Marseille, card 13 has no title and the Fool has no number.

TABLE I: MAJOR CARD TITLES AND HEBREW LETTERS

CARD		FRENCH SCHOOL				ENGLISH SCHOOL	
1	The Magician	I	LE BATELEUR	Alef	א	1	Bet
2	The Popess	II	LA PAPESSE	Bet	ב	2	Gimel
3	The Empress	III	L'IMPERATRICE	Gimel	ג	3	Dalet
4	The Emperor	IIII	L'EMPEREUR	Dalet	ד	4	He
5	The Pope	V	LE PAPE	He	ה	5	Vav
6	The Lover	VI	L'AMOVREVX	Vav	ו	6	Zain
7	The Chariot	VII	LE CHARIOT	Zain	ז	7	Khet
8	Justice	VIII	LA JUSTICE	Khet	ח	11	Lamed
9	The Hermit	VIIII	L'HERMITE	Tet	ט	9	Yod
10	The Wheel of Fortune	X	L'A ROVE DE FORTVNE	Yod	י	10	Kaf
11	Force	XI	LA FORCE	Kaf	כ	8	Tet
12	The Hanged Man	XII	LE PENDU	Lamed	ל	12	Mem
13	Card 13	XIII		Mem	מ	13	Nun
14	Temperance	XIIII	TEMPERANCE	Nun	נ	14	Samekh
15	The Devil	XV	LE DIABLE	Samekh	ס	15	Ayin
16	The Tower	XVI	LA MAISON DIEV	Ayin	ע	16	Pe
17	The Star	XVII	LETOILLE	Pe	פ	17	Tsadi
18	The Moon	XVIII	LA LUNE	Tsadi	צ	18	Kof
19	The Sun	XIX	LE SOLEIL	Kof	ק	19	Resh
20	Judgment	XX	LE JUGEMENT	Resh	ר	20	Shin
21	The World	XXI	LE MONDE	Tav	ת	21	Tav
	The Fool		LE MAT	Shin	ש	0	Alef

CHAPTER · 6

THE MAJOR CARDS

111

I

LE · BATELEUR

Card 1: The Magician

Bateleur is an archaic French word meaning a street conjurer, a juggler, a sleight-of-hand artist, a popular showman, or, sometimes, a charlatan. The man dressed in fancy garb looks like a street magician in a performance. Some of the objects in his hands and on the table can be recognized as conjuring tools. Others may be hidden in what looks like a strange bag. The raised hand has been sometimes interpreted as directing the wand toward higher powers above, but it may be just a conjuring trick to divert attention from what the other hand is doing.

THE MAGICIAN STANDS AT THE GATE

Mystical traditions often describe a gatekeeper who stands between the ordinary domain and the other reality of magic and sorcery. Before embarking on a journey to the otherworld, it is customary to ask for permission and blessing from the gatekeeper. In the tarot this figure can be represented by the Magician, which opens the major suit. We can think of the elongated form over the horizon between his legs as the gate to a magical reality. The card can be used to focus our attention when we start an experience that goes beyond earthly reality; for example, a magical ceremony or a session of guided imagination.

The street magician is an ordinary man of low social status, but once the show starts he appears as a mighty wizard using mysterious powers to change events in real life. We can also think that he is, in fact, a real magician who disguises himself as a humble street conjurer. In this regard the card can hint at the idea that thought creates reality, meaning that our ideas and our will can change life events. It can also refer to the use of sorcery, usually for good ends, as well as indicate a person who performs mystical and magical rituals.

THE MAGICIAN STARTS SOMETHING NEW

As the first card of the suit, the Magician can signify a beginning. For example, it can represent the process of embarking on a journey or the start of a new initiative. The colorful illustration and the Magician's young face with the flowing curls give the feeling of a good start. The hat with a brim open upward reflects a willingness to learn and develop. The foot on the left side points toward the past, and it is enclosed from all sides. The foot on the right touches an open white surface, which represents a step toward a yet undefined future.

In a deeper sense we can see in the card the starting point for the journey of life. The elongated form between the legs can be seen as the birth canal from which the Magician has stepped out. Also, the white shape between the Magician's legs and the table is suggestive of a female pelvis. The marks on the ground could be the first footsteps leading from the actual moment of birth. The card can thus refer to the phase of infancy in which we develop a self-consciousness of our existence as a single individual, which is also hinted by the number one. It can also symbolize the ego or indicate an immature, self-centered personality.

THE MAGICIAN USES TOOLS

Some tools on the table are more recognizable than others. Three among these recall the minor suits' symbols: a cup, a knife (which can suggest swords), and circles resembling coins. Along with the wand in the Magician's hand, we can see the symbols of the four suits, which represent the domains of earthly life. The card may symbolize the tools and means that are at the querent's disposal. It can suggest the acquisition of new professional skills or it may indicate improvising and using existing means in a creative way.

The wand and the strangely shaped object in the Magician's right hand may be masculine and feminine symbols, which he points one toward the other. The Magician tries to make opposites meet. However, with precise measurement, we can see that the continuation of the wand's line passes above the other shape and not straight through it. This may indicate a task that hasn't been achieved or the experience of missing a goal because of imprecision or sloppiness. One can also see here a missed encounter between an ovum and a sperm, meaning failure to become pregnant.

THE MAGICIAN CREATES ILLUSIONS

The Magician wearing fancy clothes is a charming and seductive figure. But his appearance might be an illusion, a calculated show of tricks. He can represent a person with personal charm, a charismatic and persuasive figure, or an extroverted personality. The card can also refer to a public performer, an actor or someone involved in show business, a salesperson, or a public-relations professional. He can also be a charlatan, a manipulator, or a con artist.

A more philosophical view might link the card with the mystical idea that earthly reality and the idea of a separate "I" are an illusion, some sort of magic show that our consciousness plays to itself. The card's number expresses the idea of individuality. The table and the arrangement of the tools are objects and situations that we perceive in the illusory show of this world. The ground under the Magician's feet is material reality, the supposed basis of our existence. But we can notice that the ground does not continue outside the table's legs, so maybe it is also part of the great illusion.

THE MAGICIAN SEES ONLY ONE PART

Above the table the Magician displays confidence and skill. But under the table his feet point to opposite directions, implying hesitation and indecision. The presence of the table, which hides the pelvis, might also symbolize a blockage of sexual or creative energy.

The Magician seems to be unaware of what goes on at the basic levels of his being, which can also be related to influences from his early childhood. His field of vision is incomplete: the table extends outside the card frame, and the bag may contain additional tools that he is unaware of. The card can thus indicate a lack of psychological self-awareness or inner confusion hidden under a confident appearance. It may also symbolize an ignorance of basic but possibly significant factors. On a positive note, it can indicate untapped potentials and opportunities.

LA·PAPESSE

CARD 2: THE POPESS

In English decks this card is called "the High Priestess," but *la Papesse* in French means "the Popess." The card may refer to the legendary story of Pope Joan (Johanna), which was well-known during the late Middle Ages. According to the story, Johanna was a philosophy teacher in ninth-century Rome. Because of the social conventions of that time, Johanna had to teach disguised as a man. Her great wisdom made her popular, and soon she became known as the greatest teacher in Rome. At that time the pope died and Johanna, still passing for a man, was elected to replace him. She served as pope for several years. But her secret was revealed when she gave birth during a procession, and the angry mob stoned her and the baby to death.

THE POPESS IS A WISE WOMAN

The Popess holding a book brings to mind the goddess of wisdom in various mythologies, such as Athena in Greece, Sophia in Hellenistic sects, and Saraswati in India. The title band at the top of the card is exceptionally narrow, which makes the tip of the Popess's tiara extend high when compared to other cards. This may indicate a higher kind of wisdom or intuition from a sublime source. The turn toward the left, signifying the past, hints at the possession of ancient or traditional knowledge. The book indicates her ability to understand and express it in words. The book is open, but it is partly hidden by the robe: the Popess is willing to share her knowledge with others, but one has to make an effort in order to receive and understand it.

The card can signify ancient wisdom, possibly with a feminine character. For example, it may be the kind of knowledge that traditionally passes between women, such as popular folk magic or methods of natural healing. Of course, it can also refer to a man who applies such knowledge. The Pope Joan story may also be read as highlighting subversive knowledge, which undermines the established conventions and the existing power structures of society.

THE POPESS IS A SPIRITUAL MOTHER

According to the writings of the Gnostic sects in early Christian times, the ancient goddess of wisdom, Sophia, is the mother of the male god who created the world and then forgot who gave birth to him. This is the ancient figure of "the Mother of God," which in Christianity became Mary, the mother of Jesus. In traditional paintings of the Christian annunciation, Mary appears with a book similar to the one we see in the card.

The theme of motherhood also appears in Pope Joan's story. But the covered body and the book give an impression of distance and intellectuality. The card may refer to motherhood expressed not as warmth and hugging, but as wise advice and guidance. It can also indicate a cold and detached mother. It can refer to an actual mother or represent a spiritual mother acting as a guide or teacher.

THE POPESS SETS BOUNDARIES

The Popess is conspicuously more dressed than other clothed figures in the major suit. The chest area is heavily covered, the pelvis and the legs are completely hidden under the robe, and the visible face is wrapped all around. In the symbolic language of body parts, the Popess expresses herself only in the intellectual domain and does this, too, in a controlled and limited manner. The other domains of body, desire and feeling, are blocked and repressed. The screen behind her back suggests the idea of virginity, further linking the figure to Virgin Mary.

The card can symbolize a closed and protective attitude or a lack of sensuality. It can also signify keeping oneself spiritually clean, puritan conservatism, or bigoted views of sexuality. Psychologically, it can indicate the setting of firm barriers of the self, whether to define the limits of the ego or to avoid intimate contact. It can also express setting moral barriers to oneself or to others. In practical matters the card can express knowledge and understanding, but not real action.

THE POPESS HIDES HER POWERS

Pope Joan's story is about a woman who has to conceal her femininity and her strengths in a world of men. This is a situation that can also be relevant today. For example, the card may represent a woman adopting "masculine" attitudes in order to be accepted in a business or professional environment. It can also indicate difficulty in accepting a relationship where the abilities or the social status of the woman surpass those of her partner. In the case of a man, the card may describe social pressure that prevents him from expressing traits that are considered feminine.

On a more general level, the card can express a need to conceal personal characteristics, such as sexual orientation, unaccepted views, or anything that is considered out of the ordinary or illegitimate by societal standards. Alternatively, it can symbolize a timid or modest person who does not boast about their qualities and virtues.

THE POPESS KEEPS A SECRET

The veiled nature of the card is expressed not only in the clothes but also in the screen behind the Popess, as if she is guarding something hidden behind it. The Popess card can refer to personal secrets, covert moves, or discreet matters that should not be openly revealed. It can also indicate a mystery or hint at a spiritual secret that has to be guarded from the unworthy. In a negative sense it can indicate excessive secrecy and a difficulty to open up or expose oneself.

The Popess card can also refer to the reading itself. As a figure who knows secrets "from behind the veil," the Popess may represent the reader. The card can also signify that the querent is hiding something from us. As a last card in the reading, it can indicate that the answer to the query is hidden behind a veil, so that it cannot be revealed at this point.

III

L'IMPERATRICE

CARD 3: THE EMPRESS

The heraldic eagle is a common symbol of royal European families. A scepter with a cross over a sphere combines elements that are also linked to traditional royalty. These elements appear in the Emperor card as well, indicating that the two figures belong to the same family and are possibly married. As an hereditary emblem, the eagle shield can represent legitimacy, tradition, and family heritage. The scepter can stand for power and authority. While the Emperor holds both at a distance, the Empress embraces them. This difference could indicate that the Emperor relies on external means of control and domination, while the Empress's activity flows from her own personal being and gut feeling.

THE EMPRESS PROMOTES FERTILITY AND GROWTH

If the Popess is the goddess of wisdom and spiritual mystery, the Empress can represent another traditional female divinity: the goddess of earth and fertility. This figure of "mother earth" goes back to the Paleolithic era and can be found in various cultures around the world. Many tarot authors have linked the card with this idea of feminine nature, discussing it as symbolizing matter made alive through sensuality and passions.

We can see suggestions of sensuous fertility in the wide and rounded lower part of the body, in the secure sitting position, and in the large scepter coming out from the pelvis. The little white form on the belly can be a symbol of feminine sexuality or a seed in the womb. The number three also suggests fertility, creativity, and growth. It is emphasized by the triangular composition, with an apex in the chest decoration and two sides marked by the slanting green shapes at the card edges.

In this aspect the Empress card can represent a process bearing fruit through natural evolution. In practical matters it expresses advancement, positive developments, or a feeling of abundance and plenty. The card also can be used as a focusing tool for the success of projects that are still in a developing stage.

THE EMPRESS IS AN EARTHLY MOTHER

The link to the mother goddess and the suggestions of female fertility can also give the card a literal meaning of motherhood. The eagle coat-of-arms stands for the imperial family, and the Empress is holding it close to her heart. We can also see the image of the bird as a young sibling, symbolizing a child that the Empress is nurturing. The touch of her fingers on his body indicates a close relationship, with much warmth and emotion. Yet we also can see it as indicating an excessive and even annoying involvement on the part of the mother in her offspring's life.

In this aspect the card can refer to a warm and protective mother figure. This can be either the querent's original mother or a strong and dominant female figure in their life. It can also refer to a female querent who is a mother herself. The card may also express maternal impulses or a desire for a child.

THE EMPRESS COMBINES NATURAL AND ARTIFICIAL

The lines and shapes of the Empress card appear more natural and flowing than those of the Emperor. Also, her hold on the shield and scepter is softer and more relaxed compared to the rigid grip of the Emperor's hand. Even the back of her seat seems soft and unfinished, perhaps resembling some primitive wings.

Still, the Empress is not all nature. Her clothes combine rounded and flowing lines with sharp stripes and angles that look worked and artificial. At the bottom left side of the card we see soft and flowing earth marks, and at the top left the back of the throne is drawn in a live and organic line. Yet on the right side, the floor shapes and the external line of the throne are straight and upright. Thus, the card illustration combines both natural and artificial qualities. The Empress expresses organic forces of nature and fertility but does so within an artificial framework of society and government.

The card can symbolize a touch of softness and natural warmth within a system or an institution that functions according to fixed laws. For example, it can be an emotional or human touch in the cold, calculated setting of a commercial company. It may also signify a "back to nature" trend set against a modern way of life.

THE EMPRESS ACTS WITH PASSION

The large scepter leaning on the bosom and slanting to the right hints to the suit of wands and the domain of desires and creativity. It can signify an action "from the guts," motivated by a passionate drive and not by calculated reason. But we can also interpret the eagle as a symbol of the intellect, as it appears in the World card. The eagle appears about the middle of the body, indicating that in this card rationality is not the dominant factor but rather is integrated with feelings and passions. The eagle's gaze is directed toward the scepter base, as if the intellect serves to control and direct the expression of desires.

THE EMPRESS EXPRESSES FEMALE POWER

A natural interpretation of the card is to see it as the figure of an Empress—that is, a woman in a strong and dominant position. The card may reflect her social position, such as a manager or a commander, or it may indicate a strong, self-assured personality. In contrast to the Popess, who conceals her femininity, the Empress displays it openly, as a source of power.

Still, there are also some masculine traits in the Empress. On her neck appears a trace of an Adam's apple, and the large scepter growing from her abdomen can be seen as a phallic symbol. We can see in these traits a further manifestation of self-confidence. The Empress is not afraid to appear unfeminine when making her voice heard in a commanding manner or when she employs power and authority to impose her will.

CARD 4: THE EMPEROR

The helmet-shaped crown brings to mind the warrior nobility of the Middle Ages and indicates that the Emperor is both a sovereign and a fighter. The heraldic eagle represents the Holy Roman Empire, which conferred authority and legitimacy on the medieval kingdoms and principalities of central Europe. The object in the Emperor's right hand is a combination of two traditional royal symbols. European kings were often portrayed as holding a scepter in one hand and a spherical orb surmounted by a cross in the other. The scepter symbolizes power and authority. The orb represents the earth, and the cross above it indicates that earthly rule is subordinate to Christian or spiritual law.

THE EMPEROR RULES OVER MATTER

In medieval terms, the emperor's figure represents the earthly authority of the state as opposed to the spiritual authority of the church. The card's number also symbolizes the stability of the material domain, and some have also interpreted the crossed legs as a hint to the shape of the numeral 4. The card can represent authority in the earthly domain, such as a government official, a military commander, or a company manager. As such, it may refer either to the querent or to their superior. It may also indicate a stable material status or a rich person. More generally, it can refer to the querent's source of income, such as their workplace.

THE EMPEROR IMPOSES HIS WILL

The authoritative posture and the strong grasp on the scepter brings to mind an imposing person, one who gives orders and expects others to obey. The scepter as a phallic symbol can represent male domination; it can also be used as a mace in battle. But we can see it as a reference to the suit of wands, symbolizing desire and creativity.

The card can signify a strong personality, self-confidence, assertiveness, and leadership. On the negative side, it can express a dictator, a tyrannical personality, or a constant need to be in control and run other people's lives.

The card can also indicate a macho attitude toward women. Like the eagle in the World card, the Emperor's eagle can also represent the intellect. Its appearance under the seat indicates that the Emperor bases his position on reason, but his actual power and domination depend on his ability to use force.

THE EMPEROR IS AN EARTHLY FATHER

The Emperor's masculine authority can symbolize a traditional fatherly image. As in the Empress card, the eagle shield may represent the family. The Emperor lays the shield behind him, as if he sees his function as protector and provider and not as someone who has to be emotionally involved in family affairs.

The card may refer to the querent's role of fatherhood or to the querent's own father. It can also signify someone functioning as a father figure; for example, someone who serves as a patron or benefactor. The card may also indicate conservative values of honor, virtue, and discipline, or maybe a stern, authoritarian education.

THE EMPEROR IS READY TO FIGHT

The military helmet and the strong hold on the scepter, with the closed fist (which looks as if he is ready to punch), give the card a warrior-like and tough character. His sitting posture is also not relaxed. He looks as if he is ready to get up and fight at any moment. The card may express determination, assertiveness, self-confidence, and willingness to fight and protect one's ground. It can also express a belligerent and aggressive attitude or symbolize someone who is readily provoked and prone to anger. The card can also refer to military and security-related issues. The tense sitting posture can indicate fear of real or imaginary enemies, which makes the querent always stay on guard.

THE EMPEROR CONTROLS HIMSELF

The left hand holding the belt looks as if the Emperor is holding himself. One can also see a similar significance in the crossed legs. It is as if the right leg is blocking the left. In pictures of early medieval kings, crossed legs indicated a king acting as a judge or dictating laws—a situation requiring discipline and self-containment. The cross above the orb and the scepter also indicate putting spiritual and moral values above personal desires.

In accordance with the traditional nobility codes of honor, the Emperor's power of leadership is supposed to be based on self-discipline and impeccable behavior, yet one can interpret the crossed leg as a blockage. We can also further link it to the gaze that is turned to the left. The Emperor's dominion relies on past achievements, which are often those of his predecessors. Thus, his attitude is primarily conservative: it is difficult for him to relinquish the advantages of his status and move forward.

THE EMPEROR CONCEALS HIS WEAKNESSES

If we look only on the upper left quarter of the card, we see clear shapes reflecting the Emperor's power and control. But on the right side the lines are more rounded and the contours of the earth are ambiguous. The lower part of the shield might even be seen as positioned over a hole in the ground. One can read this as signifying the abyss or the depths of the soul. It can also represent softness and vulnerability that are not shown on the surface.

From this point of view, the card may describe a person hiding his personal fears and weaknesses behind a tough or powerful appearance. For example, it can be a person who fears opening up to an intimate relationship and revealing their vulnerability, so they put up defenses and react aggressively to anyone trying to reach them.

CARD 5: THE POPE

Le Pape in French refers to the Catholic Pope, whose attributes appear in the illustration. The Pope's right hand with its two straight fingers forms the Latin gesture of benediction used by Catholic priests. The small crosses on the hands suggest the gloves that are usually worn by popes. Three crowns, symbolizing the church's dominion on earth, have appeared on the papal tiara since the middle of the fourteenth century. An earlier version had only two, as in the Popess card, which could thus be understood as "an old story." Until the fourteenth century, popes also had a beard. Another traditional attribute of the Pope is the triple-barred cross, usually linked with the holy trinity.

THE POPE GIVES COUNSEL AND ADVICE

The unclear shapes in the lower part of the card look like two small figures with their backs to us. Their heads are shaved in the tonsure form, designating members or aspirants of the Catholic clergy. The Pope seems to be teaching and guiding them, and they may be his students or disciples. The yellow circle on the left may be a hat taken off in respect. The uncovered heads can also symbolize willingness to learn and receive advice.

The Pope card may represent a figure of authority offering guidance and advice to the querent. If the card is straight, it may indicate good advice that should be listened to. The card can refer to someone already influencing the querent or indicate that advice is needed. As with the Popess, the Pope can also refer to the reading itself. The difference is that the Popess represents the mysterious and intuitive aspect of the reading, while the Pope represents the elements of guidance and therapy.

THE POPE IMPARTS KNOWLEDGE

As head of the church, the Pope represents a system of knowledge and values with a long tradition and well-established institutions. The card may refer to any such kind of institutional knowledge. For example, the Pope card can symbolize a school, a university, a hospital, or a court. It can refer to learning or teaching in such an institute or to a procedure that takes place in it.

The card can also indicate advice from a professional expert, such as a medical doctor, a therapist, a lawyer, a coach, or any other kind of certified advisor. In legal matters it may refer to the court as a mediator, rather than to a sharp act of judgment, as we can see in the Justice card. In matters of therapy and healing it indicates conventional and institutional methods rather than alternative approaches based on intuition.

In a couple's relationship the Pope card may represent an official procedure of status recognition. However, it can be either marriage or divorce. If it is an existing couple in difficulty, the card can also represent them seeking help from a marriage counselor.

THE POPE IS A SPIRITUAL FATHER

The origin of the word *pape* is "father," which is the common mode of address for a priest. In symbolizing the figure of a father and a teacher, the card may refer to a person who has had a meaningful role in the education or the personal evolution of the querent. It can also indicate a religious leader, a spiritual guide, or a guru. In other cases the card may refer to the actual father and describe him as a person of high ideals, a moral role model, or a cerebral and distant parent. The card can also represent a part of our own personality, expressing our moral conscience, the education we received, and the values that we absorbed in our childhood.

The Protestant members of the Order of the Golden Dawn, who wanted to eliminate the Catholic reference, called the card "the Hierophant." *Hierophant* is a combination of Greek words meaning "showing sacred things." In ancient Greece it was the title of the high priest in secret rituals known as the Eleusinian Mysteries. There are also some new decks in which the card is named "the High Priest," but its basic meaning remains the same.

THE POPE POINTS TO HEAVEN

The Pope's right hand points upward in a benediction gesture, marking a diagonal line of progress and ascent. Yet the line passes through the staff with the cross, which symbolizes institutionalized religion. It is as if the

Pope indicates that the road to salvation passes through the church that he represents.

Still, unlike later cards of the suit, what we see here is not the heavenly sphere itself but only a man pointing to heaven. The Pope's guidance can be an enlightened one, and the card can represent an inspired counsel. But it can also represent someone who expresses their own prejudices and limitations, pretending that they represent heaven's decree or an objective reality. For example, the card can symbolize unfounded claims made in the name of religion or purporting to be based on objective science.

THE POPE IDENTIFIES WITH THE SYSTEM

The flesh-colored gloves that the Pope wears indicate that it is difficult to separate the person and personality of the Pope from the institution that he represents. From this point of view the card may symbolize a person who identifies with the values and the norms of the system of which they are a part. One can see here a positive image of a person who sincerely applies what they preach. But it also can be a bureaucrat or someone who blindly serves the interests of an established system—for example, a public institution or a commercial firm. The card can also represent a person who upholds conservative, traditional, and conformist values.

THE POPE SHOWS PREFERENCES

The two disciples in the card don't receive equal treatment from the Pope. He turns his attention toward the disciple on the right and seems to ignore the one on the left. Accordingly, the disciple on the right raises his hand, and the one on the left points downward. The card may represent the act of preferring someone for a justified reason, but it can also express inequality, discrimination, and prejudice. For example, it may be an institution preferring those who conform with the norms and rejecting the ones who are different and dissenting. The card can also indicate a preference for one child over the others in a family. The light blue shape under the raised hand of the disciple on the right might be a hidden knife, which hints at betrayal by the one who was preferred.

CARD 6: THE LOVER

In new English decks the card is called "the Lovers," but the French name, *L'amoureux,* means "the lover"—a singular term. The cupid above the central male figure may suggest that he is in love, but the women on his sides can be linked to a story about the mythological Greek hero Hercules. When Hercules was young, he pondered which way he should choose as his life path. One day he had a vision of two women standing at a crossroads. The woman on his left was young and seductive, symbolizing the path of easy satisfactions and sensual pleasures. The woman on his right was older and modestly dressed, symbolizing the path of wisdom, virtue, and self-control.

THE LOVER IS IN A RELATIONSHIP

The Lover card underwent many changes in meaning and design in the two tarot schools. Perhaps this is a sign of confusion and complexity, as the illustration mixes two different themes. The card's name and the cupid's arrow suggest the idea of love, but the story of Hercules speaks about choice. There is also much diversity in the mythological reference attached to the card. Several authors link it to the story of the prince Paris's choice between three goddesses that led to the Trojan War, although there is no direct suggestion of this in the illustration. In the Golden Dawn deck the illustration was replaced by an image of the hero Perseus saving the princess Andromeda from a sea monster, and the card was named "the Lovers" in plural. Waite, who didn't like pagan references, redesigned the card with the biblical figures of Adam and Eve.

The English school emphasized the love aspect of the card and interpreted it as a romantic relationship, either literally or as a metaphor of heavenly love. Cupid's arrow indeed suggests the idea of falling in love, whether a new love in the querent's life or a romantic spark rekindled in a mature relationship. But the three figures with the entangled arms and the mutual touching can also indicate a complex relationship involving several people. For example, one woman may be the man's wife and the other may be his mistress. It may also be that the mature figure is his mother, pushing him with one hand to find himself a bride, and weighing on his shoulder with the other hand to make him stay with her. One can see other situations as well, and we should remember that a male figure in the card can represent a woman and vice versa.

THE LOVER IS AT A CROSSROADS

Many authors from the French school emphasized the aspect of choice, and some even named the card "the Two Paths." The feet pointing to both sides do hint at a dilemma, and the card may represent the querent at a crossroads, not knowing which way to go. The hands touching him may signify external influences acting from different directions. His body leans more toward the young woman, but his head turns toward the older one. In the language of body parts, this means that his desires and emotions tend to the first direction, while his reason tends to the second. As in Hercules's story, one can see in the card a difficulty in choosing between the path of desire and the path of wisdom, maybe in romance or in other matters.

THE LOVER MAKES A MEANINGFUL CHOICE

The French school linked the card to the form of the letter Y, whose inverted shape is signaled by the man's body and legs. Followers of Pythagoras in ancient Greece regarded the Y shape as a symbol of the choices a person makes in their youth. The bottom line going upward is the course of childhood. At the bifurcation point in the center everything is open, and a small push to the right or to the left may decide which road the person will take. But once life advances along one of the two branches, it becomes difficult and eventually impossible to go back and reverse the choice.

The hand on the young woman's belly may hint at future pregnancy; that is, the creation of a new life depending on the lover's choice. The illustration presents conflicting indications as to the question of whose hand it is—his or hers. Perhaps we can understand it as the common hand of both. The card may indicate a choice with significant long-term implications, such as the choices that a person makes as a young adult or the joint decision of a couple to have a child. The card can signify a meaningful decision in other areas as well.

THE LOVER IS INFLUENCED BY THE PAST

The mature woman on the left represents the influences of the past. The man's gaze to her side may indicate that the querent's way of thinking is still rooted in old patterns. The card may describe a difficulty in freeing oneself from the influence of a parent or a past figure of authority, or in general a difficulty in disengaging from existing relationships and old habits. It may also be that the querent has made a decision in the past and is now pre-occupied with doubts and regrets instead of accepting it and moving on.

THE LOVER FOLLOWS A HINT FROM HEAVEN

In the traditional story Hercules chooses the path of wisdom repre-sented by the older woman. Accordingly, his story was popular in the Mid-dle Ages as a didactic parable advocating restraint and the postponement of satisfactions. But the card illustration shows several hints in the opposite direction. The cupid may be an angel. His arrow pointing to the right starts from the center of a white circle in the sky, a symbol of purity and higher consciousness. Maybe the arrow is a sign from heaven, directing the man toward the young woman and to a shared future with her. Her hand is posed on his heart, hinting that she is the one who wins his affection, and the foot turned in her direction is more advanced than the other foot. Here the two aspects of the card are combined, with love expressing itself as choosing one partner and forgoing all other options.

If the querent faces a dilemma, the touch of the heart by the future figure and the head turned to the past can signify that it is better to decide by feeling and intuition than by rational considerations. The arrow from heaven can suggest paying attention to signs and coincidences that appear as clues to the right direction. Also, the foot farther advanced in one direc-tion indicates that we can examine small incidents and indicators that express the querent's actual choice. For example, if he is torn between two romantic partners, we might consider which is the one that he calls more often or maybe finds excuses to visit her neighborhood. Though appar-ently insignificant by themselves, such small choices can hint at the orien-tation of his heart.

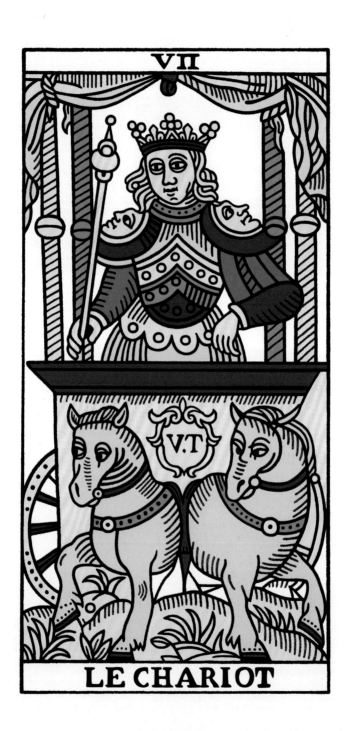

CARD 7: THE CHARIOT

Some authors have linked this card to the sun god, who in various traditions rides his chariot across the sky. Others have seen the armed rider as Mars, the Roman god of war, who is also riding a chariot. But the illustration on the card resembles medieval representations of a popular story about Alexander the Great. After having conquered many countries, Alexander decided to subdue the sky. He harnessed two gryphons—legendary flying animals—to his chariot and held a spear with a piece of meat over their heads. The hungry gryphons tried to reach the meat and, flying upward, they carried his chariot with them. On the way up, though, a flying wonder-man appeared and warned Alexander to give up his plan. Alexander lowered his spear, and the chariot landed safely on the ground.

THE CHARIOT CELEBRATES A VICTORY

The armored rider with his spear looks like a warrior. But the calm atmosphere and the decorations hint at a march of triumph rather than the act of going to war. This makes historical sense: war chariots kept their symbolic role in victory parades long after they became obsolete in actual fighting. The crown on the rider's head may also be a symbol of victory rather than a mark of royalty.

The card may represent someone who has just overcome a difficulty or a clash with an adversary. Now he can enjoy his victory in a strong and secure position. The card may describe a victory that has already been won or the possibility of a future victory. The warrior's garb indicates that victory comes to the one who is daring and ready to fight.

There are various views as to the meaning of the letters V.T on the chariot's front plate. They differ between decks and may be the initials of one of the artisans who produced the printing plates. Still, they can be given meanings if associated with something relevant to the reading.

THE CHARIOT IS IN MOTION

The card's number, seven, combines a solid structure (four) with movement (three). We may also see such a combination in the square chariot and the triangular shape of the rider's body. But the chariot has a clear structure only in its upper part. The lower part of the illustration is asymmetrical and has many strange features, which give it an intangible and dreamlike appearance. This may indicate that the solid structures of status and power suggested by the image have no real basis.

The ethereal nature of the chariot base gives the impression of floating in the air. This feature makes the illustration more dynamic, in contrast to the symmetry and heavy solidness of the upper part. The chariot is a solid structure, but its role is to serve as a vehicle of motion. In this regard, the card can refer to an advance toward a desired goal. The querent has means and resources that can help him, but they can also turn out to be a burden hindering his progress. The Chariot card may also represent a desire to go on a trip or matters related to vehicles.

THE CHARIOT IS A STATUS SYMBOL

In ancient times a chariot was a symbol of high rank or a token of excellence endowed by the ruler, as in the biblical story about Joseph in Egypt. Nowadays, too, a luxurious car is considered a high status symbol. The chariot's square shape and the four poles in its upper part hint at prestige and domination in the material world. A fleur-de-lys shape, which was the symbol of the French royal house of Bourbon, appears above the front plate of the chariot and in the crown decorations. The Chariot card can thus represent honor and prestige, aspiration to a high social status, or benefits gained through service to those in high positions. It can also signify snobbery, opportunism, and a desire to advance at whatever cost.

THE CHARIOT IS PROTECTED FROM OUTSIDE

The armor, the crown, the spear, and the chariot body create a solid and sturdy enclosure around the rider, protecting him from all sides. Only his hands and face are exposed, and they give an impression of fragility and weakness. The card can express an appearance of confidence and power that is enhanced by external symbols of success, but which hides a weak personality inside. Perhaps the querent is relying too much on external means instead of making use of his inner resources. The card can also signify dependence on material or technological mechanisms to the detriment of the human factor. In relationships, the overprotectiveness of the rider can signify a reluctance to loosen up and open oneself, or an emotional block caused by fear of intimacy and self-exposure.

The card can also refer to vanity and arrogance, which are expressed in the story of Alexander. The rider's hand posture can be a pretentious attempt to imitate the confident hold on the belt and scepter of the Emperor. In this aspect the card can also express overconfidence and failing to acknowledge one's own limitations, which can lead the querent to dangerous situations. Sometimes it can simply be the natural ambition of a young person, self-assured and overly optimistic as if he is going to conquer the world.

THE CHARIOT GOES WITHOUT CONTROL

The Indian Upanishad scriptures compare the undeveloped man to a chariot whose parts act unguided, as if of their own will. In this metaphor the rider is the conscious mind, and the parts of the chariot are the various parts of the individual's personality. We can see something similar in the card. The rider is holding no reins in his hands, and it seems that the horses are pulling the chariot as they wish, leaning to the left side of the card. The two face masks on the shoulders may represent conflicting thoughts or opposing wishes. Perhaps the querent doesn't know where he wants to go, and meanwhile the old habits pull him toward the known and familiar. It may also be that instead of setting his own targets, external factors, such as his status and assets, determine his course.

CARD 8: JUSTICE

Christian morality in the Middle Ages borrowed from Greek philosophy the idea of four cardinal virtues: Justice, Force, Temperance, and Prudence. The first three appear as figures in the tarot, and one of them—Justice with a sword and scales—is still used as a popular symbol of the judicial system today. The scales originated with Maat, the Egyptian goddess of justice, who would weigh the heart of a deceased person against a feather. If the heart was found to be lighter, it would be seen as pure and the person could proceed to a happy afterlife. Maat's scales were subsequently adopted by Themis, Greek goddess of justice. In medieval Christian paintings of the Last Judgment, the sword and the scales are two attributes of Archangel Michael. He fights the forces of evil with his sword and weighs people's actions with his scales in order to decide whether they should go to heaven or to hell.

JUSTICE IS BALANCED AND FAIR

The straightforward meaning of the card refers to issues of law and justice. It can signify legal procedures or the figure of a judge, and generally it indicates that justice will prevail. The scales express judicial deliberations weighing pros and cons, but they can also indicate a fair verdict. In situations not related to courtrooms, the card may describe a well-balanced decision that takes all factors into account. The scales may also symbolize "distributive justice," by which everyone is given their just and equal share.

JUSTICE IS SHARP AND CRITICAL

The sword wielded in the right hand may stand for the retributive justice of criminal courts, which gives punishments for crimes and transgressions. The image of the sword may signify pain or damage suffered by the querent as a consequence of their wrongs. It can also indicate a critical and judgmental attitude, which can be interpreted either as a high moral standard or as hypocritical self-righteousness. The card can also signify an "internal judge," which again can be manifested either as a developed conscience or as guilty feelings and a desire for self-mortification. We can also see in this card the figure of a judgmental and critical parent. The straight look in the eyes may be a call for introspection and self-examination.

JUSTICE CUTS AND DECIDES

Just as a court is supposed to reach a clear and sharp verdict, the sword in the figure's hand can signify a need to cut and decide. The card can describe a clear-cut decision, perhaps reached after a long weighing of pros and cons. Maybe such a decision was already made or the card can encourage the querent to finish their long deliberations and commit either way. The sword on the left side may also indicate a decision to cut away and disengage from the past.

JUSTICE ACTS WITH REASON

The structured and cerebral nature of the number eight is expressed in the orderly sitting posture and in the straight perpendicular lines that appear in the upper part of the card. The domain of intellect is also emphasized by the sword and the crown on the head. The name of the card refers to the French word *juste* ("just"), which means both justice and precision. The card may represent clear and rational thinking or a scientific outlook resting on precise theories and concepts. It can signify an action calculated to conform with socially accepted laws and norms. One can also see in it a rigid and conformist attitude that does not go beyond the limits of the existing order.

JUSTICE CONTROLS THE PASSIONS

The precise and artificial nature of the upper part of the card, which is more eye-catching on first sight, contrasts with the wavy earth and the soft lines of the clothes in the lower part. The protected chest signifies emotional closure, but the prominent and well-grounded pelvis expresses strong desires and creativity. The encounter between the two parts takes place at the height of the scales, where the order dictated by the upper part controls and directs the organic flow of the lower part. One can see here the domination of mind over passions. In this context the wielded sword may express a strong degree of self-discipline, but it can also represent sharp self-criticism, which strangles creativity and expression.

JUSTICE TIPS THE SCALES

Both the sword and the crossbar of the scales are not exactly aligned with the card frame but tilt slightly to the right side, which symbolizes the future. This inclination does not happen by itself: one can clearly see that the figure's elbow touches the balance, pushing it down on the right side. Going back to the ancient symbolism of the scales, perhaps we can take the weighing pan closer to the sword as the scale of fault, which is full of transgressions. The figure of Justice intervenes and tips the scales to the side of merit, which represents the good deeds.

In this aspect, the card can signify the need to add a human touch beyond the strict application of the law so as to tip the scales to the positive side. More generally, the card can signify a touch of grace intervening favorably in a set of rational considerations. In a similar spirit, the Mishna says, "Be judging every human to the scale pan of merit." On the other hand, if the card is inverted, we can see it as signifying unfair and crooked judgment.

VIIII

L'HERMITE

CARD 9: THE HERMIT

The name *hermit* comes from a Greek word meaning "desert." The arid landscape, the mantle, and the hood link the card to the ancient Christian tradition of solitary monks who lived in the desert and took vows of self-deprivation and penance. A beard and long, uncut hair are traditional marks of asceticism in various traditions. The lamp-like object in the Hermit's hand brings to mind the story of the Greek philosopher Diogenes. Despising accepted norms, Diogenes chose to detach himself from respectable society and live in absolute poverty, sleeping in an old barrel. Once he was seen in the busy Athens marketplace, walking in broad daylight with a lit candle in his hand. When asked why, he said that he was looking for a human.

THE HERMIT IS LOOKING FOR THE TRUTH

When Diogenes says he is looking for a human in a marketplace full of people, he speaks about what he considers a true human being—that is, an honest and virtuous one. The hermit in the religious tradition is also searching for something that represents truth, such as divine grace or mystical enlightenment.

The Hermit can express a sincere search for something of value, with readiness to pay a price, such as isolation or self-deprivation. This can be a psychological journey in search of an inner truth about oneself or a spiritual search for religious or mystical truth. In a wider sense the card may describe a search in general; for example, looking for a person or a lost object or maybe searching to find a path.

The well-developed upper front of the Hermit figure's head can signify wisdom. The three horizontal lines on the forehead resemble a symbol called *vibhuti*, which is worn by followers of the Hindu god Shiva. The spot where the symbol is drawn is the "third eye," representing enlightenment and a mystical view of truth. There are various interpretations for the three lines, one of which speaks about three levels of reality: material, mental, and spiritual. In tarot symbolism they can also represent the three layers of the major suit cards: heaven, earth, and the abyss. The Hermit may be looking for a true vision that encompasses all three. A similar form of three horizontal lines appears on the Pope's staff and can be given a similar meaning.

THE HERMIT IS FOCUSED ON HIS GOAL

The idea of a religious hermit represents a total commitment of someone who devotes their life to a single cause. Accordingly, the Hermit's gaze and posture in the card are totally concentrated in the direction of his search. Above the hand holding the lamp appears a circle with a point at the center, symbolizing a focus. The colored shapes and lines of the illustration also lead the eye to the same focal point. The fingers of the hand create a sharp shape pointed forward. This may express determination and focus or rigidity and a refusal to compromise with reality.

The card can represent determination to reach a desired goal and willingness to make sacrifices for its sake. But the turn in the left direction may also express a conservative attitude that looks for solutions within the existing frame of ideas. One can also see in the card hard-headed stubbornness, ideological extremism, or religious fanaticism.

THE HERMIT GIVES UP SATISFACTIONS

The simple habit and the monk-like appearance of the Hermit indicate that he is ready to give up comfort and material pleasures. The card can thus signify self-deprivation, asceticism, or maybe just a simple and modest lifestyle. This can be either a choice for life or a temporary stage that the querent undergoes. The reasons can also vary—perhaps it is a period of economic difficulties or maybe he has in mind some goal that requires concessions in the short term.

The image of a monk or hermit also suggests the idea of celibacy and deprivation of sexual satisfactions. More generally, it points to giving up satisfaction of any kind of desire—for example, a need to go on a diet and deprive oneself of tasty food. Still, if it is about sex, the curving stick in the Hermit's hand may refer to the suit of wands and represent crooked desires. Perhaps, as the strange yellow shape at the groin area may hint, the Hermit hides some strange and deviant passions under his puritan mantle.

THE HERMIT EXAMINES THE PAST

With the concentrated look to the left, the Hermit may be observing and examining the past or turning his gaze inward. For example, he may be trying to comprehend his past experiences and understand how they affect his present life. It can also be an attempt to find out what actually happened, as in the work of a historian, a psychologist, or a detective. In practical matters the card expresses a period of self-examination, hence inactivity. It also can be a temporary stop in order to better understand the deeper layers of the situation.

THE HERMIT MOVES CAUTIOUSLY

The concentrated look with the raised lamp in front of the eyes indicates that the Hermit examines everything meticulously. This is why various interpreters have seen this card as an expression of Prudence, the fourth cardinal virtue, which is missing from the major suit. It seems as if the Hermit checks the area well before making any move. In a positive aspect the card can describe a cautious attitude. In a negative aspect it can signal an overly suspicious character and difficulty in trusting others. The hidden feet and the turn to the left can also indicate too much caution, hindering the Hermit's advance.

THE HERMIT AVOIDS CONTACT

The literal meaning of the card's name is a solitary person who avoids contact with others. The mantle sleeve around the lamp also creates the feeling of keeping one's light to oneself. The card can represent a person with an independent thought, who doesn't care too much about what other people think of them. This is exactly the example that Diogenes offers. In a less favorable sense the card can describe loneliness, closure, fear of intimacy, and difficulty in maintaining human contact. In romantic matters the card may represent a period of solitary living or a feeling of alienation in an existing relationship. Perhaps the querent is overcritical and obsessively searches for faults in other people, or they may be searching too intensely for an ideal partner and using it as an excuse to avoid real contact.

L'A·ROVE·DE·FORTVNE

Card 10: The Wheel of Fortune

The name of the card refers to Fortuna, the Roman goddess of luck. A wheel appears in various traditional sources as a symbol of the ups and downs of life. The Talmud also says that "it is a wheel that returns in the world." Medieval paintings show Fortuna's wheel with four human figures. One is ascending, and beside it is the caption "I shall reign." The second, at the top, is sitting on a throne with a crown and a scepter, and its caption is "I reign." The third is descending, with the caption "I reigned." The fourth is lying under the wheel, and his caption is "I have no reign." A similar image of a turning wheel is also at the origin of the word *revolution*, first used in France to indicate the casting down of the old monarchic regime.

THE WHEEL PULLS UP AND BRINGS DOWN

The traditional symbol of the wheel is often used as a message of consolation. Life is a series of successes and failures, and even if we are now on a descent, ascent will eventually follow. But the wheel is round, and the change of positions in this card works both ways. Whoever or whatever is down now will move up, and whoever is up will come down. From the position of the animals in the illustration we can understand that the right side of the wheel is going up and the left side is going down. This fits the interpretation of the sides as past and future. If there are neighboring cards in a spread, the card on the right indicates a rising factor, while the card on the left indicates a falling one.

In Renaissance thinking, fortune (Fortuna) was opposed to virtue as the main factor determining the course of human life. In this view, changes symbolized by the wheel are due to capricious luck, not to personal merit. Arbitrary fortune shown in this card is also different from destiny, which drives events toward a goal that is fixed in advance. It is also possible to see the card as a roulette, or a lottery wheel, and interpret it as a reference to gambling.

The three figures with animal and human parts can represent the strange combinations of animal drives and human considerations with which we react to life's changes. The animal going up may be a donkey, symbolizing opportunistic ambition. The descending animal may be an old and wrinkled monkey, showing the ridiculous figure of vain grandiosity whose day is past.

THE WHEEL IS DANGEROUS AT THE TOP

The creature with the crown and sword at the top looks like a sphinx, a legendary ancient animal whose body combined the four living creatures of the World card: a bull, a lion, a man, and an eagle. The sphinx supposedly has it all, but the surface on which it sits looks unstable. He may be about to fall and become like the dethroned king in the traditional paintings. But we can also think that it is not moving with the wheel; rather, it is waiting for whoever reaches the summit in order to drop the sword on them. From this point of view, the card can describe danger awaiting whoever reaches the highest position.

The wheel and the device to which it is attached are unstable. The ground lines look like water waves, and the back part of the axis is missing. Perhaps the card is warning the querent not to take anything for granted. The mechanisms by which things have been moving so far may lose their basis, and one should not assume that the same wheels are going to turn in the same way indefinitely. For example, the card can symbolize the machinery of a bureaucratic system working under predictable laws. On the face of it, its wheels appear unstoppable. But an unexpected change in conditions or an exception that doesn't fit the fixed rules may disrupt them and thus render the system powerless.

THE WHEEL MOVES BY ITSELF

In medieval paintings one can sometimes see Fortuna turning her wheel. But in the Tarot de Marseille there is no one holding the handle. The two animals on the sides are also not moving the wheel; rather, it is the wheel carrying them in its motion. Maybe the querent's situation changes for better or worse, but this happens as a result of random external forces that they cannot control. This may be due to pure luck or because bigger events are happening, and the querent can only be influenced by them. One way or another, as things stand now, the querent is not a master of their own fate, yet sometimes it's a good idea to check the next card at the handle's side: after all, maybe we will see there someone or something turning the wheel and manipulating the querent's situation.

THE WHEEL TURNS AND RETURNS

The turning wheel can represent processes that repeat themselves time and again, like the number ten, which closes the first cycle of numbers and starts a new decade. We can also compare it to the circular Chinese drawing of the two elements: yang, the active and outgoing, and yin, the passive and inward-drawing. In the natural course of events, the yang element grows until it reaches its apogee, in which the yin appears. The yin grows in its turn, reaches its summit, and gives place to a new phase of yang, and so on. The revolutions of yin and yang are manifest as cycles of change, such as day and night, summer and winter, advance and retreat in life, or inner cycles in the body and mind.

The Wheel may represent astrological and biorhythmic cycles, periodic changes of mood, or bodily cycles, such as wake and sleep or the monthly cycle of female fertility. It may also represent the repeating schedule of daily life routine; symbolize time cycles like weeks, months, or years; or point to the cycle of generations in a family (for example, psychological problems repeating themselves one generation after another). We can also see it as a signification of past or future incarnations in the cycle of death and rebirth.

Another meaning we can see in the card is the closure of circles and a return to the starting point. For example, it can signify a return to a place or to a personal relationship that was significant in the past. One may also see here a vicious circle from which the querent is unable to break free, or a feeling that the querent's life is moving in circles without any real progress.

It is also interesting to compare the card to the biblical verse in Ezekiel 1:14 that speaks of a to-and-fro movement: "And the living creatures ran and returned." The living creatures in Ezekiel's vision that ride upon magical wheels have four faces each. These are the faces of the four animals composing the sphinx in the card.

THE WHEEL HAS A FIXED CENTER

Tibetan Buddhist paintings show a wheel divided into six slices representing forms of life, such as animals, people, demons, and gods. This is samsara, the wheel of existence. According to the Buddhist view, every creature dies and is reborn time and again, going up or down in the wheel according to actions in previous incarnations. A person who performed good deeds will be reborn at a higher, more pleasant domain, but sooner or later they will fall once again. The wheel of samsara also operates in a single lifetime, where it represents the endless cycle of desire and satisfaction: desire seeks satisfaction, but once reaching it, new desires are born. We can see in the samsara wheel an idea similar to the Wheel card. Interestingly, at the center of the Tibetan drawing there are also three animals: a pig, a snake, and a rooster, representing respectively the "three poisons" of ignorance, anger, and craving.

According to the Buddhist view, the ideal situation is not when one reaches a good position on the wheel, but rather when the up and down movement in the wheel stops altogether. Such a situation is called enlightenment, or nirvana. In the card we cannot see the wheel stopping, but its central point is a place that does not move up or down. Maybe this is the center of the circle the Hermit is looking at. The card may be encouraging the querent to find a fixed point of tranquility within that does not move with the ups and downs of mood changes. It may also hint at methods of meditation and spiritual exercises, whether in the Buddhist or in other traditions, which are meant to stop the wheel by giving up desires rather than satisfying them.

CARD 11: FORCE

Fighting a lion is a common symbol of force and courage. The Bible mentions Samson and David fighting lions, and the Greek mythical hero Hercules kills a lion as one of his twelve tasks. The female figure may come from another Greek tale about the nymph Cyrene, the daughter of a mortal king. One day, when tending her father's sheep, Cyrene fought and killed a lion who threatened to devour them. The god Apollo, who was passing by, watched the fight and fell in love with her. He took her to the Libyan coast, where he made her a queen of the area known to this day as Cyrenaica. A female goddess riding a lion or a tiger is also known in India, where she appears as the mighty fighting goddess Durga, or Kali in a darker aspect.

FORCE ACTS GENTLY

The Force card clearly represents strength and domination, but it is not the tough, masculine domination that we see in the Emperor, with his hard grip on the scepter. The Force figure is a woman; her posture and hold on the animal's mouth seem soft and gentle, and the lion's docile gaze upward may suggest a pet rather than a wild beast. Perhaps it is a situation of taming and mastery through collaboration, rather than a fierce struggle against a cruel adversary.

The card expresses self-confidence and personal strength, without the need for violence or forceful oppression. Still, the hierarchy of control is unambiguous: it is the woman taming the lion and not the other way around. If the querent is in a strong or dominant position, the card may indicate that others respect their authority and there is no need for excessive use of force. Rather, things can be organized and moved in a gentle and friendly way. Alternatively, if the querent is in the lion's position and is subject to a superior force, the card may indicate a choice to cooperate rather than to rebel and fight.

FORCE DISPLAYS SELF-CONTROL

In traditional pictures of a man fighting a lion, the man and the lion often face each other as opponents, but in the Force card the woman and the lion are facing the same direction. The lion even seems to be growing from the lower part of her body, as if he is an extended part of her. Perhaps the lion represents not an external agent, but her own wild animal impulses. One can see it as an image of self-control, where a person dominates and tames their own natural wild impulses. For example, she may be controlling her anger or restraining herself from acting on impulse.

The head topped with a wide hat and what looks like a crown represents the intellect, guiding the hands and taming animal desires. A line on the neck separates the head from the rest of the body, and the tightly laced bodice covering her chest indicates blocked emotions. In a positive sense, this can signify the detachment necessary to control emotions and desires. In a negative sense, it can indicate a disconnected rationality and losing touch with one's feelings and passions.

FORCE TAMES HER PASSIONS

A lion appears also in the World card, where it represents the suit of wands and the domain of desire. In the Force card it looks as if it is growing out of the woman's pelvis, so it is natural to interpret it specifically as sexual or creative impulses. The lion's open mouth can symbolize the female sexual organ. Its sharp teeth bring to mind the obscure but recurrent symbol of a "toothed vagina," expressing male fear of female sexuality. This sense of danger evident in the card may also refer to the perils associated with uncontrolled bursts of passion.

The lines of gaze of the woman and the lion meet at some point to the right of the card. We can think of them as converging at some future goal. In this aspect their joint efforts create a mighty power that is difficult to stand against. The six spikes on the woman's hat resemble the six teeth in the lion's mouth and may indicate that she is turning the fierce passions into part of her strength. The collaboration between the different parts of the figure's being can also indicate that the querent summons all their internal resources together in order to face a task or overcome a challenge.

FORCE ALLOWS OPEN EXPRESSION

The woman holds the lion's mouth delicately, touching it with her fingertips. It is not clear whether she is trying to open it, close it, or just maintain it as it is. We might understand this as an action that does not block desires altogether but rather maintains their expression under control. As the lion can also symbolize creative urges, we can see in the card an active but controlled attempt at creative expression.

FORCE TAKES A RISK

To hold a lion's mouth, even if one controls it, requires alertness and constant attention. One may also think that there is something devious in the lion's look, as if it is waiting for the right moment to free itself and bite. The finger inside the open mouth may signal playing with danger. The card may thus describe courage and daring, but in a less positive sense it may represent rashness and careless risk-taking. The card can also symbolize a threat or an inner conflict that is currently held under control at the price of constantly felt tension.

There is very little ground at the bottom of the card, and none of it on the right side. Underneath the missing ground there are parallel lines in the title strip, which give it a dark aspect. This may be the abyss representing deep layers of the soul, and the lion's legs are growing out of it. We can understand from this image that passions originate in deep levels that are beyond the rational mind's control. The woman's foot appears to have six toes. Its wide spread may signify an attempt to hold to the ground as firmly as possible. This impulse might be the result of feeling that one is on the edge of the abyss. On the other hand, it may be that the wild lion of passions is connecting the figure to a basic source of vitality that exists beneath the detached intellect and blocked emotionality.

CARD 12: THE HANGED MAN

In ancient times hanging a person upside down was a form of torture combining pain and humiliation. Often it was used on people with unorthodox beliefs. In the Roman Empire it was applied to Christians, and in medieval Spain to Jews and Muslims. But in the Hanged Man's inverted view *everything* is upside down: suffering for your faith isn't a humiliation, but a great honor. Many authors saw this card as a representation of Jesus on the cross or connected it to other sacrificed gods, such as Odin in Norse mythology. Odin hanged himself on the world tree Yggdrasil, looked down into the depths of existence, and thus discovered the magical runic letters. The card can also remind us of a bungee jump, whose origins are in a rite of passage of native islanders in the Pacific Ocean.

THE HANGED MAN RECEIVES A PUNISHMENT

In some old Italian decks the card is called "the Traitor." This may be a reference not to Jesus but to Judas Iscariot, who hanged himself on a tree after betraying Christ. In such a view, the querent may be receiving punishment for an improper or unacceptable action they have done. The punishment might be inflicted by an external source or the querent might be chastising him- or herself for real or imaginary faults.

Even if we forgo the traditional link between hanging and punishment, the Hanged Man is clearly in an unpleasant situation. The wooden frame encircles and isolates him from the surroundings and from other people. The red tips of the cut branches indicate sharpness and aggression, pointed outward (to others) and inward (to himself). The card can also describe a feeling that "everything is upside down," meaning that one doesn't understand anymore what is going on in one's life.

THE HANGED MAN MAKES A SACRIFICE

The mythological link to a god who sacrifices himself motivated many authors to see the card as an expression of giving up one's personal interests for the sake of a higher cause. In some new decks this interpretation is emphasized by a calm expression and a halo of light around the

head. Perhaps the querent accepts the process of undergoing difficulties or renouncing vital interests for the sake of someone else, for some political or ideological cause, or as part of some process of spiritual initiation.

THE HANGED MAN REFRAINS FROM ACTION

The hands of the Hanged Man may be tied behind his back or held there by choice. Either way, they signify a passive acceptance of whatever comes. The hanged posture and the surrounding wood frame give no space for maneuver. The twelve tips of the branches may symbolize a whole range of possibilities, like the full circle of the zodiac. Their cutting can signify giving up all possible ways of action. There is pain involved with the relinquishing of all initiative, as the red tips—which look like blood drops—indicate.

The card may describe the querent's being in a helpless and paralyzing state. Alternatively, the querent may be reacting to a complex situation by giving up any action and accepting whatever happens, even if it turns out to be the inverse of what they expected. The card can thus indicate surrender and reconcilement with reality as it is. Alternatively, it can describe the emotional state of regarding oneself as a passive and helpless victim, either to avoid taking responsibility for one's situation or as a means for emotional extortion.

THE HANGED MAN SEES THE WORLD UPSIDE DOWN

The Hanged Man's position seems distressful, but this is only a matter of perspective. As he is hanging upside down, his point of view is the inverse of the normal perspective. The card has no landscape except for the green ground on the sides, which can also resemble treetops. This may hint that it is impossible to decide which is the correct point of view—the Hanged Man's or the accepted views held by people outside his frame. We can also find some similarity between this card (number twelve) and the central figure in the World (twenty-one) in an inverse position.

The card may describe a unique person who sees things in their own way. It can also be encouraging the querent to think in original and non-conformist terms, which may be opposed to the common logic. If an inverse card is beside the straight Hanged Man card, it may be that from the special perspective of the querent, what is usually seen as a handicap or a crisis can look like an advantage or an opportunity.

THE HANGED MAN ACCEPTS BEING DIFFERENT

When the Hanged Man is held inverse, we have supposedly returned to the normal situation with the head up. But now the figure gives a very strange impression. The figure remains enclosed and isolated, with a sense of lacking a hold on the ground. We can see here a futile attempt by someone to be "normal" and to conform to common values at all costs. In contrast, in the upright position with the head pointing down, the card depicts him recognizing the fact that he is different so that the standard solutions are not valid for him. Instead of making hopeless efforts to "straighten himself up," he accepts himself as he is and strives to make the best of his unique qualities.

THE HANGED MAN EXAMINES THE DEPTH

The horizontal axis of earthly reality is completely blocked by the wood frame on both sides. The vertical axis is also blocked from above, and the only direction open is through the hole in the ground. This can mean that the only way to advance is to refrain from action and to engage in a profound self-examination. It can also hint at deep knowledge, such as the mysterious runes in Odin's story, or "the depth of the matter" in some situation.

Symbolically, hanging with the head down means giving up all previous assumptions, including the self-evident distinction between up and down. This means that unlike the Hermit, who seeks truth while taking for granted his existing beliefs, the Hanged Man is ready to put everything in question. The uneasy position and the isolating frame indicate readiness to pay the price of personal difficulties and social reclusion. Similar to the passage rite of the bungee jump, this also can be some kind of test or initiation preparing the querent for the transforming experiences in the following cards.

CARD 13

In new decks card 13 is called "Death," but in traditional decks it has no name. The skeletal figure with a scythe is the popular figure of the grim reaper. It is not the medieval Angel of Death, who was portrayed as a body full of eyes, but clearly it represents some personification of death. A scythe appeared in the hand of the Greek Titan Cronus (the Roman Saturn), who represented both time and harvest and was king of the Elysian islands of the blessed dead. In Greek and Roman cultures, a skeleton symbolizing inevitable death carried a hedonistic message: "eat, drink, and be merry, for tomorrow we shall die." In the Christian Middle Ages, a skeleton was used to convey the opposite message: earthly life is ephemeral, so we should better prepare ourselves for the eternal life in the afterworld.

CARD 13 CUTS THE PAST

The skeletal image, the big blade of the scythe, the scattered body parts, and the overall dark appearance of the card suggest the idea of death cutting and terminating life. The yellowish shade of the black ground above the scythe's blade expresses the total nature of the cut, as it colors everything where it passes. Still, it is a traditional rule that we should observe—never to predict the death of somebody who is alive. At most, the card can indicate the influence of a death that has already occurred on those who are alive. For example, it can describe coping with loss or a period of mourning.

More generally the card can represent the end of something. For example, it may be the end of a chapter in life, cutting off a relationship, moving away to start a new life elsewhere, resigning or being fired from a job, and so on. The sharp and decisive character of the card indicates an abrupt termination rather than a gradual decline. It also gives a feeling of inevitability.

The pair of male and female heads on the ground, one of them crowned, can represent the parents or other figures of authority who were significant for the querent. Stepping on the woman's head and passing the blade on the man's head may indicate a rebellion against their influence or cutting off emotional dependence on them.

CARD 13 IS COPING WITH CHANGE

The black ground, the skeleton with the scythe, the severed limbs, and the grim significance of the number thirteen all give the card an unsettling and fearsome character. This expresses the fact that any meaningful change in life always involves an emotional crisis. Even when it is a positive change, such as cutting ourselves off from a situation that is bad for us, it is still a move away from the known and the secure toward a new and scary domain of uncertainty. This aspect is made stronger when the card is inverse, with the black ground on top signifying the querent's difficulties in facing the change.

The gloomy appearance of the card can be unsettling for a querent who is new to tarot cards. Therefore, if card 13 appears in the reading, it would be better to refer to it right away and clarify that it is about change and not necessarily about death. For a person wishing to disengage from past patterns and start something new, card 13 is a good sign. We can also notice that the skeleton is wielding the scythe not in front of a live person, but over heads and limbs already spread on the ground. Thus, it may indicate the end of something that has already lost its integrity and vitality.

CARD 13 HIGHLIGHTS THE ESSENTIAL

Card 13 is the first card in the suit showing a completely naked figure, but it is in an extreme and blatant way "naked to the bone." The skeleton, which remains when other parts of the body have decayed, is a constant and stable element. The neck bone is divided into four parts and may thus represent the stability of matter. Old Jewish scriptures speak about the *Looz* (essential) bone, which remains after the decay of all the others. This is the seed from which the body will grow once again in the final resurrection. Some identify it with the neck bone and others with the base of the spine, which is marked red in the card.

The card may describe a shock or a crisis that exposes the true nature of things. It can also symbolize maintaining the essential and giving up the superficial. For example, it can be a financially difficult period that makes it necessary to relinquish luxuries and superficial pleasures. The hardy skeleton also may be a sort of "moral backbone" that reveals itself in a time of crisis.

CARD 13 PUTS THINGS IN PERSPECTIVE

In the popular book *Journey to Ixtlan* by Carlos Castaneda, a Native American sorcerer teaches the author that "death is an advisor." As many cultures express in their own terms, an awareness of the inevitability of death gives us a correct perspective on what is really important in life. In ancient Rome it was customary to call out *memento mori* ("remember death") in a triumphal parade, to remind the victorious hero that he is only a mortal. In a similar spirit, Buddhist monks meditate on a human skull or in a cemetery in order to be aware of the temporary nature of human existence.

The crowned head at the bottom of the card can express the idea that in front of death everybody is equal, kings and simple folk alike. In this aspect card 13 can indicate a mature and balanced view of reality that is able to distinguish between what is important and what is not.

CARD 13 OPENS A NEW PATH

Contrary to the morbid association of the card, the illustration is full of movement and dynamism. The skeleton faces right, indicating an advance toward the future. The cut limbs on the ground may remind us of the vision of dry bones in the book of Ezekiel: disintegration followed by rejoining and resurrection in a new form. The scythe's blade can also be seen as some sort of path curving upward in the future direction. We can understand that from the perspective of the present situation and the existing structures, the card expresses ending and loss. But the disintegration of the old clears the ground for something new to be born. In this respect, card 13 indicates not only the end of past structures, but also the possibility of a new beginning.

CARD 14: TEMPERANCE

The word *temperance*, of Latin origin, means "pouring or mixing liquids to obtain an average blend." Often it is used specifically for pouring water into wine. As a figure of speech it indicates a moderate behavior without exaggeration, and in this sense it became one of Christianity's four cardinal virtues. "To temper one's wine with water" is a popular French expression that originally meant calming down after being angry. Today it is used for one who makes concessions about principles, either in a positive or in a negative sense. In the Catholic Mass water is poured into wine to symbolize the dual nature of Christ as both human and divine. A figure pouring from one vessel to another appeared in the Middle Ages in depictions of the miracle of Cana, where Jesus turned water into wine for the benefit of wedding guests.

TEMPERANCE FINDS A MIDDLE WAY

The liquid flowing between the two vessels brings to mind the original meaning of the card title: a mixture of two liquids, implying a compromise between their opposite qualities. Other elements of the illustration also express a combination of two opposites. The lower half of the figure's body leans to the right, and the upper half to the left. The dress combines the opposite colors red and blue. The figure's wings suggest an ability to fly, but it also has a wide base solidly planted on the ground. The Catholic mixing of water and wine to symbolize the dual nature of Christ can also be seen as reconciliation between two incompatible elements.

Originally, Temperance as a virtue meant balanced behavior that finds the middle road without being swept to any side. This is the doctrine of the "golden mean" advocated in ancient Greece by Aristotle: always keep the right measure between excess and deficiency in anything. Similar ideas were developed in Buddhist and Confucian philosophies. The medieval virtue of Temperance was often interpreted as moderation and restraint in the satisfaction of desires, and later it was linked especially to alcohol consumption. Eventually it was identified with complete abstinence, which is clearly contrary to the original meaning.

XIIII

TEMPERANCE

The card can indicate a compromise between two opposites. For example, it can describe a reconciliation between conflicting parties or finding a middle ground between different interests. It may also indicate a person who serves as a mediator. In case of a dilemma, the card may describe a middle road, which combines the advantages of both options. More generally it can mean moderate behavior without exaggeration to any side.

It is also interesting to note the evolution between the three cardinal virtues. In the Justice card the cerebral order of the top part wields a sword and forcefully subdues the natural life flow of the bottom part. In the Force card the higher element is still master over the lower one, but this is done in a soft way that allows expression. In Temperance, too, we can see a high part and a low part, each with its own vessel, but in this card the two parts are united by the liquid flow.

TEMPERANCE DOES THE IMPOSSIBLE

The liquid seems to defy the laws of physics by hanging in the air, and yet the figure apparently manages to pour it without losing a drop. We can even imagine that it is some sort of magical liquid that can flow back and forth between the vessels. The angelic wings, the flower on the forehead, and perhaps also the link to the miracle in Cana may hint at extraordinary abilities. The Temperance card may indicate a precise and skillful action that achieves something that would normally seem impossible. We can also link this reading to the previous one and interpret the card as a compromise reached between sides that apparently seemed irreconcilable.

TEMPERANCE PROCEEDS WITH PATIENCE

The general atmosphere of the illustration is serene, and the act of pouring the liquid back and forth appears to be slow and patient. The card can describe patience, perseverance, and long-term efforts. It may also indicate a slow pace of events, preparations that go on and on, or unending hesitations between options without taking a real step. The card's calm and flowing nature, along with the angelic appearance of the figure, may also express patience, acceptance, and forgiveness toward inner conflicts and weaknesses in others and in oneself.

TEMPERANCE GENERATES AN INNER FLOW

The stripe of liquid flowing before the figure's abdomen may represent not an external but an internal flow. This can bring to mind methods of traditional medicine that regard life processes as a flow between opposite elements. For example, medieval Western medicine spoke about four liquids (humors) in the body, where the wellness of body and soul was seen as being dependent on their correct and balanced mixing. A similar concept of wellness exists in Chinese medicine, which speaks of the energy of life (chi) flowing between the active element (yang) and the passive element (yin). In this regard the card may refer to alternative and holistic medicine or to natural methods of body and mind therapy. For example, it can refer to Indian yoga, Chinese tai chi, or to New Age methods of self-balance and inner harmony. It can also indicate healthy nutrition and a well-tempered lifestyle.

TEMPERANCE DISTILLS ITSELF

Various authors have linked this card with spiritual alchemy, which interprets the alchemical writings as an allegory of a personal transformation from rough matter (the normal state of consciousness) to the philosopher's stone (pure and enlightened consciousness). The miracle in the village of Cana is also some sort of alchemy whereby humble water becomes exalted wine. Such an interpretation does not speak of blending but of distillation, a process of making liquid more refined and pure. The figure generating the flow across her middle may be engaged in such a process of self-distillation. The angel's wings and the flower on her forehead may symbolize superior, benevolent intelligence and may also indicate that the distillation is driven by a pure and spiritual element in her being.

Still, the flow in the card is directed only inward. The immobile figure rooted in the ground expresses lack of actual movement, and the raised elbows may be fending off other people from invading one's personal space. This can indicate excessive preoccupation with oneself and with one's own inner processes, which leaves no place for practical advancement or close contact with others.

CARD 15: THE DEVIL

Le Diable in French may be the Christian Devil, which stands for absolute evil. But it can also be a mischievous and unruly—but not totally malevolent—demon or imp. New decks in the English tradition have adopted the first interpretation and show a frightening demon. But in the Tarot de Marseille the figures are smiling, and they look bawdy and shameless rather than evil. The animal-like feet and horns resemble medieval descriptions of the Devil in popular beliefs and witch-hunter's manuals. But they may also relate to Pan, the Greek god of shepherds who represents the wild forces of natural passion. The image closely resembles an old Babylonian tablet known as the Burney relief, kept in the British Museum and dated around 1800 BCE. Some believe it represents Ereshkigal, queen of the underworld.

THE DEVIL MOCKS CONVENTIONAL LOGIC

The Devil (card 15) is sometimes linked to the Pope (card 5), with a similar structure of one large and two small figures. But we can also see its upper part as a distorted mirror-image of the Justice card. The Pope and Justice represent the socially established and accepted values, while the Devil represents their opposite. The stuck-out tongue echoes the male sexual organ at the center of the card, expressing mockery and defiance of social conventions and norms. The large figure is also full of contradictions: a human body with animal elements and a male sex organ with female breasts.

The Devil can represent anarchism, subversion, and defiance of conventional norms. It can also stand for inner paradoxes and contradictions that go beyond the traditional logic and the simple binary classifications of good and bad, male and female, or human and animal. It can express a borderline behavior that strains the limits of respectability and acceptance. For example, it may represent an audacious display of a libertine or licentious lifestyle. It can also indicate a desire to experience forbidden things, or original and deviant thinking that defies conventional norms.

THE DEVIL EXPRESSES IMPULSE AND PASSION

Nudity appears in many major suit cards. But only in the Devil, with the exposed sexual organ directly in the center, does it refer explicitly to sexuality. The blatantly lustful nature of the card suggests an unrestrained expression of desires. For example, the two little devils or imps, one male and the other female, may be two partners in a stormy and passionate liaison. Their animal features and their gazes directed at the tip of the main figure's penis express a relationship centered around sex and impulsive desire. At the same time, the ropes tied to their necks symbolize a difficulty in breaking up. More generally, the card can express any irrational behavior motivated by desires and passions.

One can also see the bondage and the object wielded like a whip as an indication of sexual domination or sadomasochistic experiences. It is not even clear that the penis and the breasts are genuine: perhaps they are worn as artificial accessories, indicating that although everything is exposed, nothing can be taken at face value. The card can thus express fantasy, imagination, and inventiveness in sexual matters. Going back to the symbolic link between desire and creativity, we can also see in the card a creative impulse breaking forth and going beyond the conventional limits.

THE DEVIL GROWS FROM THE ABYSS

The black area at the bottom of the card represents the abyss, which also appears in other cards. We can interpret it as deep layers of dark feelings, past traumas, fear, and pain. The sense of movement in the card is upward, so that it may represent forces originating in the hidden depths of the soul and coming out into the open. The wild, impulsive behavior of the Devil may be an expression of an underlying personality disorder or a plea for help in a situation of emotional distress. The card can also represent the influence of dark impulses such as anger and aggression, indicating the release of "the devil within you."

The upward movement also has its enlightened aspect. The two little imps seem to hint at plant growth, their feet resembling tree roots and their horns resembling branches. We can also note their tails, which symbolize an animal-like character. Compared to them, the large central figure has more human aspects, and its wings even suggest an angelic potential. We can also relate it to the myth of the Devil as a fallen angel and interpret the upward movement as a return to its original dignity. In this regard, the card can express a process of personal growth from a state of pain and emotional suffering.

The little imps might also represent parents, and the larger figure may bring to mind a smiling and cross-eyed baby's face. The parents are still bound by their necks to the darkness from which they came, but the next generation already manages to rise from the painful past and express its forces of life and creativity. In this aspect, the Devil card can indicate a process of reparation and healing from past family trauma.

THE DEVIL IS BOUND TO SATISFACTION OF DESIRES

Another paradox in the Devil card concerns the notions of freedom and bondage. On the one hand, its open display of sexuality and desire appears as a free and liberated act of self-expression. On the other, this is the only card with slave-like figures bound by their necks. This is the inherent paradox of desire: acting on it can be perceived as liberation from inhibiting norms but also as bondage-like addiction to pleasure and satisfaction. The card can represent any kind of compulsive or addictive behavior; for example, addiction to sex or drugs, eating disorders, and so on. Often such dependency is denied by the addicted person, who claims to be in control and acting on their own free choice. The large figure dominating the bound imps can also represent a relationship of abuse and manipulation, exploiting others for egoistic ends, or a negative influence of someone who seeks their own personal satisfaction.

THE DEVIL GENERATES HIS OWN UNDOING

The upright object in the large figure's left hand may be a burning torch, and the red color of the wing's tip might indicate that it is also being set ablaze. The torch may hint at the suit of wands, representing passions and burning desire. Unrestrained desire may lead to satisfaction and pleasure, as the tempting smile of the big figure suggests, but it also has its price. The card may describe some self-defeating conduct that will eventually harm the querent or a bad influence that can lead them to failure. Still, one may think that if the card represents a one-time liberating experience and not a constant way of life, it may be worth the price of a small burn to one's wing.

CARD 16: THE TOWER

A tower is a masculine symbol of power and domination. When it is hit by lightning it becomes a symbol of pride suffering a blow. Some authors have seen the card as referring to the Tower of Babel, whose builders were punished for their vain attempt to reach heaven. The three windows, the crown on the top, and the lightning may refer to the story of St. Barbara, who was a pagan king's daughter. To prevent her from converting to Christianity, her father locked her up in a tower that had two windows. Determined to convert, Barbara carved open a third window as a symbol of the Holy Trinity. Her angry father had her executed, but then a lightning bolt struck him dead. The colored circles in the air are not related to this story. They resemble medieval pictures of the manna that came down for the Israelites when they were crossing the desert.

THE TOWER KNOCKS DOWN SOLID STRUCTURES

The image of a tower hit by lightning, with figures that appear to be falling to the ground, suggests the idea of a sudden blow that strikes and destroys a solid construction. The card can therefore signify a sudden collapse of a structure or framework that appeared stable. For example, the two figures may represent a relationship or a partnership that is breaking apart. As the positions of their bodies indicate, the partners are now going in separate ways. The card may also describe losing one's position in a workplace, the crumbling of beliefs and opinions, an economic or political crisis, and so on. The crown on the tower can indicate that even those with power and authority are not protected from downfall.

The disintegration of solid structures can also be positive. The stone walls of the tower may be some sort of prison in which the querent was locked up, but now they can go free. The card can signify a liberation from confinement, which can be either the removal of external barriers or an inner emancipation from limiting and paralyzing ideas.

THE TOWER OPENS UP TO HEAVEN

The French card title, *La Maison Dieu*, translates literally as "the house god" (with faulty grammar in the original). This suggests some sort of temple rather than a punishable defiance against heaven. The spiritual significance of a temple is a material structure that opens up to receive heavenly grace. This might explain the colorful undefined shape spilling out of the circular object whose tip is just visible at the top right-hand corner. We can see it as divine energy entering the tower from above.

The Tower card can represent some sort of miracle or a sudden divine intervention in the earthly domain. The flesh-colored tower may also represent the physical body, with its upper crowned part symbolizing the head. In this interpretation the human being is a sort of living temple receiving influences or messages from higher levels, as in a divine trance or prophecy. More generally, the card can indicate a sudden revelation or insight, like an idea that strikes us as a lightning flash and dramatically changes our vision.

The opening of the tower's top to the penetration of energy can also be seen as a symbol of feminine sexuality, while the masculine tower with the circles flying around can suggest a male orgasm. The two short windows and the elongated third one also suggest the shape of male genitalia. The card may thus signify a passionate sexual union or, more generally, a state of ecstasy that can move us beyond the normal experience of reality.

THE TOWER IS BUILT SLOWLY
AND FALLS APART QUICKLY

The tower is made of bricks laid layer by layer. If we consider it a temple, then the lightning strike of divine grace isn't an unexpected catastrophe. Rather, it is the moment in which the purpose of the building is realized. In this sense we can see in the card a continuous process reaching a critical point at which everything suddenly starts to move. For example, it can be a sudden realization of a project after long and laborious preparations. Seen in a negative sense, the image could convey tension that accumulates until it explodes—for example, a hidden personal resentment that builds up and suddenly reveals itself as an open quarrel. One way or the other, the stormy nature of the card indicates an intense and dramatic turn of events.

THE TOWER SUSPENDS THE LAWS OF REALITY

It is not clear whether the two figures are actually falling from the tower at all. The one on the right may just be crawling around from behind the tower, and the figure on the left could be hovering in the air, his hands just touching the ground. This may look like a temporary suspension of gravity—that is, of the ordinary laws of reality. We may interpret it as a critical point of realization that changes everything. Even if it was planned and expected, when it finally happens it is a shock that can generate a feeling of fantastic reality where, for a moment, anything is possible.

The card may describe a period of personal upheaval during which the querent cannot be sure about the limits of the real. They can experience difficulties in adapting and feel as if everything is upside down, but they may also see new and promising possibilities that do not exist in a normal situation. In other words, one can seize the moment when the old rules fall apart in order to turn a crisis into an opportunity.

THE TOWER RETURNS TO THE GROUND

The tower is an artificial structure that rises upward, while the figures in the card look like they are returning to the ground. Their hands are extended almost as if to touch the plants. Alternatively, if we interpret the colorful little circles as manna, their hands may be gathering pieces that have fallen to the ground. Perhaps we can see the high-rise tower as symbolizing fantasies of grandeur and far-fetched plans. The figures are returning to the solid ground of reality with modest but productive plans and aspirations. In this respect the card can encourage the querent to focus on small-scale but realistic goals instead of far-reaching but uncertain plans. The card can also suggest a return to a modest but decent way of living, without excessive luxury beyond the querent's actual means.

CARD 17: THE STAR

The Star is the first of three cards having a similar structure: a celestial object in the upper part and a dreamlike scene in the lower. The big star resembles the compass rose found on old maps. Its central position may also refer to the North Star, which is the fixed point around which all the other celestial objects revolve. Some authors identified the seven small stars as the Pleiades group. In Greek mythology the Pleiades were seven nymph sisters who attracted the attention of the lustful hunter Orion. To save them from his pursuit, the god Zeus transformed the seven sisters into doves. Flying upward, they reached the heavens and became stars. Various mythological stories also tell about someone falling in love with a goddess or a woman who is bathing in the nude—that is, in a situation that combines cleanliness and vulnerability.

THE STAR REVEALS THE TRUTH

The sun, the moon, and a star are a common combination of symbols in Renaissance alchemy, and in alchemical emblems they are depicted in a form very similar to that of the cards. In the alchemical symbolic system the sun is the masculine principle, the moon is the feminine principle, and the star expresses the mystical union between them. This combination is also significant in medieval cosmology, which identified the celestial objects with crystal-like spheres ("orbits") nested within one another. The sphere of the moon was the closest to Earth. The sphere of the sun was in the middle. The sphere of the fixed stars was the farthest from Earth and the closest to the divine realm.

The calm and flowing character of the card illustration, along with the symbolic vision of a star as something pure and sublime, has motivated many authors to link the Star card with images of nature fantasy, such as the garden of Eden or the fountain of youth. These authors saw the nude figure in the card as a symbol of honesty and truth: nothing to hide, all is revealed.

In contrast to some new decks in which the woman's body is idealized, in the Tarot de Marseille it has physical distortions, especially in the lower part, but this does not spoil the pleasantness of the illustration. We can interpret it as readiness to show or to accept things as they are, with all their weaknesses and flaws. The openness in the card can also symbolize innocence and pure intentions.

THE STAR WASHES HERSELF CLEAN

In both Western and Eastern religions, bathing or pouring water on oneself is considered a symbolic act of self-cleansing and spiritual purification. It is often stressed that the water should preferably come from a natural source. The figure on the card is washing the lower part of her body. This may signal purification from feelings of sin and guilt linked to the body and to sexuality.

The naked figure and the open landscape express the renouncement of artificial and sophisticated structures and a return to the simple and natural. For example, it can signify a moment's withdrawal from the modern pace of life and the usual everyday occupations. It can also represent a ritual or a personal experience that gives a feeling of self-purification and cleansing from negative influences. It can also represent actual experiences of physical or emotional nakedness.

THE STAR REMOVES COVERS AND LIMITS

The removal of limits in the Star is expressed not only by nakedness, but also by the blending of details in the lower part of the card. The flow of water from the vessel on the right blends with the woman's thigh. The details of the landscape on the left complement the vessel and create a complex and strange shape. Near her right hand a patch of landscape has the same color as her body. The border between water and land is also unclear. In this respect, the card expresses a softening of rigid limits and clear-cut separations, giving rise to a sense of flowing and adaptation.

The card also may indicate a difficulty in setting limits for oneself or for others. Still, in spite of the removal of fixed borders, the figure maintains distinctions between what is part of her (the flow on the abdomen and the sexual organ) and what is not (the flow from the other vessel, which is held at a distance from the body). In other words, limits are made very flexible but not completely lost. The North Star above her head can also indicate that she is maintaining her focal point, even though she is not looking directly at it. This means that she is doing the right thing intuitively and from gut feelings.

THE STAR GIVES GENEROUSLY

The liquid coming freely out of the vessels can signify a willingness to give and share with others. This can be seen as either generosity or wastefulness and squandering. The figure pouring from the vessel into a kind of pool may also refer to a popular French expression "bringing water to the river," which means an unnecessary investment of efforts on something that is already there.

One can also think that the naked figure in the open scenery is too exposed and vulnerable. The bird on the tree might be the silhouette of a dove, referring to the story of the Pleiades fleeing their pursuer. Alternatively, its black color may indicate uncertainty and danger. In this aspect, the querent may find themselves exposed and defenseless in front of a threat.

THE STAR FLOWS DOWN TO EARTH

In a more mystical interpretation, we can see the large star as a symbol of divine or cosmic consciousness and the small stars as its reflections in the minds of individual persons. The small star above the figure's head is her own "higher self," an intermediate level between her personal individuality and the cosmic consciousness. Various traditions describe such a presence hovering just above the head, such as the crown chakra in India or the Shekhina that one respects by covering the head in Judaism. The comparison between a multitude of humans and the stars is also common; for example, in Abraham's vision in the book of Genesis.

We can imagine something like divine plenitude or affluence flowing from the central star through the streaming hair and then taking the form of water poured from the vessels on the earth. In this regard, the card can represent the idea of cosmic energies flowing down to earthly reality, such as in spiritual therapy methods like Reiki or healing, or channeling of messages from higher beings.

THE STAR SHINES WITH HOPE

The figure's rounded abdomen may indicate pregnancy. The pleasant nature of the card and the willingness to take a risk by exposing oneself express a feeling of optimism. The main star also suggests the Star of Bethlehem, which announced the birth of the Christian savior, or it may give the feeling that somebody is guarding you from above. We can see the card as a message of hope, encouraging us to let matters flow naturally and expect something good to come out of it.

One can also connect the card with the Hebrew word *mazal*, which means "luck." Originally it referred both to the stars and to something liquid and flowing, a combination that is also expressed in the illustration. In this sense, the card can signify luck from heaven.

CARD 18: THE MOON

The moon image in the card is taken from alchemical symbolism, where it represents the female principle, which absorbs and contains. Traditionally the moon is linked to the idea of a repeating cycle (lunar phases, menstrual cycle) and to matters related to water (tides). A link between the moon, water, a crustacean, and traditional ideas of femininity also appears in astrology, where the moon rules the sign of Cancer (the crab), associated with the element of water and representing the womb, motherhood, and home. In medieval cosmology the moon's orbit is a border zone between the earthly domain and the heavenly spheres. In popular belief full-moon nights are often related to rites of sorcery and to "lunatic" behavior.

THE MOON EVOKES A DIFFERENT REALITY

The lined light-blue areas in the card give the impression of a moonlit landscape, where things look different than in broad daylight. The animal figures and the strange buildings create a mysterious, enchanted, unsettling atmosphere. They might hint at the nocturnal reality of dreams, where deep and strange contents rise and flood the mind like the crustacean emerging from the pool. The animals, the floating drops, and even the ground between the dogs seem as if they are attracted upward. This expresses the quality of attraction ascribed to the moon in alchemical symbolism.

One cannot really touch the moon, and the sharp rays suggest that it is better not to try. The card may express a feeling of longing for something beyond normal reality. It can also represent an attraction to a dangerous ideal or toward a person who is emotionally unreachable. The card can also be related to the French popular expression "the dog barks at the moon," indicating a futile attempt to oppose something over which you have no influence.

The medieval significance of the moon as the border zone of the earthly domain can link the card with an inclination toward the occult and the supernatural reality of magic and sorcery. The Moon card can also represent an altered perception of reality, such as in dreams or with psychedelic drugs.

THE MOON AWAKENS HIDDEN FORCES

The lowest part of the card can be seen not as the bank close to us, but as the bottom of the pool. It is made of raw rocks, in contrast to the upper side, which is an artificial and worked-out structure. The upper edge might represent the constructions of rationality and psychological defense mechanisms that usually block subconscious contents. Under the moonlight these lose their power and the hidden contents are revealed. The card may describe the awakening of vague but strong emotions or actions motivated by deep feelings rather than rational considerations. It may also refer to the reading itself, which may arouse charged contents like painful memories or repressed emotions, warning us as readers to be careful and sensitive.

In the wider sense, the card may describe underlying factors hidden from "daylight" perception. The crustacean and the dogs (or maybe wolves) are dangerous animals, and the card may express a hidden danger. The two dogs barking at each other may also symbolize a quarrel whose real motives are different from what is seen on the surface.

THE MOON LOOKS BACK TO THE PAST

The left side of the card, symbolizing the past, appears to be more dominant than the right side. The moon's face is turned to the left. The left dog is in a higher position, with its tail raised, while the right dog's tail is drooping. The left tower looks open and lit up, while the right tower looks closed and shaded. The upper edge of the pool is inclined so that the left side is higher than the right side, and the crab is slightly facing the right, as if it is attacking the dog on this side.

The Moon card can describe past influences emerging and impacting the present. The depth of the pool suggests that these influences are from the distant past, not the recent past. For example, it may be about people or events that we encountered long ago, or early childhood experiences. It also may be related to past life incarnations, previous generations of the family, or the influence of distant historical events. The symbolic connection between the moon and motherhood, along with the animals drawn toward the moon, might express an unfulfilled need for motherly love in the querent's childhood. The card may also describe a person preoccupied by memories and constantly thinking about the past. Alternatively, the card may indicate a need to take a step back in order to move forward later on.

THE MOON DESCENDS TO THE DEEP

The unsettling nature of the card—with the dogs, the strange landscape, and the rising crustacean—may express a difficult struggle with contents that are emerging from the deep. But the advanced position of the card in the suit sequence indicates that the querent has the maturity and personal resources needed for such a struggle.

The movement in the card is upward. Maybe this represents the mythical theme of descent to the underworld in order to rise again with new powers and insights. The Moon can also signify tackling a problem by going deep down to its roots instead of contenting oneself with superficial solutions. It can also encourage us to look for the basic elements of a complex and confusing situation.

THE MOON DISCOVERS FIRM GROUND

The Moon card can express emotional decline and depression or even hint at the symbolic link between the moon and madness. But if we see the rocks in the lower edge of the card as the bottom of the pool, then one can't fall indefinitely. Deep down there is a solid and reliable foundation. The card may encourage the querent not to resist or repress dark feelings, such as pain, anger, or fear. Instead, they may let themselves experience the feelings, confident that deep down in themselves there is a solid base that can be trusted.

Advancing from left to right, we can see that above the pool, the horizontal axis of the card is blocked and offers no way toward the future. But at the lower edge we can see a change from the barren and shaded rocks on the left to the clear and fertile ground on the right. At the midpoint between the two sides the solid bottom almost disappears, but the lowest wave of water adds its yellow color to the rocks. This can represent getting help from others just at the most difficult moment, or it can be a golden coin symbolizing hidden treasures that can only be retrieved by going deep down.

The symbolic link between the moon and repeating cycles (waxing and waning) or tides (ebb and flow) may suggest that present hardships are just like a descent before a rise. The trouble will pass away, and by enduring it we will become stronger. The narrow passage of rocks at the bottom can also remind us of Rabbi Nachman of Breslov's saying, "Know that this world is a very narrow bridge, and the essential thing is not to be afraid at all."

CARD 19: THE SUN

The sun plays a central role among the heavenly bodies, both in medieval astronomy, where its apparent motion is the basis for all celestial movements, and in modern astronomy, as the center around which all the planets revolve. In alchemical symbolism the sun has a masculine and fatherly character, radiating out and emanating light and warmth. In the era of absolute monarchy in France, the sun was regarded as a symbol of the king, who emanates his grace on his subjects. In astrology, too, the sun is considered the ruler of the royal sign Leo. The two children in the card are often identified with pairs of twins appearing in myths of various cultures. Sometimes they are the direct children of the father of the gods or of the sun god and are regarded as heroes who fight for the forces of light. In Indian mythology they are called the Ashvin twins and possess healing powers.

THE SUN SHINES LIGHT AND WARMTH

The warm and bright colors, along with the gesture of touching between the children, give the card a bright and optimistic character. The straight radial lines around the sun create a smooth surface that blunts the sharp tips of the rays. It seems as if the sun is expanding until it almost touches the children's heads. This is especially noteworthy when compared to the porcupine-like contracted shape of the Moon.

Like the life-giving sunlight, the card can express affluence and blessings coming from above. It may represent the positive influence of people in high positions, an influx of healing energy, or the help of higher forces, whether natural or supernatural. In practical matters it can signify a comfortable situation, prosperity, and success.

THE SUN GIVES SPACE TO THE CHILD

The two young figures can signify children or refer to childhood. We may also think of the partially walled space bathed in sunlight as a child's playground. In this aspect, the Sun card may refer to the querent's children (not necessarily two), to the querent's childhood, or to children in general. It may also describe childlike traits or be an expression of one's inner child—playful, creative, and imaginative. Alternatively, the card can signify impulsiveness or lack of patience, innocence and naivety, sincerity and spontaneity, curiosity, fresh thought, or a capacity for learning and adapting. One also can see the card as a hint to New Age workshops or to similar activities that encourage participants to express childlike aspects of their personality.

The card can also indicate a refusal to grow up and to take on adult responsibility; for example, a person who is overly dependent on his parents or generally dependent on patronage and external help. We can also see it as "a fool's paradise," in which the querent is living without facing real life. Jodorowsky sometimes interprets the Sun as a father in heaven—that is, an idealized father figure. For example, it can indicate a father who was absent during childhood, so he is not felt as an earthly or tangible presence. It can also express a persistent feeling that someone is watching and supervising your actions from above.

THE SUN SETS MEASURED LIMITS

In the Sun we can see exposure and openness, but also limits and coverings. The children are almost naked, but they have a loin cloth. Behind them there is a wall, but it is low and one can jump over it. The card may express a moderate degree of openness that keeps boundaries but also permits personal contact. For example, it may represent a friendship without sexual involvement or a close relationship that still leaves some space between the partners. It can also express an education or a style of management based on setting boundaries but keeping them moderate and with a human touch.

THE SUN FINDS A PARTNER

Many authors see the two children as twins, although clearly they are not identical ones. Maybe we can just see them as brothers, whether in a biological or a metaphorical sense. The feeling of brotherhood is expressed in the gentle and warm contact between them, with a hug and a touch in the heart area. The sunlight and the nudity indicate that they are not hiding any weapons or bad intentions from each other. The protected space also creates a feeling of intimacy and security.

The card may express a feeling of warmth and mutual trust between siblings, partners, or friends. It can indicate a need to find a suitable partner for a planned project. The card may also indicate finding a "twin soul" with whom one can find emotional support. In a negative aspect the childish figures and the loin covering may express a sexual block in a romantic relationship.

THE SUN SHOWS A WAY

The figure on the left has something that looks like the remains of a tail, which may hint at an animal-like and undeveloped character. His groping hands might indicate that he is searching for his way. The figure on the right has a more alert and focused look, and he may be guiding and leading the other one. Under his feet there is a white surface open toward the future, as in the Magician card. The Sun may describe someone who gives support and guidance to the querent, leading them in a good direction. This guidance is given from an attitude of equality, not from up high, as in the Pope card.

The tail and the collar rings also resemble similar features of the two imps in the Devil card. Maybe we see here a more enlightened phase of a relationship between two people. Alternatively, they can be two aspects of the querent's personality. Carl Gustav Jung spoke of the "shadow personality," which represents the dark aspect of the subconscious mind. Our initial tendency is to reject those parts and deny their existence, but in the Sun card we can see the more developed part accepting and containing the dark side, gently leading it toward the light.

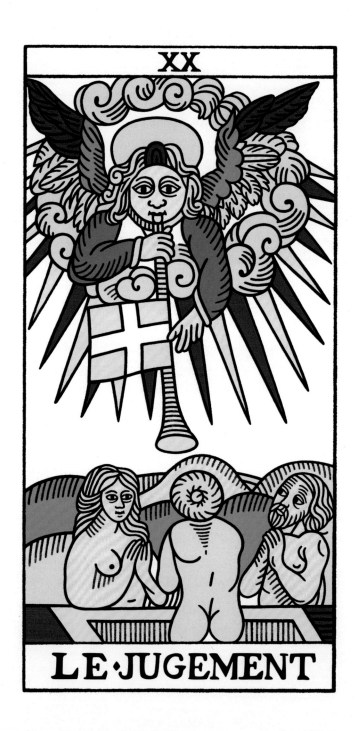

CARD 20: JUDGMENT

The card image is clearly inspired by the Christian idea of the last judgment originating in St. John's vision from the book of Revelation. In that vision seven angels blow their trumpets and announce global disasters. After a series of extraordinary events, the dead rise from their graves to stand final judgment, and finally heaven and earth become united. Pictures of the last judgment usually emphasize its terrible aspect and the fate of those sentenced to hell, but the Judgment card seems lively, illuminated, and optimistic. It may refer to the resurrection of the dead ones, but the attributes of judging them (sword and scales) appear in Justice and not in this card. Jodorowsky reads the name of the card as *le juge ment*, meaning "the judge lies." In his view this indicates that every judgment is false.

JUDGMENT SIGNALS AN AWAKENING

The original Greek name of the book of Revelation is *Apocalypse*, which means "lifting of the veil" or "revelation." The Christian day of judgment is the end of worldly history and the manifestation or revealing of heaven on earth. We can see a connection between the idea of the end of history and the two final cards of the major suit: Judgment, referring to the apocalyptic events, and the World, which can be a perfect vision of reality made divine.

The difference between the two is that the World card is more symmetrical, delimited, and stable. It may signify the end of a process on the practical level, reaching its completion in a state of equilibrium. In contrast, Judgment shows drama and movement that is directed mainly along the vertical axis. Perhaps what we see here is a completion of inner processes like a spiritual or an emotional quest. Such a completion is not a closure but a revelation and awakening that opens us to a new experience of life.

The Judgment card can indicate a moment of revelation, an awakening, or a new understanding. For example, it can signify a new insight that changes our understanding, a paradigm change, or a personal transformation. It can represent a significant turning point in a therapy process or some sort of enlightenment and spiritual awakening. The dramatic nature of the card indicates a quick pace of events, indicating a special moment rather than an ongoing process. It can also represent a meaningful insight obtained from the reading itself.

JUDGMENT OPENS THE SKY

The cross on the flag can be a Christian reference, but the cross is also an ancient symbol that predates Christianity, and thus we may give it another interpretation. It can symbolize the meeting of the two axes in the cards: the horizontal axis of earthly reality and the vertical axis of inner experience. The trumpet can be seen as a kind of tube that is an open path to the sky above. The line pattern on the back of the middle figure imitates the trumpet shape in an inverted way and expresses active acceptance of what comes from above. The tonsured head resembles the two aspirants in the Pope card and indicates that the figure has undergone a path of spiritual learning. The head and the hill behind it may also remind us of an eye observing us, a mystical symbol of higher wisdom that has survived from ancient Egypt to modern times. Sometimes it is drawn inside a triangle, and we can see such a shape between the three faces in the card.

The card may describe a moment of grace in which spiritual reality manifests itself on the earthly plane. For example, it may be the peak moment of a magical ritual or a mystical experience that blurs the limits between ordinary and extraordinary reality. It can indicate an awakening to a higher level of consciousness or to the understanding that there is something above and beyond material existence. It might also signify the opening of the gates of heaven—that is, a moment in which we can make a wish that will come true.

JUDGMENT ILLUMINATES THE ABYSS

The three figures on the ground can be a child with two parents. If this is so, the card may be showing an ideal family triangle where the parents assume their role with adoration and devotion. Their contact with the child's body indicates closeness and support, and their nudity expresses an egalitarian attitude that respects the basic humanity of child and adult alike. We can see here a reparation and recovering from problems originating in the relationships with the parents. Alternatively, the card can represent the querent's assumption of responsibility as a parent. If the card is inverse, it can indicate an unhealthy relationship between parents and child.

The opening in the ground is the abyss, which has appeared in the previous cards but is now illuminated and open to the sky. The white surfaces around the pelvis may express purity and cleanliness in sexual matters. One can also see the angel with the raised wings and the tongue extended outward, as an elevated version of the main figure from the Devil card. Like the Christian day of judgment that is the world's redemption, the card may express some sort of redemption or emotional reparation—that is, healing of the soul's suffering and illumination of its dark sides. The connection between the angel and the figure in the middle may also represent an encounter of the querent with their personal angel or with a sublime and benevolent part of themselves.

JUDGMENT REVEALS WHAT IS HIDDEN

The nudity, the figure coming out of the hole, and the bare ground indicate that whatever was buried and hidden is now revealed and exposed. The Judgment card may indicate the revealing of a secret previously kept by the querent or from them. The trumpet resounds far and wide, and it may indicate that private matters become common knowledge. The card may express public exposure and fame or, alternatively, defamation and gossip. It can also symbolize mass media and the spread of information.

JUDGMENT CELEBRATES A NEW BIRTH

The central figure emerging from the earth between the two parental figures can hint at a baby coming out of the womb. The card can refer to the circumstances of the querent's birth or to a new baby in the family. In a more general sense, one can think of the birth of something new in the querent's life. Whatever is born is accepted with approval and support, but its face is still hidden; we cannot know exactly what will come out of it. The card may also describe a rebirth, a personal transformation, that opens a new chapter in the querent's life.

CARD 21: THE WORLD

Medieval depictions of "Christ in majesty" show him surrounded by a pointed oval aureole called a *mandorla* ("almond" in Italian), which resembles the wreath of leaves in the card. In the four corners around the mandorla appear the four living creatures mentioned in the books of Ezekiel and Revelation: a bull, a lion, a man, and an eagle. In Christian tradition they are called tetramorph and symbolize the four evangelists. The central figure resembles a twelfth-century illustration by the mystic Hildegard von Bingen called "cosmic man," surrounded by a circular halo and the four wings of the cardinal directions. The card also resembles South Indian depictions of the god Shiva Nataraj ("king of dance"). Shiva, whose dance animates the universe, is shown dancing inside a round wreath with one leg raised in the air.

THE WORLD UNITES ALL THE ELEMENTS

The concept of cosmic man refers to a traditional mystical view of the human body and soul (the microcosmos) as a small-scale image of the universe (the macrocosmos). In the microcosmic scale the living creatures can represent the four domains of the minor suits: body, desire, emotion, and intellect. The central figure can symbolize the unifying consciousness represented by the major suit. In the macroscopic scale, the figures correspond to the five elements of ancient Greece, medieval philosophy, and Hindu tradition. Four of them make up the material world as well as the human body: earth, fire, water, and air. The fifth element, called ether or akasha, represents a more sublime level of existence. Putting it all together, we can say that the World card depicts a complete image of the universe, of the human being, and of the tarot deck that represents them both.

The card can symbolize a harmonious integration between different areas of activity. For example, it can be a simultaneous advance in several directions or a good balance between different life domains. In practical matters it symbolizes realization and success. One also can see it as referring to the world in a literal sense, such as a trip abroad, foreign connections, or issues involving other countries.

THE WORLD PRESENTS A PERFECT VISION

The image of the World can be connected with the preceding card, Judgment. In the book of Revelation, after the judgment of the dead, Christ appears in majesty as king of the world, surrounded by the four living creatures. This is the moment when the universe reaches its final perfection, and in the card we can see an image of perfection in the symmetrical and balanced illustration of the card, which puts everything in its proper place. In this aspect the World expresses an ideal vision of perfection that can motivate the querent to move forward, evolve, and find better solutions. Alternatively, it can represent a tendency to see the world or oneself in terms of an ideal image far removed from reality. As the last card of the suit, it can also represent perfection in the sense of completion and signify the positive outcome of a project or the closure of some process.

THE WORLD MOVES BETWEEN OPPOSITES

A recurrent idea throughout history is that everything that happens in the world is driven by the tension between two opposites: light and dark, for example, or hot and cold or high and low pressure. Such ideas appear in the teachings of the ancient Greek philosopher Heraclitus, in the Chinese concept of yin and yang, and in the modern physical theory of heat and energy (thermodynamics).

The dance of the central figure in the card can also be driven by such an opposition, expressed as the polarity between male and female. The hand on the right is holding a masculine wand. The hand on the left is holding a sort of semi-hidden receptacle, a feminine shape that may suggest a womb. The hand on the right is pushing at the wreath as an active gesture, while on the left the figure approaches the wreath at several points without touching it. As in the correspondence table in chapter 7, we can also see two living creatures on the right as representing the hard (male) suits and those on the left as the soft (female) suits.

The card may indicate a movement driven by tension and opposition between two poles. For example, in case of a clash between two adversaries, the card can indicate a third party who stays protected in the middle while taking advantage of the situation. In case of a dilemma between two options, it can signify that the best course is not to commit oneself one way or the other, but to draw benefits from both.

THE WORLD DANCES INSIDE A FRAME

The four living creatures are believed to be of Babylonian origin, representing the astrological fixed signs. These are like four stable points holding the celestial wheel of the zodiac in place. The fixed signs are Taurus (bull), Leo (lion), Scorpio (which is sometimes represented by an eagle), and Aquarius (a bucket shown in the hands of a man). At the upper edge of the wreath we can see two tiny triangular shapes with a dark right half, perhaps two rays of a hidden star. Noticing the resemblance between the upper part of the dancing figure and the figure in the Star card, we may also think that it is the North Star.

In the medieval worldview the zodiac and the North Star belong to the sphere of fixed stars, which provides a stable frame of cosmic laws for the ephemeral life on Earth. In this aspect the card gives an image of movement taking place inside a fixed framework. For example, it can represent a person experiencing a rich and dramatic inner life while externally following an uneventful conventional routine. It can also represent someone carving themselves a private niche for free expression within a heavily regulated environment, such as a workplace or an organization.

The dancing figure also resembles a ninth-century Carolingian illumination of David playing the harp. He is depicted as dancing with one leg bent backward and is surrounded by an almond-shaped aureole and four figures of the cardinal virtues. This and the hint to the dancing Hindu god Shiva can link the card to dance, performance, and bodily expression.

THE WORLD IS CLOSED WITHIN ITSELF

The dancing figure is contained in some sort of an enclosure, which protects but also limits it. The card may thus indicate that the querent is trapped in a situation where everything looks fine from the outside. For example, it can be the golden cage of a well-paid job that doesn't allow real advancement or personal evolution. The wreath separating inside from outside may also symbolize disconnection and estrangement between the inner feelings of the querent and their external life situation. For example, it can represent a feeling that "I don't belong here" in marital life or at work.

The navel of the dancing figure can bring to mind the ancient Greek concept of an *omphalos*, the world's navel. Together with the separating wreath, it can indicate that the querent feels themselves to be at the center of their own private universe. In a positive aspect it can indicate emotional independence and self-sufficiency. In a negative aspect it can mean narcissism, a feeling that the whole world revolves around you, and social isolation.

THE WORLD PREPARES SOMETHING NEW

As the last card of the suit, the World represents a closure. But the illustration also resembles medieval medical depictions of a human embryo, with a folded leg and spread arms inside a round womb. The hand touching the wreath on the right side can also be expressing a desire to come out and be born. In this respect, the card may describe a process of reaching an apparent measure of stability, while inside there are already the seeds of change. It may also indicate pregnancy, whether literally or metaphorically as a project or an idea in preparation.

THE FOOL

The French word *mat* means "dull, not shiny." Sometimes the card is also called *le fou*, "the insane." This sounds like an unflattering title, and the card shows a wayfarer or vagabond in a strange outfit, fancily decorated above but shabby and torn below. Still, various spiritual traditions link madness with sanctity and higher wisdom. In the Bible and in the Jewish Midrash tradition, the terms "prophet" and "man of spirit" are often associated with "madman" or "fool." The Daoist and Zen philosophies in China and Japan portray an ideal sage behaving like a mindless madman. Influenced by such ideas, many authors see the Fool card as a symbol of sublime spirituality, and in the Golden Dawn system it represents the highest degree of consciousness.

THE FOOL IS ROAMING FREE

The illustrated figure may remind us of the classic village fool being chased by dogs. The natural landscape suggests that he is outside the structures and the accepted norms of society. One can understand the image of the Fool literally, meaning that the querent is acting foolishly and risks making themselves a laughingstock. But we can also see the card as an expression of total freedom: from the laws of reason, from worldly obligations, and from caring about others' opinions. His progression toward the right represents advancement, and the figure of the Fool—who seems not to care where he's going—expresses uncertainty and an open future.

The Fool card can indicate freedom from bonds and from attachment to fixed frameworks. For example, it can symbolize a period of aimlessly roaming about without a clear goal, a long journey, or an attitude of non-commitment that leaves all options open. In a less positive sense the card can represent a person who has difficulties in choosing and committing themselves—for example, to a fixed place of residence or relationship or professional activity. One might also consider that the lower end of his staff is stuck in the ground, so he is going round in circles.

In new English-school decks the Fool is walking carefree along the edge of a cliff. This can indicate a lack of responsibility in a dangerous situation

LE ·MAT

or "fool's luck," which protects him from harm. This detail is absent from the Tarot de Marseille card, but the colorful and cheery nature of the illustration also gives an optimistic feeling of avoiding misfortune along the way.

THE FOOL BELONGS AND DOES NOT BELONG

The Fool card has no number, a fact that has made some authors suggest that it isn't really a part of the major suit. Though empty, the number band at the top nonetheless gives it a typical major suit structure. Perhaps, like the village fool who is part of society but also an outcast, the Fool both belongs and doesn't belong to the major suit. The card can indicate a maverick or "odd bird," someone (or something) that is unusual, deviant, and impossible to classify. It can also encourage the querent to free themselves from conventional patterns and look for uncommon solutions outside of the box.

THE FOOL GIVES UP CONTROL

A yellow hem, a belt, and a rod separate the Fool's figure respectively into legs, pelvis, chest, and head, symbolizing the four domains of earthly activity. There is also some breaking apart between the various sections, as if each of them acts on its own. The man's upward gaze gives the impression he's not paying attention to the road. The exposed buttock scratched by the animal (a dog or a cat) may symbolize a weakness or a vulnerable point of which the querent is oblivious. Being on the left, the animal may also be something from the past disturbing the querent, haunting or prodding them to move forward.

We can interpret the card as lack of organization, chaos, and carelessness. But in a situation of uncertainty, perhaps it is better to adopt the Fool's attitude: give up control and embrace spontaneity, refrain from too much planning, and adapt oneself to changing circumstances. As someone who lives outside the power structures of common society, the Fool can also indicate lack of interest in things like self-promotion, ambition, and domination of others.

THE FOOL LIVES HERE AND NOW

The three sections of the rod resting on the Fool's shoulders may represent past, present, and future. The sack hanging from its end can symbolize the heavy burden of past memories or the assets and tools acquired through experience. The Fool carries his past along with him, so that at any moment he can reinterpret and give it a new meaning. The receptive spoon-shaped rear end of the rod may indicate readiness to add new insights to old ones. The white front tip may express an undetermined future, but the hand touching it indicates that the Fool's actions are shaping and directing it.

The philosophies of Dao and Zen, which recommend focusing on the present without useless concerns about the past or the future, speak in similar terms. In addition to the "wise fool" figure of a careless and free-spirited bum, both refer to the concept of emptiness, which may remind us of the missing card number. The Chinese word *dao* means "way," thus suggesting the image of a walking figure such as we see in the card. The Fool card can indicate someone who lives for the moment, paying attention only to what is happening here and now. If the card turns out to be the last one in a spread, it can signify that the outcome is unknown because it is not yet determined.

THE FOOL CAN BE ANYONE

In traditional tarot games every card had a fixed value except for the Fool, which could replace any other card. In ordinary card games a similar role is played by the joker. Like the Fool in the tarot, the joker is also commonly depicted wearing a clown outfit with round bells and a pointed hat with a ball on its tip.

The Fool card may represent somebody acting like a clown or a joker, treating any issue with humor, and not caring much about the scorn of others. But we can also link it to the common playing card joker, with its unfixed value, and interpret it as a sign of flexibility and adaptability. For example, it can be someone who adapts themselves well to a wide range of situations or avoids being labeled by expressing different aspects of their personality in different situations.

But the Fool can also be you or me or any other person walking the path of life. The card can be a reminder that in front of the great mystery of existence, we are all mindless fools. And in complicated situations that bring people to the reading, maybe it gives a simple and sobering message: let go of big questions and sophisticated plans, stop worrying about the past and the future and issues far removed from your reach, and just live.

CAVALIER·DE·BATON·

CHAPTER 7

THE MINOR SUITS

Each one of the four minor suits contains fourteen cards and has its own suit symbol: coin, wand, cup, or sword. The structure of the suits is very similar to ordinary playing cards, except for an additional court card in the tarot. In fact, the common ("international") playing card suits are simplified versions of the tarot suits, whereby the coin has become a diamond, the wand a club, the cup a heart, and the sword a spade. These changes were not universal, however. In Spain and Hungary, for example, local playing card suits still carry symbols similar to those of the tarot.

There are three kinds of cards in each minor suit:

- An ace card, which is generally considered as number one in the suit. The illustration of an ace card shows a single exemplar of the suit symbol, large and rich in its details.

- Nine number cards, which run from two to ten. Each one of these shows the symbolic suit object in the corresponding number. For example, card number three in the suit of cups shows three cup icons.

- Four court cards with human figures, which represent four ranks in the social world of the Middle Ages: a page, a knight, a queen, and a king. Each card shows the symbolic suit object, and usually the figure is holding it.

Many conventional tarot books group the aces and the number cards together as pip cards, where the word "pip" refers to the small icons of the suit symbols that appear in the card illustrations. However, in the Tarot de Marseille (and, in fact, in most of the new decks as well) the illustrations of the ace cards resemble each other while being quite different from the number cards of their respective suits. We can understand this as a statement that "being an ace" is more significant than "being of this or that suit." In this book we consider the traditional card illustrations as the key to their meanings, so we shall treat the aces and the number cards as different types and discuss them in separate chapters.

The Suit Symbols

The symbolic objects of the suits are mentioned in various traditions as having a mystical or magical significance. For example, in the Christian Mass the coin and the cup appear as the bread and wine of the Eucharist: a sacramental bread, round and flat like a coin, and wine that the priest drinks from a chalice. The shape of the coin is also similar to traditional round charms with symbols and letters carrying a magical power. The cup appears in the book of Genesis as a silver cup that Joseph uses for divination. In the English legends of King Arthur, the Knights of the Round Table go searching for a sacred cup, the Holy Grail.

The wand appears as a tool for performing magical acts; for example, by Moses and the Egyptian priests in the book of Exodus. Today it is still used in popular magic shows. The sword appears in the hands of superior beings such as war gods in various traditions or the archangel Michael in Catholic lore. It also appears as the flaming sword placed with the cherubim to guard the way to the Tree of Life in the book of Genesis. Magical swords are a common motif in many legends—for example, the sword Excalibur in the Arthurian myth.

In the English-school decks the suit of coins is sometimes called "pentacles," with the illustrated coins inscribed with a five-pointed star, or pentagram. But this is a new addition meant to emphasize the connection between the coins and a specific kind of magical amulet. The coin cards in the traditional Tarot de Marseille deck show a flower with a fourfold symmetry, not fivefold. This shape is also magically significant, as we shall discuss in the next chapter.

A common view links the four suit objects with the four social classes that are typical of traditional society; for example, in medieval Europe or in India. The wand, which appears in some cards as a green branch, represents the class of peasants and farmers. The coin represents merchants and urban artisans. The sword represents the fighting nobility. The cup represents the clergy.

THE SUIT DOMAINS

Each minor suit has its own specific character and domain of action. When cards of a specific suit appear in a reading, they can represent either an issue arising in its domain or an attitude typical of its character. For example, the suit of coins is related to questions of money and material possessions, but it can also indicate a practical and possessive attitude in another domain, such as in a romantic relationship.

The list of suit domains given here is derived from the teachings of Jodorowsky, which are not very different from other conventional approaches. More information on the character of each suit can be learned from the discussion of the ace cards in chapter 8.

COINS: BODY

material and physical, practical and conservative

The suit of coins indicates money, the workplace, and the space we live in. It also represents the body, health, and food matters. The nature of the suit is stable and conservative, like the round coin (as seen from above), which is enclosed in itself and does not evolve in any direction. The suit is characterized by practical thinking, preference for concrete and tangible things, and preservation of what is already there.

WANDS: DESIRE

passionate, outgoing, energetic, creative, conflictive

The suit of wands expresses sexuality, growth, self-expression, and giving birth to new things. It can represent creative impulse, stamina, energy, and a desire to advance and to dominate. It can also indicate complications, difficulties, and struggles. In Mamluk playing cards, which are probably the origin of the minor tarot suits, the wands appeared as polo sticks used to hit balls in a horse-riding game. We can see this as an indication of matters related to games, recreation, or competition.

CUPS: EMOTION

sentimental, romantic, social, spiritual

The suit of cups is related to emotions, to human relations, and to mystical feelings of devotion. We may think of the cup as being filled with water (life-giving flow), wine (joy, drunkenness, illusions), poison (negative feelings, hatred), or being empty (dryness, emotional block). It may appear straight (positive emotions) or upside down (negative emotions). The nature of the suit is romantic, nostalgic, and suggestive of things beyond the tangible world.

SWORDS: INTELLECT

rational and verbal, decisive, aggressive

The suit of swords expresses ideas and thoughts, an ability to focus, decision making, and also the possibility of hurting oneself and others. In common language we often use the image of the rational mind as a blade that cuts and separates things. For example, we may speak about a sharp mind, a piercing logic, or an analytical ability. The word *decision* also derives from *cutting off* in Latin, signifying a choice of one option and cutting off all the others. The nature of the suit is sharp and determined, calculated, and ready to fight, and it also may be cold and cruel.

SOFT AND HARD SUITS

Even a superficial look at the illustrations of the minor suit cards shows that they are divided into two groups. One group we can call the "soft" suits: the coins and the cups. The other group is the "hard" suits: the wands and the swords.

The soft suits can be regarded as having receptive, feminine, and favorable characteristics. Their symbolic objects are round, enclosed, and containing, and the dominant colors of their number cards are yellow with some red. This gives the cards an enlightened and pleasant feeling, suggestive of gold objects, riches, and pleasure.

The hard suits can be regarded as having an outgoing, masculine, and challenging nature. Their symbolic objects are long and narrow, suggestive of rigidity and penetration, and they can serve as weapons. Their number cards are colored mainly in red and black, emphasizing toughness, struggles, and clashes. They are also composed of long intermeshing parallel bars, suggestive of closure and complicated entanglements.

This distinction between soft and hard is very clear in the design of the number cards. It is also significant in the ace cards and is still present in the court cards. From this we can understand that it was clearly present in the minds of whoever created the minor suits. Other indications of this exist elsewhere. In ordinary playing cards the symbols of the soft suits (diamonds and hearts) are red, while the symbols of the hard suits (clubs and spades) are black. In traditional methods of fortunetelling the soft-suit cards are often considered as more beneficial than the hard-suit cards.

In the soft suits each suit symbol has one basic shape that repeats itself throughout the suit. There may be some differences in detail, and the object size becomes smaller as the card number increases. In particular, the objects in the Ace of Coins, the Ace of Cups, and the 2 of Coins are considerably larger and much more detailed than in other cards. But the coin is always shown as a flat circle with a fourfold flower-like decoration, and the cup is a goblet with a hexagonal base and a wide ring around its stem.

In contrast, each of the hard-suit symbols has two different shapes. The wand can be either a naturally shaped green branch or a worked-out straight rod. The ace card shows a natural branch. In the court cards the shape of the wand gradually develops from a branch in the page card to a rod-shaped lance in the king's hand. In all the number cards the wand appears as a straight, smooth rod with a wide blade at each tip. We can interpret the two shapes as two aspects of the wand suit. The natural branch expresses growth and creation. The artificial rod expresses conflicts and difficulties.

The sword may have either a straight or a rounded shape. In the ace and in the court cards it is straight. In the uneven number cards there is one straight sword, and in the ten card there are two straight swords. But the other swords in the number cards appear as an even number of rounded arches with wide blades at their tips. The round swords are arranged so that they cut off the center of the card from its edges. We can interpret this also as two aspects of the sword suit. The straight sword represents penetration, determination, and breaking through, while the round sword represents separation and limits.

CORRESPONDENCES

Various traditions maintain the idea of a symbolic quartet—a set of four symbols that together represent something whole and complete. The four minor suits are often correlated with such symbolic quartets. The most popular association is with the four elements of Greek and medieval philosophy: earth, fire, water, and air. There are different opinions as to which suit corresponds to which element, but most tarot readers accept the Golden Dawn scheme: the coin is earth, the wand is fire, the cup is water, and the sword is air.

Other symbolic quartets associated with the four suits include the four cardinal directions and the four living creatures at the corners of the World card. Again, there are different opinions on the exact correlations. Another correlation that was mentioned in chapter 4 links the suits to four body parts: feet, pelvis, chest, and head.

Tarot theorists who believed that the cards were originally connected with the Jewish Cabbala have correlated the suits to the four letters of the Tetragrammaton, the unpronounceable Hebrew name of God. These letters are in their turn linked with other quartets in Cabbalistic symbolism, which provide further correspondences for the suits. For example, the four letters are correlated with four worlds that are different layers of Neoplatonic emanation, as mentioned in chapter 5.

We can also think of correlating the suits with the fourfold systems that were dominant at the time when the tarot emerged. For example, as we mentioned earlier, the four suits might represent the four classes of traditional society. Another possibility is to correlate the four suit domains with the four natural kingdoms in Aristotelian and medieval philosophy: mineral, vegetable, animal, and human. The kingdom of mineral is pure matter, which is the coin. The kingdom of vegetable introduces sexuality and fertility, symbolized by the wand. The animal kingdom sees the gradual development of emotion, represented by the cup. And finally, with humans appear language and rationality, which correspond to the sword.

Such systems of correspondences can be useful in different situations. For example, when discussing the symbolic language of body parts in the tarot figures, we referred to the corresponding minor suit domains. We can also do a "tarot meditation," concentrating one by one on the four ace cards. Going from bottom to top, with each card we concentrate on the corresponding body part while reflecting on the corresponding domain in our life. If we want to construct a magic circle for a ritual or a meditation session, we may want to mark the four cardinal points with ace cards, and for this we need a correspondence between the suits and the cardinal directions.

The idea of correspondences also raises the question of the suits' ordering. Is there one true way to list them in sequence? Different sources present the suits in different orders, but looking at the suit correspondences, we may think that a standard ordering could represent the evolution of natural kingdoms (mineral, vegetal, animal, and rational), which is also going up with the body parts (legs, pelvis, chest, and head). This would give the ordering as coins, wands, cups, and swords. We can call this the symbolic ordering of the suits.

Still, as the division into soft and hard suits is expressed so strongly in the illustrations, the study of the cards becomes simpler when suits of each kind are grouped together. Therefore, when presenting the cards in the next chapters, we shall arrange the suits in the following order: coins, cups, wands, and swords. Note that this "didactic" ordering is used here only for the practical purpose of learning.

The following table shows the minor suit correspondences used in this book. It is based on the Golden Dawn system, which is today widely accepted, with some additional elements from Jodorowsky. The suit arrangement is by the symbolic (evolution) ordering.

For each minor suit, the listed correspondences are the suit name, French title, playing card suit, life domain, body part, living creature (from the World card), element, and cardinal direction.

TABLE 2: **MINOR SUIT CORRESPONDENCES**

SUIT NAME	FRENCH TITLE	PLAYING CARD SUIT	LIFE DOMAIN	BODY PART	LIVING CREATURE	ELEMENT	CARDINAL DIRECTION
Coins	DENIERS	Diamonds	Body	Legs	Bull	Earth	North
Wands	BATON	Clubs	Desire	Pelvis	Lion	Fire	South
Cups	COUPE	Hearts	Emotion	Chest	Human	Water	West
Swords	EPEE	Spades	Intellect	Head	Eagle	Air	East

READING THE MINOR SUITS

Many readers find that the twenty-two major cards of the Tarot de Marseille are sufficient for a deep and productive consultation. Still, we may think that it is not for nothing that the tarot has kept all its suits throughout its long history. There must be some symbolic power in the complete tarot deck, and we may want to tap its full potential.

There are several possible ways to integrate the minor and the major suits in a reading. One way is to treat the two kinds of cards on the same footing: to shuffle them together and to lay them down side by side in the same spread. This was the accepted way of using the complete deck in the English school and its New Age derivatives. The opposite way is to keep the major and the minor cards separate. For example, one can think of doing a two-part reading, first with minor cards only and then with the major cards. I sometimes do a similar thing when I use the court cards as a projection tool to begin a reading, as described in chapter 9.

A third possibility, which is a middle way between the first two, is to shuffle together the two parts of the deck but treat them differently in the spread layout. For example, suppose we have some experience with the major cards and are just beginning to use the minor cards. In this case, we may want to rely more on the majors and use the minors only for supplementary information and background. A possible way to do so is to use the minor suit cards as a background layer for the basic three-card spread.

To do this, we start by shuffling the complete deck. Then we draw cards from it one by one in the usual way. But we don't stop after three cards as before. Instead, we fill the three positions of the spread in the following way: we lay the first card, which comes out from the shuffled deck in the first position at the left side. We lay it open (that is, faceup). If the card is from one of the minor suits, we draw another card and put it on the first one so that it covers it completely. If it is again a minor card, we draw yet another one to cover the first two, and so on. We continue piling cards on top of each other until a card from the major suit turns up. Once this happens, we leave it on top and move to the second (middle) position.

Now we repeat the same procedure, piling minor suit cards on top of each other until a major suit appears. Then we pass to the third (right) position and repeat again. Finally, we end up looking at three cards from the major suit. Under each one of them is a pile of minor cards whose size may vary. It is possible, of course, that in one position or more the first card that came up is a major card, in which case it has nothing under it.

The reading of the spread can now be done on three levels. First we can read only the top cards from the major suit, as in the usual basic spread. In fact, this is the case during most of the reading sessions. The top cards hide the cards beneath them, and what we see in front of us is the basic spread of three major suit cards. Sometimes we may even be tempted to stop at this level if we see a clear answer from the three top cards. However, it is important that once we have drawn cards and laid them down, we should refer to them, even if briefly. Failing to do so would almost always result in a negative reaction from the querent.

On the second level we don't read each minor suit card separately but only pay attention to their general distribution. We can do this even before learning each minor card in detail. First, we note the number of cards in each of the three piles. If there are many cards underneath the top one, it is "a big bundle." This means complicated issues, many factors involved in the matter, or a great load that burdens the querent. In contrast, if the top card appears alone or maybe with one card underneath, it means that what we see is what there is. We can take things at face value and don't need to look any deeper.

Now we can check how much of a given suit is present. For example, if one of the piles (or maybe the whole spread) contains many coin cards, it may indicate matters related to the material and physical domain, practical considerations, or a lot of money. On the other hand, many cups can indicate emotional matters, a romantic attitude to the question, or special attention that should be paid to human relationships. A large number of hard-suit cards (wands or swords) expresses hardship and struggles. A large number of soft-suit cards (coins or cups) indicates a more relaxed atmosphere, an easy situation, or a supportive environment.

Another thing to notice is the kind of minor cards. Aces indicate energy, a strong drive, or an initiative expressed through the cards on top of them. Many number cards can mean a lot of details and small issues that the querent has to deal with. The court cards present human figures with a specific social status. If many of them appear in the spread, it may indicate many people involved in the matter or consideration related to status and social relations. Since the court card may also express the querent's way of action or their attitude, a large number of court cards may indicate that various attitudes and drives are at play within the querent's mind.

Finally, we may notice the appearance of several number cards with the same number or several court cards of the same rank. A recurrent number may say something related to the numerological meaning of the number. For this we may use the list of number meanings in chapter 4. We can also interpret it as an indirect hint to the major card carrying this number. Alternatively, the number itself may be meaningful; for example, the number three can indicate three people involved in a situation or a time span of three months.

Several court cards of the same rank can signify an attitude or a position typical of this rank, as explained in chapter 9. For example, several page cards may indicate lack of experience or insecurity in the querent. Several king cards may express a mature and responsible attitude or a recognized and distinguished standing. It can also indicate the completion of a process and readiness to embark on new adventures.

On the third level, which we can apply once we know the minor cards well enough, we can read the cards under each of the three majors as a story or process. The story is read according to the order in which the cards were laid down, leading to the major card on top. One can also take each pile and spread its cards in a row from left to right in order to see the whole story in a glance. After having read them, then we can put the cards together again and proceed to the next pile.

It is also possible to use this method with only some of the minor suits, especially when we are still in the process of learning them. For example, we can start by adding the four aces only to the twenty-two majors. An ace card would give a special emphasis to the card covering it and infuse it with energy and drive according to its suit domain. Then we can put in the court cards, adding a human dimension with feeling and motivation. Finally, we could add the number cards, which can give us a detailed story of actual events.

As an example, consider the following spread. For some time, the querent has been preparing herself for a change in her professional occupation. She is apprehensive about possible negative reactions from her environment toward the new direction she has chosen. In a basic spread with a minor suits background, the cards on the facing page came out.

Card 13 on the left expresses a sharp and abrupt change. The skeleton looks at the faces in the World and the Moon cards and moves toward them with his scythe. It has nothing underneath: for better or worse, change is coming; there is nothing more to say. The old road has come to an end, but the card says nothing on the next move.

Left: Card 13 with nothing underneath;
Center: 2 of Wands, 7 of Coins inverse, 3 of Swords, The World on top
Right: King of Coins, 2 of Swords, 10 of Swords inverse, The Moon on top

The 2 of Wands, looking like a crossroads, represents the question of where to go now. The central coin in the 7 of Coins looks protected and well placed, maybe expressing the possibility of remaining in the comfortable and secure zone of the old occupation. But with the card inverse, it may be under pressure. The straight sword in the middle of the 3 of Swords symbolizes the other option: it breaks out from the protected space between the two arches and advances to a new domain. The World on top, with a dancing figure within a close space that resembles the curved arches of the swords card, indicates that, for the moment, the querent remains secure in the existing zone and doesn't make a move to break out.

The King of Coins holds a coin that he already has on his lap, symbolizing assets that have accumulated in the old professional domain (such as experience and status). But his gaze is toward the future. The flower in the center of the 2 of Swords is still contained within the boundaries, not breaking them. But in the 10 of Swords the two inverted swords stuck in, and the general feeling of heaviness, make it too difficult to remain in the present space. The Moon, with its strange and intimidating landscape, expresses the challenge of confronting the unknown. But the solid ground at the bottom indicates that with such a move, the querent can connect to a deep and stable basis of her inner strength and underlying powers.

From the spread as a whole, we can understand that the main motive of the querent now is her hesitation to take the risk of moving forward to a new and uncertain domain. As long as she can remain reasonably comfortable in the boundaries of the present condition, the urge to move forward and change will remain unrealized. But in a broader perspective, it is possible to see that the old course has already reached its final stage. It has no place for future development, and its only advantage is the comfort and protection of the existing situation. At a certain moment the querent will be under pressure that will not allow her to remain where she is now. This will be the moment when she dares to move forward, challenge the unknown, and find her deep strengths.

The Row Spread

When we first begin to study the tarot, we may want to rely on the major cards as the backbone of the reading because we know them best. Still, when we know fairly well all the deck parts, we may want to do an open reading with all the cards shuffled together. The natural way to do so is to lay the cards side by side, majors and minors alike, and look at the resulting picture, as we do in the basic three-card spread. However, as most minor cards in the Tarot de Marseille are not very rich in details, it is difficult to have a deep and meaningful reading with only three cards. The obvious solution is to lay a larger number of cards in a horizontal row, so that their combination is interesting and complex enough. As before, we do this moving from left to right.

The number of cards that we use can be decided in advance. Usually, a row of seven cards from the complete deck would not be too complex to read as one coherent story, and as an odd number it would have a well-defined center. We can also lay six cards and separate them into two groups of three in order to compare two options or ways of action side by side. We can also decide on a longer row if we feel that it would be more suitable for our style of reading.

Another possibility is not to decide in advance but to lay the cards, one after another, until we feel we have enough. This option gives us more freedom, but it also has its drawbacks. We may be tempted to stop the spread just when we reach a card that we like. In other words, we may end up getting whatever answer we wished for in the first place.

As an example for a row spread, the following cards appeared in a spontaneous reading with a new deck of cards that were shuffled for the first time. This fact may explain why there are so many coin cards. Still, I considered the spread as valid because in a reading everything is a sign.

2 of Coins, 3 of Coins, 4 of Coins, King of Swords...

The three cards on the left together form a shape that can express expansion. Starting in the space between the two large icons in the 2 of Coins, it goes through the 3 of Coins in the middle and ends in the wide gap in the middle of the 4 of Coins. As these are coin cards, they may refer to some issue about money and livelihood. The querent has made some progress in this area and achieved a certain degree of stability, which is hinted at by the square array in the 4 of Coins.

Now the king in the middle cuts the process with his sword and turns his eyes in a new direction. Instead of material and practical concerns, he is interested in an internal process of self-transformation, as indicated by the two major cards. With the Moon he goes through a challenging period of exploring dark layers in his soul. This process blends, through the lines of water and earth, with the magical flow of the Star. In this pair of cards we can see a road that is dark at the beginning but further on becomes enlightened.

The naked figure who generously spills her water seems to be oblivious of questions of gain and loss. It is as if she gives up material concerns to gain emotional integrity. But later on in the process the 6 of Coins appears, again with a focal point in the middle and with joyful leaves all around. The number six is connected to the first three cards: six is the sum of two and four, and echoes the three between them. One can also see its two coin

(continued from left) The Moon, The Star, 6 of Coins

triangles as a visual combination of the three coins on the second card and the triple fleur-de-lys shield on the third card. It appears that the time-out that the querent is taking from material issues, and the embarkation on a process of self-exploration, finally leads him to the economic comfort that he was initially looking for.

As another example for a seven-card row spread, consider the following story. The querent holds a medium-level position in an established company but hasn't had a promotion for some years. In the past she's made some mistakes that were turned against her by competing colleagues. This has made her feel bitter and socially isolated in the workplace. Still considering herself the victim of unfair treatment, she also understands now her own role in making it happen. She asks how to proceed from here.

The following cards came out in a seven-card row spread:

9 of Coins, King of Wands, King of Cups, The Popess...

The single coin at the center of the 9 of Coins represents the querent's present position, blocked and isolated in a narrow space. The King of Wands, who may be stabbing his own heel, symbolizes the self-defeating actions in the past. The King of Cups holds his cup firmly as he turns a covered ear to it and looks away toward the future. He can represent the current resolve to control personal emotions and issues, which may have been behind those self-defeating moves, and look ahead for a new chapter.

The Popess, book in hand, may represent the reader and her cards. The very act of seeking advice now expresses the querent's new phase of self-awareness. The veil behind the figure represents uncertainty; the future is not yet defined because the querent has a choice.

The three cards behind the veil represent three options. The 6 of Swords has a central plant adapting its form to the shape of an enclosed space. This represents the passive option: accepting the present situation as it is and trying to make the most out of it while avoiding a clash with the sharp swords around. The Justice card represents the overactive option: coming forward with your own sword, demanding what is rightfully yours, and being ready to fight for it. But the brightest-looking option is the middle one, the 5 of Cups with a central object echoing the single coin of the first card. Not isolated any more, now it is surrounded with plants and flowers, all streaming toward and from the other cups. In this option the querent

(continued from left) 6 of Swords, 5 of Cups, Justice

doesn't make an active move now. Instead, she puts her effort in building better personal ties with her fellow workers, winning friends through gifts and gestures, and gradually turning people in her favor. In this way she will be in a better position when the next opportunity for promotion arrives.

CHAPTER 8

THE ACE CARDS

Each minor suit begins with an ace card that presents the suit symbol as a large image rich in details. In ordinary card games, an ace card can have two values: it can be both the lowest and the highest card in the suit. In much the same way, the tarot ace card has a double function in the suit. On one hand, the ace is number one, the beginning of the suit. On the other hand, the ace represents the suit symbol in its most developed form, and thus it summarizes the nature of the entire suit.

In a reading we can interpret an ace card in both ways. As number one, the ace card expresses the beginning of a process or a new initiative related to the suit domain. For example, the Ace of Coins may be a new business venture, and the Ace of Wands can indicate the beginning of a creative project. As the card that summarizes the whole suit, an ace can symbolize an attitude or a significant factor expressing the character of the suit. For example, the Ace of Cups may represent a sentimental and romantic attitude that motivates the querent, while the Ace of Swords may describe a cerebral attitude, a cutting decision, or the act of focusing on a goal.

As mentioned in the previous chapter, various mystical and magical traditions employ the idea of a symbolic quartet that represents four aspects of some wholeness. The function of the ace card as representing the energy of the suit makes it possible to take it out of the deck and use it as an emblem or amulet representing one element of the quartet. For example, we can set up a magical circle for a ritual or a focusing and visualization session by laying around us the four ace cards in the four directions corresponding to the suits. We can also perform an exercise in which we focus on one of the ace cards in order to strengthen our inner forces in the corresponding suit domain. We can also make a copy of the ace card and carry it with us, and so on.

The Four Aces: Wands, Cups, Coins, and Swords

ACE OF COINS

The three other aces present objects that stand upright, but the coin appears as if it is lying flat on the ground. According to Jodorowsky, this expresses the more basic nature of the coins relative to the other suits. The coin is the ground from which the other suits grow, just as the material reality is the basis of all life functions: without a body, there is no place for desire, emotion, or intellect.

The four-petaled flower at the center of the coin may signify the structure of the complete tarot deck. The circle in the middle represents the major suit, and the four petals are the minor suits. The round coin may also symbolize the Earth as it was thought of in ancient times: a flat and round plate, but marked by the four cardinal directions. In alchemy and astrology the symbol of the Earth is a circle divided into four equal quadrants, which represent the four material elements: earth, fire, water, and air. In traditional Western magic it is also customary to perform rituals within a circle around which the four cardinal directions are marked.

The Ace of Coins thus can be considered as containing within it the potential for growth, not only for its own suit but for the other suits as well. The plant decorations above and under the coin are still turned inside, but they seem to be ready to open and might hint at the suit of wands, the next suit in the order of evolution. The aspect of growth is also reflected by the presence of the number three: three lines on each petal of the central flower and three kinds of triangles in the external part of the coin.

The Ace of Coins is almost symmetrical in the vertical axis, meaning there is only a minor difference between the straight and the inverse position. For example, in the upper right-hand side the flower isn't completely painted, the space above the coin is a little larger than the space under it, and the pattern of dots at the center of the coin looks different when the card is inverse. Still, as the basic structure is the same, usually we do not distinguish between a straight and an inverse card. This may express the neutral nature of money and matter: both have an objective measure

(for example, in kilograms or dollars) that does not depend on our moral preferences. Therefore, we cannot speak about them as good or bad by themselves.

INTERPRETATION: The beginning of a business or an economic venture. Devoting attention and effort to material matters, such as bodily health, property, the workplace, or the living space. A stable and solid base for future growth. A practical attitude that remains close to the ground and to tangible matters. Materialistic considerations. A significant sum of money appearing in the querent's life.

ACE OF CUPS

The base of the cup in the card illustration looks as if it is emerging from a water-covered surface, and the whole image gives the impression of pushing upward. The three jagged shapes in light blue at the middle of the card may be streams of water pouring from the cup or perhaps wings carrying it up to the sky. The vertical structures at the upper edges resemble the towers of a fortified city or a religious structure, like a cathedral. They are pointing to the sky or to heaven, but they also fall short of actually touching the card frame. We can see here an aspiration to grow out of the material realm and reach something beyond ordinary reality, an aspiration that can never be fully realized.

In the Christian tradition a liquid-holding cup appears in various places as a symbol of a mystical aspiration or of sanctity, such as the chalice of holy wine or the grail of Arthurian legend. But the receptacle on the card looks rather like a reliquary of the kind used to keep relics of Catholic saints. In Judaism a similar shape can also be found in Havdalah receptacles, which contain perfumes and are used to separate the sacred time of the Shabbat from worldly existence.

The suit of cups represents the domain of emotions and love. The religious element in the card's design may express the idea of earthly love as a reflection of heavenly love. In other words, love and devotion toward God are a higher aspect of similar feelings shared between human beings. This idea plays an important part in mystical currents of many religions, such as Christianity, Judaism, and Hinduism. We can find another hint connecting earthly love with the divine realm in the Lover card from the major suit.

There are differences between the left and the right side of the cup, especially a difference in the shading, which makes the right side more open and illuminated. Still, generally speaking, the card looks fairly symmetrical and schematic, with straight lines and square angles. This may seem strange for a card that is supposed to represent emotions. Indeed, in some other traditional decks, the cup shape looks softer and rounder. One possible explanation is that the objects of the other three suits can be used alone as they stand. In contrast, the cup is only a receptacle that serves for something else, namely the liquid it contains. In a similar way, we may think that the ace card does not represent emotion itself, which is subtle and intangible. Rather, it symbolizes the human structures that provide space for emotion and love, such as a family or a couple relationship.

> **INTERPRETATION:** A new love. Intimacy, mystery, the warmth of hidden feelings. Focusing on romantic affairs or on emotional issues. Yearning for someone who is absent or longing for something unattainable. A romantic, spiritual, or idealistic attitude. Feelings of mystery. Devotion and submission to something beyond yourself.

> **inverse:** Negative feelings, an emotional block, misguided aspirations, a deception in romantic matters.

ACE OF WANDS

The ace cards of the two hard suits show a hand coming out of a strange yellow-tipped shape and holding the suit symbol. Both aces also contain colored drops that give the cards an energetic, vibrant, and bursting character. But in the Ace of Wands the grip is gentler than in the Ace of Swords, with the soft and accepting side of the hand turned toward us. One may understand that the Ace of Wands has a softer nature, which is also expressed in the illustration of the wand.

In the Rider-Waite deck the Ace of Wands has a strong masculine aspect, with a clear phallic shape of the central object, but in the Tarot de Marseille the wand shape has a double nature: it is both a stick and a tube, meaning that it is both masculine and feminine. The lower part of the wand is straight and upright, and it stresses the masculine aspect. In the upper part the external lines of the wand are soft and rounded, and the tip shows an opening that is suggestive of a female sexual organ.

The green wand becomes wider in its upper part, expressing vitality and growth. The drops spreading at the sides signal an outgoing flow. These aspects emphasize the relation of the suit to creativity, desires, and life force. The cut stubs of the branches may seem like blood drops, but their shape is also similar to the colorful drops surrounding the emblem. We can interpret them as initiatives in various directions that do not lead to long-term achievements (meaning they are cut off), but they still inspire and generate a general atmosphere of energy and creation. This signifies the plentiful and extravagant nature of the life force, which spreads its resources in all directions. The evident fingernails express the process of struggling and coping with difficulties. On the stem above the severed branch on the right is a sort of hidden thorn, which may symbolize the dangers of an uncontrolled burst of passion.

When the Ace of Wands card is straight one can see it as a plentiful force of life, full of dynamic impulses, energy, and creativity. When the card is inverted the drops are converging and the wand, with its side branches, becomes narrow and squeezed between the fingers. In this position it can

symbolize a block or a limitation of impulses and desires, especially in the sexual or creative domains. But it can also signify concentration that aligns impulsive drives toward a specific goal.

> **INTERPRETATION:** A period of growth, drive, and energy; moving forward with passion. Start of a creative project or a generally creative period. Dissipation of resources in all directions. Active sexual life, a new partner, or multiple sexual affairs at once. An attempt to advance in different directions simultaneously, letting the results decide which one to follow in the long term. Acting on desire and impulse without thinking too much about the consequences.

> inverse: Restriction, a creative block, lack of energy, repressed sexual drives.

Ace of Swords

The large sword rising through the middle of the card gives it a sharp and decisive character. The crown is decorated with two branches, which can be a palm on the right and a bay laurel on the left. Both are known since ancient times as common symbols of victory. The red tips of the cut branches resemble blood drops and may symbolize sacrifice and hard struggle through which victory is achieved. The crown can also refer to the head and highlight the suit's link with the domain of intellect. A crown with two similar branches appears at the bottom of the 2 of Cups.

The irregular shape at the bottom left, from which the hand emerges, resembles a similar shape in the Ace of Wands card, but in the Ace of Swords the yellow serrated edge looks sharper and more angular and agitated. In addition, the hand is growing from the edge of the shape, while in the Ace of Wands it emerges from the center. This might express the intuitive feeling that impulses and desires originate in deep levels within our mind. In contrast, rationality and the intellect conform to laws that we learn and absorb from our environment. This means that they are felt as something external that we assimilate.

One can also see the wavy lines as a symbol of the brain. Today we know that impulses and desires come from central parts of the brain. In contrast, rationality and language are processed in the outer cortex. This means that passion and desires come "from inside," while rational thinking is imposed "from the outside." Clearly, the original creators of the tarot couldn't have been explicitly aware of this fact, but they might have felt it intuitively. We can also note the difference between the natural, flowing wand and the artificial, rigid blade of the sword. Again, this may express the difference between passions and rationality.

When the card is straight one may think of the sword as being held in our hand. In such a situation the card can indicate a sharp and precise action, clear thought, efficient planning, or the ability to make an incisive decision. However, when the card is inverse we can think that the sword is being thrust into us. This may represent negative ideas and fixed preconceptions that hinder and damage the querent. Alternatively, it can indicate being hurt by someone. We can also see the inverse card as encouraging the querent to "turn the card around" and take deliberate and decisive action in order to change their situation.

> **INTERPRETATION:** Sharp thinking; a clear definition of goals. Power and control of the situation. An ability to skip lengthy deliberations and decide one way or the other. Cutting away with the past, with negative influences, and so on. A fighting spirit, courage, victory, glory. A new initiative characterized by determination and precise planning. Separating between beneficial and damaging things. Ambition and competitiveness.

> inverse: Confusion, negative thoughts, unproductive perceptions, self-punishment, cruelty, hurt, defeat.

THE COURT CARDS

RANKS AND SUITS

Each of the four minor suits includes four court cards, which represent four ranks, or positions, in the aristocratic hierarchy of the Middle Ages. In ascending order of status, these are:

- A page, marked *valet*. The French term indicates a subordinate, and in the context of the other cards he can be either the knight's servant or his apprentice (a squire). In either case he is a young man of low position, but as an apprentice he may rise in the future to be a knight himself. All the pages in the cards are young men standing with their feet on the ground.

- A knight, marked *cavalier* (an old spelling, today it would be *chevalier*). All the knights are mounted on horses (*chevals* in French).

- A queen, marked *reyne* (today spelled *reine*). The queens are crowned and seated on thrones, with their feet hidden under robes.

- A king, marked *roy* (today: *roi*). The kings are also crowned and seated on thrones, but their posture seems unstable and their feet are showing.

Three of the four tarot court ranks also appear in ordinary playing cards: a knave or jack (who replaces the page), a queen, and a king.

The court cards may, on first sight, resemble the major suit cards, as they also display human figures and carry card titles, but there are important differences between the two card types. First of all, while in the major suit there is no clear pattern in the organization of the cards, the court cards can be arranged in a well-ordered four-by-four table: four ranks in each of the four suits. This gives the court cards a much more orderly and schematic structure.

Another difference is that in the major suit there are many mythological and symbolic figures, and as the suit develops these figures gradually lose their social function, as well as their clothes. By contrast, there appears to be no explicit mythological or mystical references in the court cards. All their figures are dressed, and their ranks identify each one of them with a definite social status. This means that the resemblance between the court and the major cards is felt most strongly at the major suit's beginning, which represents the everyday life of earthly existence, and much less in the abstract cards at the major suit's end.

The symmetry of the four-by-four table makes it possible to see a correspondence between the ranks and the suits. The four pages are standing on solid ground, which links them to the suit of coins. The knights mounted on horses express dynamism and movement typical of the wands suit. Also, the horse touching their pelvic area can represent the animal forces of desire. The original form of wands as polo sticks in the Mamluk playing cards can also be linked to the horse-riding polo players. The female figures in the queen cards express the domain of emotion represented by the suit of cups. And finally, the kings' domination, resolution, and mature wisdom correspond to the combative, decisive, and intellectual suit of swords. As with the body parts, in this correspondence the suits are arranged from lowest to highest by their symbolic ordering of evolution: coins, wands, cups, swords.

In studying the court cards, it's a good idea to lay them all down in the square table form—that is, in a four-by-four array—with the ranks as rows going from bottom to top (page, knight, queen, and king) and the suits as columns going from left to right. Now we can look at the card images and note their common features and differences. We can lay the suits in columns from left to right according to the symbolic ordering just mentioned, but in order to notice the design features that distinguish the soft suits from the hard suits, it is better to arrange them by suit types: coins and cups, followed by wands and swords (see table on following page).

Ordering the columns in this way, we can notice that many figures in the hard suits look warlike and inclined to action, while figures in the soft suits generally look more peaceful and relaxed. The kings of the hard suits look young. They wear armor and hold their weapons with confidence. The pose of their bodies hints at imminent movement toward the right. The kings of the soft suits, on the other hand, look older and more settled. They are also looking toward the right, but their posture suggests caution and restraint.

As for the queens, they look closed and defensive in their posture, and in some way they are all armed. In the hard suits they hold their big weapons in a threatening manner. In the soft suits, though, they only have a sort of rod resting on their left shoulder. This looks rather like a defense against possible attack from behind, and they seem to be more concerned with the nonaggressive suit symbols that they hold in their right hand.

The knights of the hard suits wear some kind of armor-like decoration. It is less elaborate than the kings' armors, but still it gives them a more combative appearance than the civil clothing of the knights in the soft suits. It is only in the page cards, especially the Page of Wands, that we cannot see the more warlike character of the hard suits. But still, we can also assume that the page is preparing himself to use his wand as a mace at some later stage.

A Four-by-Four Table of Court Cards

In a reading a court card can represent the querent or another person involved in the question. Alternatively, a court card may represent a course of action or an attitude toward the issue of the query. In such a case, several court cards can refer to the same person and indicate different aspects of their attitude or behavior. We can also ask the querent directly who or what the figure in the card reminds them of. As with the major suit cards, here, too, a male figure in the card may refer to a woman or vice versa.

THE HUMAN FIGURES

Having a similar structure with fewer details, the court cards are sometimes treated as some sort of poor relations of the major cards, but this view overlooks their unique qualities. No doubt they are less sophisticated, less surprising, and less dramatic than the major cards, but this is exactly why we can see their figures as more human, friendly, and down to earth. They are not involved in extreme and bizarre situations, nor do they look up to the sky or down into the abyss. Neither do they try to represent abstract moral principles. Instead, in the court cards we see human beings leading a normal life, each of them having a definite status in society and belonging to a particular family, or suit.

For people who don't know the tarot, the major cards can appear intimidating, with their mysterious and complex "larger than life" symbolism. In comparison, the simpler and more earthly character of the court cards can make it easier for people to relate to them emotionally. Even without having studied the court cards systematically, we can look at the figures and start by asking ourselves questions: Who is this person? Why is he sitting or standing in such a way? What exactly is he doing with his suit symbol, and how is he treating it?

This possibility of looking at the court cards just as we look at ordinary people opens up new ways of using them in a reading. For example, instead of shuffling the court cards into the deck as part of a regular spread, we can use them separately to help a querent express their own feelings in their own words.

I sometimes use such a technique with querents who find it difficult to open up and share their concerns with me. First I separate the court cards from the deck and spread them with their faces up. I ask the querents to concentrate on their feelings about the issue and pick up the card whose figure echoes them most closely by posture or facial expression. Then I ask them to look again at the card, describe the features that catch their attention, and comment on their reasons for having chosen it. These include both their explicit thoughts while picking it up and the insights that they get from a closer examination of the image details. Having listened to their description and shared my own thoughts about it, I then proceed to a three-card spread from the major suit.

TABLE AND IMAGE

In chapter 5 we discussed the elements of order and chaos in the major suit. As we saw, the suit presents a complex interplay between the two. The regular four-by-four table of the court cards expresses a much higher degree of order than the haphazard sequence of the major suit. It also expresses the stability of the number four. This stability goes well with the established order of the feudal figures shown in the illustrations, but there is also a strong element of chaos. To see it, we should look closely at the images.

Each court card figure is drawn in a unique posture and with unique details. Some figures are looking to the left and others to the right, some are shown in an artificial environment and others in a natural landscape, some have their head covered with a hat or a crown while others are bareheaded, and so on. Any rule that we can try to find in such details seems to have its exceptions.

Features involving the suit and rank of the figure also show exceptions. On each card the suit symbol appears once, but the Page of Coins card shows two coins. There are also cards with an additional suit symbol from another suit, such as a wand in the Knight of Coins or a sword-like rod in the Queen of Cups.

A more surprising indication of chaos in the court cards is the titles. It is surprising because, in principle, titles such as "King of Cups" should express the ordered table structure. But there are numerous irregularities and exceptions in the written titles of the Conver deck. Most of the court cards' titles are written inside a strip at the bottom of the card, but in the Page of Coins the title is written down the side. The titles of three suits are in the singular form, but the coins are written in the plural, *deniers,* and not *denier.* In the wands suit the suit name is *baton* on three cards, but on the queen card it is written in an older spelling: *baston.* And—as in some major cards—there are also many dots and groups of vertical lines in the titles, with no apparent pattern.

These two aspects—the orderly table structure and the more chaotic image details—form the basis of two methods for interpreting the court cards. We shall refer to these methods as interpretation by the table and interpretation by the image. Many writers writing about the Tarot de Marseille in the last century have combined elements from both of them.

The interpretation by the table is based only on the suit and rank of each card. In this method each rank represents an attitude or a stage in a process, as we shall elaborate in the next section. The suit indicates the domain or the stage in which this attitude finds its expression. For example, a knight can symbolize progress toward some goal. In the suit of coins it may be about a business initiative that has already started to move toward realization. Note that the interpretation by the table does not refer to the details of the illustration; only the suit and rank that define the card's place in the table are significant. Therefore, we can reach similar interpretations from the table with decks in which the court cards are differently drawn.

The interpretation by the image is essentially similar to the intuitive perception of the human figures that we described above. We can make it more systematic by applying the symbolic language of chapter 4. In addition, we can refer to the unique features of the card title and think of possible meanings for them.

The two methods of interpretation actually have been applied already in our discussion of the ace cards. The table structure of the aces is much simpler, as it consists of only one row and four columns. Still, we rely on it when we say, for example, that the Ace of Coins can represent a new business initiative. This interpretation comes from crossing the number 1 (beginning) with the suit of coins (practical domain). On the other hand, we apply interpretation by the image when we speak, for example, about the masculine and the feminine aspects of the Ace of Wands. We get this information not from the number and suit of the card, but rather from the shape of its main object.

THE FOUR RANKS

The four ranks of the court cards can be interpreted as four phases of a process. The page represents an initial phase characterized by hesitation and uncertainty, a humble position and limited resources. The knight is already in movement toward an achievement or a goal, but his ability isn't yet fully developed and his attitude isn't completely mature. The queen represents a phase of realization. She can enjoy the fruits of her past achievements, but her tendency to preserve them may block her from advancing further. The king represents a process that has reached its peak and is now going past it. In this phase whatever has been accumulated and learned can serve as a starting point for the next move.

THE PAGES

The pages appear as youths with a soft and slightly feminine appearance. They are standing or walking on untilled ground, and their posture expresses hesitation and lack of confidence. The coins and swords pages are standing with their feet pointing in opposite directions; the Page of Cups even seems to be stumbling on the uneven ground. The Page of Wands's suit symbol is a huge trunk blocking his way. In addition, the suit symbols themselves appear almost too heavy or complex for them. The Page of Coins is holding only one coin out of two. The Page of Wands has a wand that is too large to hold comfortably. The Page of Cups is trying to look into a cup that seems too deep. The Page of Swords rests his heavy sword awkwardly on his shoulder, almost as if he is going to cut off his own head.

A page card may represent a person acting in a new and unknown field. At this stage he still lacks proficiency and has little control over his environment; therefore, he is unsure in his actions and decisions. His status as page may also indicate that he is still dependent on others better positioned than him. On the positive side, he may represent a fresh approach, someone ready to learn and improve, and can expect help from others as well as forbearance for his beginner's mistakes. A page card may also represent a person who is young in age or attitude, or signal a lack of maturity and responsibility.

THE KNIGHTS

The knights are all mounted on horses in an open and untilled landscape. The suit symbol is either held in their hand or is in front of them. The knights of the hard suits, wands and swords, have a decorated outfit or some sort of armor, and their horses are covered with large pieces of cloth. The knights of the soft suits, coins and cups, wear simple clothes, and their horses are more exposed. The knights seem a little older than the pages, but still they all have yellow curls, except for the Knight of Swords, whose hair is hidden. Each of the horses' shoes is held in place by five nails, except for one hoof with four nails in the Knight of Cups.

A knight mounted on a horse can symbolize a person advancing toward a goal. Medieval representations of the knight portray him as an embodiment of the values of honor, courage, and virtue. He is supposed to be dedicated to the service of others: his feudal lord, the church, some lofty cause or perhaps, in a romantic vision, his queen. The idea of being on a mission can suggest responsibility and commitment. The horse may also represent people that he is "riding on," meaning those under his control and in his service. It could also signify the means by which the knight is able to move and to act.

THE QUEENS

The queens are drawn as mature women sitting on a throne and wearing a crown. They are dressed and covered, their faces are serious, and their posture looks solid and stable. Each queen holds her suit symbol in her right hand, while the left is positioned level with the belly. The queens of the soft suits, coins and cups, hold a rod or a sharp scepter in their left hand, as if to protect them from an unexpected attack from behind. The queens of the hard suits, wands and swords, hold their suit object like a mighty weapon.

The queen cards may express achievements and realization, solidness and stability, a strong position and real assets. But trying to preserve their existing position, they may also be conservative and defensive, cautious, suspicious of the unknown, and unwilling to take risks.

THE KINGS

Each of the kings wears a hat with a wide brim opening upward, and three of them also have a crown. The fourth, the King of Coins, also has an implicit crown in the yellow triangles on his hat. We can interpret the open hat's brim as readiness to accept new influences and ideas, and thus to change and develop. The kings of the soft suits, coins and cups, look like mature men; they have beards split in two, and they are dressed in gowns. Their appearance symbolizes maturity and cautious wisdom, and their split beards may express the ability to see separate and conflicting aspects of a situation. The kings of the hard suits, wands and swords, are younger; their faces are smooth, and they wear armor. Their appearance and their posture suggest action and dynamism.

Each king holds his suit symbol in his right hand. Three of them also rest it on their knee. Their thrones are not symmetrical, and their posture looks unstable. Their feet turn to the left but their faces turn to the right, and it seems that they might get up at any moment. We can interpret the lower part of their body as old habits and patterns of the past, while the upper part represents readiness to move forward to the future.

The kings may express a position of power and control or a phase of maturity and experience. The old processes in which the king was involved have reached their end, and now he is ready to move in a new direction.

VALET·DE·DENIERS

PAGE OF COINS

The page is looking at the coin in his hand. He may be unaware of the other coin near his foot. This indicates that he realizes only part of his potential, while the rest may still be hidden in the ground. The focused gaze at the upper coin may indicate that the querent is concerned with what they already have. The feet pointing in opposite directions express indecision. Perhaps the page had an initial success and now, examining it, he hesitates between exploiting the current situation (the second coin) and taking a new direction (the higher foot on the right). A unique feature of this card is that the title is written down the side and not in a strip at the bottom. This gives the card a solid basis, as the page's feet are planted on the ground at a level lower (or deeper) than any other figure.

INTERPRETATION: A practical attitude, feet on the ground, but a vision that is limited to existing structures and what has already proven its worth. Even in the present situation, many advantages and possibilities may be missed because of insufficient attention. It is worth looking for these untapped potentials and benefits before embarking on an altogether new way. Hesitation, restlessness of spirit, and an unclear feeling that something is missing. Goals that we seek might be closer than we imagine, and all we have to do is to look in the right direction. A solid material base for future endeavors.

CAVALIER·DE·DENIERS

KNIGHT OF COINS

The knight looking at the coin in front of him may have aspirations or plans in the material domain. The horse marching to the right indicates movement toward a realization of these plans. But the four slices of the center of the coin lean slightly to the right, as if the coin is rolling and moving farther the closer the knight gets to it. The green wand that the knight is holding in his hand may hint at the suit of wands. It may indicate creativity and self-expression, which the knight wishes to combine with material considerations. For example, this could indicate a desire to find a job that would guarantee both personal satisfaction and a good salary. Yet the wand may also make the coin fly out of reach, meaning that personal desires can spoil practical plans. We can also think that the knight is chasing the coin, meaning that he is motivated by the thought of profit and personal gain.

> **INTERPRETATION:** Advancing toward a tangible goal that seems close at hand but somehow evades our actual grasp. An aspiration to combine creativity and self-expression, on the one hand, and material considerations on the other hand. Personal impulses might interfere with practical plans. Looking for short-term gain may lead the querent forward to find other things that they do not yet expect. Constantly chasing after money, either due to a real need or because in this frame of mind one can never have enough.

REYNE · DEDENIERS

QUEEN OF COINS

The queen's coin is the largest and the most developed of all the coins in the court cards. It is the only one that has a point at the center, similar to the focusing point in the major suit's Hermit card, and it completely fills her field of vision. The stare directed to the left side of the card and the back turned to the right signify attention to past achievements and to existing assets that the queen holds in her hand, rather than to new possibilities and future plans. The scepter in her other hand can also be interpreted as a kind of wand. It forms a fixed triangle with the point at the coin center, which strengthens the impression of a deep focus. The small white circle level with her abdomen signifies a sense of feeling at ease with her inner self, as if her center is where it ought to be. The lines of the dress flow gently toward the ground, giving an impression of stability and signaling a solid basis in the material domain.

> **INTERPRETATION:** A practical and well-focused view that has already proved itself in real achievements. Good intuitions in practical matters of money and material goods. Stable situation that still demands constant attention to maintain. Being content with what one has, feeling at ease with oneself and with one's assets and position. A conservative attitude that seeks to preserve the existing state. Resistance to change that is felt to be a threat and not an opportunity. An overly materialistic attitude that sees everything only from the perspective of tangible gain and loss.

ROY·DE DENIERS

KING OF COINS

The King of Coins differs from the other kings in that he doesn't have a visible crown. He also sits in an open, natural landscape, while the others are shown in artificial environments. This may indicate a simple and practical, down-to-earth attitude of one who avoids excessive luxury or pompousness. He also differs from the other figures in the suit who are looking intensely at their coins. Instead, he holds his coin in his lap, treating it as something secure that doesn't need special attention, while his gaze is directed to the future. His line of vision is open but well defined by the limiting lines of the hat and the shoulder. His body leans slightly back—a posture expressing reticence, caution, and critical examination of new things rather than rushing forward toward them. The crossed legs and the hand on the belt resemble the major suit Emperor card and indicate discipline and self-control.

> **INTERPRETATION:** A solid and reliable attitude toward practical affairs. Keeping things simple and useful, without excessive sophistication. A cautious and balanced approach toward suggested projects or tempting offers, not rushing forward with uncritical enthusiasm, but also not altogether blocking the possibility of development in new directions. Self-control, maturity, and responsibility, especially in business and practical matters. Modest and unpretentious behavior based on confidence in oneself and in one's achievements.

VALET·DE COUPE

PAGE OF CUPS

The page is looking into his narrow cup, but his focus remains only in the top part and does not penetrate the deep layers. The round object in his other hand may be either his hat or the lid of the cup. The act of gazing into the cup can express readiness to examine his own emotions, and the uncovered head indicates an open mind. The cloth covering the cup from behind indicates that the page is undergoing this process only with himself. The movement to the left expresses an occupation with the past, and the page's left foot appears to stumble on the uneven ground, as if he may get stuck or even fall down. The shape and coloring of the ground may also suggest a female human body and indicate perplexity and inexperience in romantic affairs. On the belt there is some sort of hidden dagger, which may indicate the ability to hurt, maybe even without conscious intention.

> **INTERPRETATION:** A fresh and inexperienced attitude in emotional matters. Sentimentality; being moved by one's own feelings but without understanding them deeply. An attempt at self-examination that remains superficial, as it is not shared with others. Hesitant steps in the romantic or erotic domain. Preoccupations with one's own feelings may disrupt practical progress. Sincere intention, but still a possibility of hidden and unintentional aggression.

CAVALIER·DE·COUPE

Knight of Cups

The knight holds out the cup in the palm of his hand as if presenting it in a romantic act of devotion. The modest clothes, the exposed natural curls, and the spare ornamentation on the horse emphasize a feeling of openness and simplicity. The cup is large and open, but also flat and lacking depth. The knight looks hesitant, and one may think that the cup isn't really positioned on his hand. It could be floating in mid-air, and the knight may just be putting his palm underneath it. The knight supposedly gives what he has, and he may be sincere, but it isn't certain that one can rely on the depth of his commitment. The direction to the left might signal giving up personal goals and ambitions.

> **INTERPRETATION:** Devotion, emotional giving, openness, and sincerity. Giving up personal goals in order to serve something or somebody one cares for. The image of a romantic knight, which might be authentic but also may be a kind of self-delusion. Devotion without hidden motives. Open expression of emotions, but they may be only at a shallow level. A romantic and idealized view of reality motivates the querent, but perhaps not in a productive direction.

REYNE DE COUPE

QUEEN OF CUPS

The queen's cup is the only closed one in all of the suit's cards (a trait that was also preserved in the new Waite deck). The closed character of the image is also expressed in her heavy headgear, the chest bound with a tight belt, and the canopy that leaves only a narrow opening in front of the queen's eyes. The queen holds the cup on her knee, with her palm in a centered position that expresses a desire to control. The scepter in her other hand looks like some sort of sword or weapon, as if the queen is wary of a possible attack from behind. The closed cup and the tight chest also indicate blocked emotionality, while the elaborate headgear and the sword-like scepter may represent cerebral self-control.

> **INTERPRETATION:** A rich but hidden inner world. Stunted and controlled emotion under an external guise of the intellect. Closing in and defending oneself; difficulties in opening up emotionally. A person who has a lot to offer, but one has to make an effort to reach them. Guarding something of value. Seeing things through the narrow perspective of past experience, possibly traumatic, without opening up to new possibilities. Being emotionally content spending time with oneself. A secure feeling in the present situation.

ROY DE COUPE IIII

KING OF CUPS

The cup in the king's hand resembles the closed cup of the queen, but it has a narrow opening, which may symbolize the controlled expression of emotions. The cup appears to be divided into two parts held together by the hand but having a small misalignment. We can see this as an emotional rupture or maybe a broken heart, but the king manages to hold the pieces together and look forward. The raised brim of the hat expresses openness and reception toward new messages. It also opens the king's field of vision to the right, signaling an optimistic look forward. While the feet point in the direction of the past, the lines of the floor converge toward the future.

> **INTERPRETATION:** Emotional maturity and the wisdom of experience. An ability to overcome past sorrows and look forward; for example, getting over a psychological or romantic crisis. A lucid and realistic outlook that can still be positive and optimistic. A restrained and careful way of expressing emotions. Openness toward new experiences and new relationships but with prudence and caution. "Nothing is more whole than a broken heart."

VALET DE BATON·

PAGE OF WANDS

The natural branch looks big and massive, and the page's hands are poised on it in an awkward way. The illustration itself is unrealistic. It has a cubist quality that connects the tip of the wand and the palms with the sleeves in a triangular shape. Another distinct form is created by the whole wand as it connects with the right-hand part of the outfit. It seems as if the wand absorbs the page's hands, meaning that the querent's actions are driven by their desires and not by their conscious control. We can also think that the page would like to turn the wand so that its wider end is at the top, but it is perhaps too heavy for him. The page faces the future, and his feet touch the bottom line of the card in a way that suggests a stable base. But the wand is rooted in the ground and may perhaps block his advance. Alternatively, he could be hiding behind the wand and observing things from a distance instead of moving forward and actively intervening in them.

> **INTERPRETATION:** Desires and drives that the querent doesn't yet know how to control and direct. Creative potential and a real intention to move forward, but more maturity and self-discipline are needed for things to happen. A task that is too heavy or that the querent still hasn't found the right way to deal with. Using sexuality as a barrier or as a defense against an emotional relationship. Keeping oneself at a distance from events, perhaps waiting for the right moment to employ one's tools or weapons.

CAVALIER·DE·BATON·

KNIGHT OF WANDS

The wand in the picture retains the natural branch shape, but it looks more refined than the unwieldy object in the page card. The knight's gaze seems completely absorbed in his wand, which might indicate that he is preoccupied with his own desires and impulses. The bodies of the knight and the horse are turned to the left side of the card, but their faces and their eyes are directed to the right. Maybe the knight is changing direction and turning to face the future, or perhaps he is just stopping to examine what he really desires. The heavily covered horse, which does not look very athletic and agile, may symbolize lack of self-awareness or the hiding of one's real motivations. The floral device on the man's knee may be a fancy decoration, suggesting a taste for luxury or vanity. It might also indicate an aesthetic sensibility that strengthens the suit's link to creativity and self-expression. Overall, the image suggests a feeling of vigor and energy but may be lacking guidance and direction.

> **INTERPRETATION:** Suitable resources and an impulse to advance, but the direction is unclear. A momentary pause in order to reexamine what the querent really wants. An excessive preoccupation with one's own sexuality, selfish desires, or creative urges. Following the instinctual drives may indicate the right direction, but more confidence and commitment are needed for a real advance. Disregard of others' needs or lack of self-awareness may hinder the querent's progress for the moment. Still, they have enough resources and energy to correct the situation and advance later on.

REYNE DE BASTON·

Queen of Wands

The queen's large wand is semi-elaborate. It represents a middle phase between the natural branch of the knight and the well-fashioned rod of the king. The object that she appears to hold in her right hand resembles an eating utensil, something between a fork and a spoon. This may hint to matters related to food, or maybe expresses the power of the queen, as though she can devour whoever is facing her. The wand, which she wields like a heavy club, and the elbows pointing outward reflect power and domination, yet the look on the queen's face is tender and well-wishing. Her flowing hair shows sensuality, and the wreath of leaves supporting her crown suggests growth and fertility. The wand rising from the pelvic area emphasizes desire, creativity, and sexuality. The single white cuff indicates clean and pure action. On the other hand, her chest constrained by the belt may signal an emotional block.

> **INTERPRETATION:** A strong and self-confident female figure. A gentle appearance or soft speech backed up by the presence of a big stick. Using sexuality as a means of power and control. Irresistible drives of passion or creativity. Matters related to food, eating, or cooking. Friendly and cooperative attitude toward others but keeping a tight guard on one's personal space. Intuition and gut feeling gain the upper hand. Generosity and benevolence by someone in a secure position.

ROY · DE · BATON ||||||

KING OF WANDS

The elaborate and artificial wand represents creative energy or drives that are fully under control. The right foot points to the past (as in the other king cards), but the heel of the left foot is raised, as if in movement toward the future. The pointed triangular shape formed on the right by the wand, the leg, and the arm and shoulder almost breaks out of the card frame. This expresses a dynamic urge to push forward. Yet it appears as if the king is about to stab his own heel, maybe to curb an overly impulsive enthusiasm that might result in a hasty move or maybe the contrary—to prod himself into moving. The look is cautious and contained between the back of the seat and the brim of the hat, but the space between them is open in an optimistic line ascending to the right. The wand may also be the missing column of the chair back on the left side, which means that the king is using past resources as a tool for new advances and endeavors.

INTERPRETATION: A mature and responsible attitude that does not get carried away by impulses and desire, but rather harnesses them toward creative and controlled action. A look forward with cautious optimism. A moment of prudent consideration before starting to move in a new direction. The previous stability has already been shaken, but a new movement still demands a self-disciplined internal push. Investing accumulated resources to advance further instead of just keeping them as they are. A self-defeating tendency of the querent to make an obstructive move each time they have a chance to advance.

VALET · D'EPEE

PAGE OF SWORDS

The page wields a sword, but he does not look like someone ready for battle. The sword rests on his shoulder, blocking his view toward the future, and he turns his face away from it. We can also think that if he isn't careful, the sword might cut off his head. Thus, the sword may symbolize not a weapon but a barrier or hindrance, such as negative thoughts. The feet pointing in both directions express indecision. They rest on the bottom line of the card in a way that hints both to stability and to lack of movement. They are also closer to the left side. In his other hand the page holds something that looks like a scabbard. This could also be a hint to the suit of wands and to passions that interfere with judgment. The little shape at the groin level suggestive of a male organ may indicate a dilemma between desire and intellect.

> **INTERPRETATION:** Hesitation, indecision. The querent has resources and abilities but still doesn't know what to do with them. Examination of the past before making a step toward the future. Fear of facing the reality of things that are to come. The future is perceived as a menace, but this can be put right with a change of approach. Hindering factors can be turned into useful tools and weapons. Confusion resulting from strong desires and misguided ideas.

CAVALIER D'EPEE ||||

Knight of Swords

The emphatic diagonals created by the horse's body, the sword, and the upper part of the knight's silhouette express strong drive and energy. But the knight is riding to the left, not the usual direction of advancement. Maybe he's moving in a wrong direction, and the right-facing mask on his shoulder expresses doubts and second thoughts. The horse's raised forelegs may indicate that the animal is also refusing to advance, and perhaps the knight is using the sword to urge it forward. Alternatively, we may think that obstinacy and perseverance will nevertheless make the knight succeed in the way he chooses. The arch shape with the plant at the bottom of the card may indicate a turning point. The dotted circles on the horse's bridle and the ground may symbolize different goals and areas of focus. The white hooves may also represent pure intentions or a detachment from the practical ground.

> **INTERPRETATION:** The querent has the energy, motivation, and resources needed to advance, but they should control their impulse to charge ahead and instead check whether the direction in which they are advancing is a good one. It is advisable to pay attention to hesitation and doubts. Willpower and obstinacy, an attempt to impose your view on the environment or on people under your charge. Determination and perseverance may lead to success in an unexpected direction. A feeling of floating above the constraints of normal reality.

REYNE·DEPEE

Queen of Swords

The two slightly asymmetrical posts behind the figure, the rounded screen between them, and the sword in the right hand resemble the Justice card from the major suit. Other similarities include the closed and tight clothing and the yellow crown. The queen's posture and her facial expression reflect suspicion. The rounded abdomen may hint at pregnancy, and the hand placed over it may be an act of protecting the embryo inside. Her gaze is to the left, as if the queen were worried about what has menaced her in the past. The sword's hilt doesn't exactly continue the line of the blade. It is as if the queen's grip is holding together disconnected parts.

> **INTERPRETATION:** A secure and protected but static situation. Entrenching oneself in an existing position. Extreme caution, defensiveness, and avoidance of risks. Worry about possible menaces that were relevant in the past. Strong psychological defenses, shunning self-exposure and closeness. Protecting oneself with sharp and rigid rationality. Something in preparation that has to be kept secret and well guarded until it is mature enough to reveal itself.

ROY·D EPEE

KING OF SWORDS

The two shoulder masks may express opposing tendencies or possibilities of action, and the vertical division of the king's chest can indicate that his heart is divided between them. The feet seem to be drifting to the left, but the king holds the sword in front of the mask on this side, as if expressing a firm decision to block this direction and turn his head toward the future. The strange illustration on the base of the chair may represent the uncertainty about the future: what sprouts now may grow and prosper, but it also may be cut. The small lines on the scepter, which starts at the king's pelvic area, look like the markings on a ruler. These may indicate passions under the control of the mind. They may also represent the intellectual capacities needed to regulate and deal with an uncertain future. The crown on the king's head seems flooded in light, expressing superior wisdom.

> **INTERPRETATION:** Willpower and a determined decision to break from past influences and face the future, even though the heart is still divided between the old and the new. A combination of sharp intelligence and openness to superior wisdom of a mysterious nature. Readiness to face uncertainty with the intellectual tools needed to cope with unknown situations. A regulated and controlled expression of desires and passions. Making plans and preparations but not moving yet.

CHAPTER 10

THE NUMBER CARDS

READING THE NUMBER CARDS

Each one of the four minor suits contains nine cards numbered from two to ten. In the Tarot de Marseille and in other traditional decks, the number cards have a relatively simple and abstract design. Each card shows the suit symbol in a number of copies equal to the card number. The suit symbol icons are arranged in a geometric array and surrounded by plant decorations. For example, the 3 of Cups shows three cups arranged in a triangle, the 2 of Wands shows two crossed rods, and so on.

Before studying their illustrations in detail, it may be difficult to tell the number cards apart. Not only do the cards of each suit resemble each other, but we also may get confused between the number cards of the wands and the swords. This is because all the wands and most of the swords are illustrated as narrow stripes with black blades at the tips. The difference is that the stripes of the wands are straight and cross over at the middle of the card. In contrast, the swords' stripes are rounded and cross over at two points—at the top of the card and at the bottom.

6 of Wands (left), 6 of Swords (right)

The simple design of the number cards can make them quite challenging to interpret at first. This is especially true for readers who have experience with Waite's and other new English decks, in which the number cards are illustrated with realistic scenes of people and objects. These scenes, completely different from the traditional design, show various life situations and have a relatively narrow range of possible meanings. This makes them easier to read for beginners. In the Tarot de Marseille, on the other hand, novice readers often postpone the detailed study of the number cards to a later stage, after having gained some experience with other parts of the deck.

Tarot authors from the French school who have written about the Tarot de Marseille number cards have often combined two different methods for interpretation. These are similar to the two methods already mentioned in chapter 9: interpretation by the table and interpretation by the image. In the number cards, interpretation by the table means that each card represents the numerological significance of its number, acting with the character or in the domain of its suit. Thus, for example, the 3 of Coins symbolizes dynamism and advance (the number three) in practical matters (the suit of coins).

The interpretation by the image is similar in spirit to what we did with the aces and the court cards. Looking at the card, we notice the arrangement of the suit symbols and the emotional tone suggested by the plant decorations. These are interpreted as symbolizing events and processes in the querent's life.

For example, we can read the following story in the image details of the 3 of Cups:

The pair of cups at the bottom can signify two lovers. The sensual red shape in the middle indicates mutual passion. The heart shape of the leaves around the red shape's tip expresses emotional bonding, but the little leaves above the heart—red on the right and white on the left—represent differences between the two partners. They turn in opposite directions, indicating the start of a separation.

The card's answer to the situation is to produce a common creation; for example, a child or a common work project. This is signified by the third cup. Now the branches turn inward again, with pomegranate-like fruits on their tips, creating the shape of a bigger heart. The outer edge of the top right-hand leaf is white, mirroring the small white leaf at the center left. It is as if the right-hand partner assimilates the higher qualities of the other, which at first were rejected.

We can also look at the story from the perspective of the third cup. The querent might have grown up as a child with such a relationship between the parents. Since he functioned as the glue holding them together, they cared for him and gave him lots of attention. But from his point of view the excessive attention could be felt as too much, blocking him from all sides and letting him develop only in a very defined direction symbolized by the top opening.

The Language of Directions

In chapter 4 we interpreted the horizontal axis of the cards, left to right, as the time direction of earthly events. The vertical axis, bottom to top, we saw as representing the inner experiences of the soul. This scheme is appropriate especially for the major suit cards, but we also can apply it to the aces and the court cards. The court cards express the vertical axis in a very limited way, as they show no sky and no abyss, but this is only natural, as they present people in practical life situations and don't refer to the psychological and spiritual dimensions.

The same interpretation for the axes is unsuitable for the number cards. On one hand, their illustrations don't show any development along the horizontal axis, as they are almost symmetrical between left and right. Instead, we can see variations in the details along the vertical axis, often with a sense of growth and advancement from bottom to top. In other words, only the vertical axis is significant in the number cards. On the other hand, the simple and basic design of the number cards suggests that we should interpret them mainly in terms of concrete and external events. This makes the interpretation of the vertical axis in terms of internal processes irrelevant for the number cards.

What we need is a new interpretation of the vertical axis that is specific for the number cards. We can think of two such interpretations, which may be appropriate in different situations.

Inspired by the upward movement in many cards, we can interpret the vertical axis in the number cards as a time direction. For this we can imagine the number cards as lying flat on the ground, one after the other, like large bricks paving a road. As we advance on the road, we pass through each card from bottom to top. In such a vision the bottom part of the card represents the past or an early stage in a process, while the top part represents the future or a later stage. In other words, we interpret the vertical axis of the number cards as a time axis, similar to the horizontal axis in the other parts of the deck.

In the number cards of the soft suits, coins and cups, we can find another meaning in the vertical axis. In these cards up and down can be interpreted in terms of power and status relations. Naturally, we would see the stronger or more influential element on top and the dependent or subordinate at the bottom. For example, the 7 of Coins may show the querent's position at work as the single coin in the middle, protected and relatively well placed. The 8 of Coins can remind us of an office building or a big organization, with management on top and employees at the bottom. In the 10 of Cups we see one big cup on top of nine small ones, and we can interpret it as a leadership position.

7 of Coins, 8 of Coins, 10 of Cups

Another feature of the vertical axis in the number cards concerns inverse cards. Some number cards are almost symmetrical between top and bottom, with only slight differences in the decoration. In these cards it is difficult to distinguish between a straight and an inverse position. Other number cards show a clear distinction between straight and inverse. For example, when a number card from the cups suit is inverse, its cup icons are turned down, which makes a big difference.

As the distinction between straight and inverse is very clear in some cards but not in others, should we consider it in a reading? My way of dealing with inverse number cards is to distinguish between the two cases. With cards that are roughly symmetrical, I usually give the same interpretation regardless of the card's position. I make an exception to this rule only if I have a spontaneous intuition about the interpretation of a minor difference in the details. On the other hand, if the illustration is clearly asymmetrical, I give a separate interpretation to an inverse card. As I do with other parts of the deck, I usually give an inverse card a less favorable meaning than if it were straight.

THE GENERAL DESIGN

Although each suit has its typical design, as we shall see in the next section, there are some features that are common to different suits. One of the most significant among them is the distinction between even and odd numbers. In the even-number cards the suit icons are usually arranged in pairs, giving the card a solid and stable character. In the odd cards a single suit icon appears between the pairs, disrupting the stable structure and creating a more dynamic and tense impression.

It is useful to distinguish here between the soft and the hard suits. In the soft suits a single pair (two icons) can indicate an alliance, a partnership, or two opposing forces. Several pairs can represent an environment or a system within which the querent operates. A single icon in an odd card may symbolize an individual person or a singular element in the situation. It can also refer to the querent's relationship with their environment. For example, a single cup can represent the querent's relationship with family, and a single coin can symbolize their position at the workplace. This expresses the fact that the cups refer to a web of human and personal relations, while the coins indicate a system based on practical and material considerations.

In the hard suits we can see the singular icon as an individual facing a challenge or opposition. The single wand in the odd-number cards can symbolize the querent's path, which is crossed by two bundles of wands, representing challenges and difficulties. Alternatively, it could be a single wand warding off an attack by others who are crossing the querent. The single sword of the odd numbers is breaking out from a limited area enclosed by pairs of rounded swords. We can see the sword pairs as limits and boundaries that block or protect the querent. As for the single sword, it can represent an initiative to break through the existing barriers and advance toward new territories.

The first and last numbers, two and ten, also present similar traits in different suits. As we shall see further on, card number ten has a unique design that somehow resembles the odd cards of its suit. Although this is more noticeable in the hard suits, we can see something of this in the soft suits as well. As for the number two cards, in the soft suits their designs are unique and show more complexity and richness of detail than other cards. In the hard suits this particular characteristic of the number two cards is not evident; rather, they have the same structure as the others.

Another trait of the soft suits' number two cards is the presence of writings that can be read as some sort of signature or acknowledgment. Traditional Tarot de Marseille makers often decorated the 2 of Coins card with a band of text displaying the name of the deck creator or publisher, the year, and the place of publication. Conver also did this in his 2 of Coins card, and in the CBD deck I added my name to his. In some older decks the publisher's details appear not in the 2 of Coins, but in the bottom part of the 2 of Cups. The Conver deck also has text at the bottom of the 2 of Cups, but it is just the letters G and M. Perhaps they were intended to convey some message, but they could also very well be just another signature. For example, maybe these were the initials of an artisan who carved the wooden printing plates.

In addition, the bottom part of the 2 of Cups shows a shield with three fleurs-de-lys or stylized lily flowers, which is the coat of arms of the royal French house of Bourbon. The shield is mounted by a crown and decorated with two branches, similar to those that appear in the Ace of Swords.

The Bourbon shield itself appears again in the 4 of Coins. There may be a connection between these heraldic emblems and the fact that cards were printed in France under strict royal supervision at that time. Still, in a reading everything is a sign, and we can interpret these details in a different context. For example, the royal symbols can represent the established powers and institutions in society. The letters G and M can hint at a name or a concept relevant to the query.

The Four Suits

The number cards of each minor suit display a typical design structure that evolves along with the progression of card numbers. When we begin to study the number cards, it is a good idea to arrange each suit in a row according to the card numbers. Looking at the nine number cards of the suit, we can have an impression of their common structure as well as of the differences that give each card its individual character.

COINS

In the number cards of the other suits, the card number appears on both sides in roman numerals. But in the suit of coins the number is not written, and to identify the card one simply has to count the number of coins.

Except for the two card with its large and detailed coins, all the coin icons in the number cards have the same design. On most of the cards they are arranged in a uniform and symmetrical pattern with pairs piled up on top of each other. This creates stable structures suggesting solidity, reliability, conservatism, and rigidity. The yellow coins give the cards an illuminated and optimistic character, and one can naturally see them as gold coins. Besides other possible interpretations, we can see large numbers of coins as indicating a large sum of money or perhaps an extensive involvement in practical or financial issues.

In the 2 of Coins card it is natural to see the two large coins as two elements. They are held together, but also separated from each other, by the snake-like band. In the 3 of Coins we can see a new coin emerging from the alliance of the pair below.

In the higher numbers we can see a system or an environment evolving through different phases. The solid square in the 4 of Coins with the royal shield at the center suggests a stable structure based on conventional norms. In the 5 of Coins a new element appears in the center, disrupting the stability and creating a space for itself.

The 6 of Coins can symbolize a more flexible and dynamic organization, deviating from the design of layered pairs and presenting a more harmonious and rounded arrangement. Adding the single element in the 7 of Coins, we can see it receiving its own place in the middle of a layered pairs structure. It is well placed but not central, and the plant decorations around it suggest harmonious integration, cooperation, and support.

The 8 of Coins shows a complex structure with a uniform and hierarchical arrangement. It symbolizes another form of rigidity, mechanical and impersonal. In the 9 of Coins we see again a single element, but now its space is squeezed and limited in the middle of the well-established structure. If we think in terms of a conflict between an individual and a system, we can see a pattern that repeats itself in the other suits as well. In the five card the single element is facing four others, but its uniqueness gives it an edge, and it is strong enough to win over them. In the seven card the single element is up against six, and the forces are equally balanced. In the nine card it is one against eight, and now they are stronger.

Finally, in the 10 of Coins we see harmony restored, with an abundance of coins. It can be individuals integrated in a system, like the two single coins along the middle axis, each of them well placed at the center of its own square. We can also see in the middle of this card a repetition of the harmonious arrangement of card number six surrounded by the solid and practical four.

CUPS

The yellow color of the cups gives the number cards of this suit an illuminated and happy character. Their red openings express passion and energy, while the shading inside the cups may hint at complex feelings. Perhaps things inside are not as simple and bright as they seem from the outside. We can also see the cup icons as golden cups full of red wine. Thus, a large number of upright cups can suggest a feast or festivity and symbolize happiness and a feeling of plenty, both material and emotional. Still, the cups can stand for deeper and sometimes darker emotions. In some cases they may be seen as full of blood or we may suspect that the wine might be poisoned.

A clear distinction between straight and inverse cards exists in all the number cards of the suit. An inverse card can signify negative feelings or emotions that play an obstructive part in the querent's life. The downturned cups in an inverse card can also indicate the loss of emotional energy, despair, or dryness and inability to experience emotions.

When we see a pair of two cups, one beside the other, it is natural to interpret them as a relationship between two people. It may be a romantic relationship or another form of alliance or partnership with an emotional dimension. Alternatively, we can see in the cups two parts of the querent's emotions (for example, a case of conflicting feelings) or relations between two groups of people.

Repeating pairs in a card can be different stages in the evolution of a couple's relationship. They can also represent several couples; for example, several generations in an extended family. In the case of bigger groups of cups, they can just represent a group without each cup necessarily referring to a particular person. For example, a row of three cups may symbolize a group of people (not necessarily three) in the querent's surroundings.

The large pair in the 2 of Cups may represent two people in a partnership or a love affair. The lower part of the card, with its reference to royalty, suggests this relationship does not exist in an empty space. It has its basis in the norms and institutions of society; for example, the perspective of an eventual marriage, which is a social institution. In the 3 of Cups we can see something new that is born from the union of the two. For instance, it can be a child or a mutual project.

The 4 of Cups shows a solid structure of personal relations; for example, a family or a group of friends with a common history and a feeling of commitment. In the 5 of Cups we see an individual placed in the middle of a group. The rich and happy plant decorations indicate a key position and positive influences. The 6 of Cups has a strong central axis, which gives direction to the columns of cups on either side. The feeling is of continuity and repetition; for example, a long-term relationship.

In the 7 of Cups the single icon in the middle is more isolated, but the lively plant decorations around it suggest a uniqueness turned into an advantage. The 8 of Cups shows two central cups between two tiers, perhaps a couple or a partnership of two with many other people meddling in their affairs. In the 9 of Cups we can see a large group in which each individual finds his proper place, without any one of them in particular standing out. In the 10 of Cups we see again the same crowd, but now our attention is focused on the large single cup above, apparently lying on its side, which may represent someone in a leading position.

WANDS

The straight rods with the black blades at both ends suggest some kind of fighting sticks. Their crossing over in the middle can symbolize conflict and struggle. Alternatively, they can be roads or pathways on which we can walk. In this perspective the black divergent tips can signify uncertainty about the continuation of the road, as it may diverge in different directions as it reaches the limits of the card. The dominant black and red colors indicate that the roads may be difficult and full of hardships and trials. On the other hand, most of the cards present plant decorations whose lines of growth lead from the center outward. Thus, the struggles and difficulties can be connected with growth, creativity, expansion, and perhaps the discovery of new horizons.

As the number of wands increases, their crossing at the center becomes larger, denser, and more dominant. In the higher numbers it looks like a mesh of crisscrossing wand sections. We can interpret this as a complex situation in which many elements and interests are entangled. In such a reading the crossed wands symbolize obstacles or opponents. The mesh can also appear as a maze of paths in which the querent has difficulties finding their way.

A single wand in the odd-number cards can look like a road, which the querent traverses from bottom to top. They enter the crisscrossed mesh at the center from below and emerge again above. This can be like passing through a period of confusion, conflict, or hardship. In the even numbers the central axis is marked by two branches above and below. We cannot see a single road passing through, and the card may represent the complex situation itself, rather than a dynamic process in which the querent enters and gets out of a difficulty.

The wands crossing each other can also be fighting sticks locked in a struggle. For example, the 3 of Wands can be one person in the middle of a conflict between two others. The 7 of Wands can be one person standing against a coalition of many. Still, in the wands suit we see only conflicting interests or opposing wills. It is not actual war in which the intention is to hurt or destroy the enemy, as we might see in the swords. Also, as the suit of wands is related to drives and desires, we can interpret the card images as patterns of desires and passions. For example, the 2 of Wands can signify two urges pushing the querent in two different directions. In the 8 of Wands we can see a web of complex, intertwined, and conflicting desires in which the querent is caught.

In the 2 of Wands the crossing of the wands is a simple intersection with no meshing. The plants growing in all directions are more prominent than the black blades. The short yellow bands separating the wands into sections have rounded ends. This gives them a soft aspect in contrast to higher number cards in which they are rectangular with sharp edges. The impression is colorful and optimistic, and it suggests a crossing of ways open to all sides.

In the 3 of Wands a single wand passes through the crossroads, marking a clear and well-defined direction. In the 4 of Wands a mesh now appears at the center, but it is relatively simple and looks solid and reassuring rather than confusing. The plant decorations are rich, suggesting growth and creative energy. In the 5 of Wands the growth diminishes, and a single wand passes through the center. It seems to be on top of the perpendicular yellow bands just above the central mesh, covering their inner edges, as if overcoming their attempt to block its way.

In the 6 of Wands the plant leaves on both sides and on top become long and narrow, still expanding but as if constrained to follow the direction of the wand bundles. The 7 of Wands shows a single wand passing at the center, but the yellow leaves with sharp metallic-like tips signal tension. Also, the central wand's segments are not exactly aligned but rather form a broken line. It is as if the central wand is passing through but with difficulty.

The 8 of Wands shows a thick central mesh that now becomes the strongest element in the card. This suggest a complex and confusing situation, like a maze of roads crossing each other, in which the querent can lose their way. The 9 of Wands shows no plant decorations, and the single wand is cut by the central mesh into two segments, one above and one below. If this is a road, it is interrupted by the mesh and has to start anew after the challenging period is over. We see again the same pattern as in the odd coin cards: in the five the single one overcomes the four, in the seven it is balanced by the six, and in the nine it is overcome by the eight. Finally, the 10 of Wands presents two joined wands entering the mesh and coming out together. It is as if loyalty binds the two and helps them pass through the opposing eight.

SWORDS

In the even cards of the suit, the swords appear as two bundles of curved parallel stripes forming an oval enclosure. At first sight, it is even difficult to recognize these shapes as swords. This could be a remnant of the origin of the minor suits in Asian countries, where curved swords, or scimitars, were common. In the odd cards an additional straight sword commands the center with its tip projecting out of the oval enclosure. The 10 of Swords is the exception with two bundles of four curved swords, plus two slanting straight swords with their tips pointing inward.

The bundles of curved swords cross over both above and below the card center, thus they separate the card into two parts, one inside and the other outside the oval enclosure. As the card number increases, the separating barriers become thicker and denser, forming a grille of sorts. In the higher numbers they begin to resemble prison bars. In the outer part of all the cards there appear four stemless flowers with five sepals each. This structure resembles the World card from the major suit, with an oblong space in the middle and four animals around it. We can also see the four five-sepaled flowers as symbolizing hands and feet.

The separation between an internal part and an external part emphasizes the cutting character of the suit of swords. It can also symbolize the role of language and rationality, which divide our experience of reality into an inner part (our mind) and an outer part (external circumstances). The hinted limbs can represent the querent's actions (hands) and the external conditions (feet, what they are standing on). Alternatively, the separation could be between an inner sphere, such as the space of private life, and an outer sphere of public activity.

The grille-like barriers formed by the intersections of curved swords can also indicate that the querent is blocked or confined inside a limited space. For example, it can be a relationship or a job that the querent wants to leave but doesn't know how. Another option is to think of the querent as actually being outside the enclosed area. In that case, what is inside can represent a hidden treasure or asset that they want to reach, or perhaps a part of their personality to which they have no conscious access.

The stripes of the curved swords are crossed over at several points by small perpendicular bands, which look as if they are holding together the bundles. Similar bands also appear in the wands number cards, but there are some differences between the two suits. In the wands suit card number two has bands with rounded edges, while in the other numbers the bands are rectangular. The rounded-band edges give the card a softer appearance. In the swords suit rounded bands appear both in two and three. In the other cards the edges are rectangular, but in the higher numbers the bands themselves become curved. Also, while in the wands suit all the bands are yellow, in the swords suit some bands are yellow and others are red. It is difficult to see a regular pattern in this coloring, but its perceptible effect is that a higher number of red bands create a stronger feeling of tension in the card.

In the odd cards of the suit, we can interpret the single sword sticking out from the central enclosure as an effort to break out and free oneself from the confined space. This effort becomes more difficult and challenging as the number of arched swords increases. When the card is straight, the tip of the single sword points upward, and then it may express success. In contrast, an inverse card with the tip down can indicate a failed or misguided attempt to overcome the barriers. Where the single sword passes through the upper bundle crossing we can see red diamond shapes, but only in the 5 of Swords can we actually see the blade passing through. A similar red shape also appears in the two crossings of card four and on the bottom crossing of card five.

The use of swords as weapons suggests an interpretation of the suit's number cards in relation to wars and combat. These can be clashes with other people, the querent's struggles against difficulties, or inner conflicts. Alternatively, we can follow the suit domain and interpret the cards as structures or patterns of thoughts and ideas. For example, the 2 of Swords with its symmetric flower developing within borders can signify a developed framework of ideas in a well-defined field, such as a scientific theory. The 5 of Swords with a single sword breaking out of the four arches can represent a breakthrough idea. The 10 of Swords with two crossed swords entangled in the dense side bundles can represent an argument that has been going on until nothing new can be said anymore.

In the 2 of Swords the inner part of the card is bounded by a single arch from each side, with a well-centered and symmetrical flower growing inside. The borders around it seem to be marking its space rather than limiting its growth. In the 3 of Swords the single sword is decorated with branches and does not seem to be hindered by the pair of arches as it passes through. This can indicate an easy victory. Alternatively, it can signify a new phase in which the protecting barriers are no longer needed.

The plant inside the central area of the 4 of Swords is shown from the side. It seems to be completely filling the available space, even touching the border as if trying to grow beyond it. We can feel the double arches as limitations. But in the 5 of Swords we see the central line of the single sword as it passes through the upper crossing and overcomes the limitations without setback.

The 6 of Swords shows again a plant branch from the side, but now it adopts the form of the available space. It is as if the plant accepts the limits imposed on it and gives up the attempt to change the external conditions. In the 7 of Swords we see a narrow and well-shaped sword. Its hilt is placed at a higher point than in other odd cards, so that it is more free to move, and a single line on its blade expresses a higher degree of focus than in the three or five cards. We can interpret it as a concentrated and determined effort to break through a considerable opposition.

The 8 of Swords shows a small flower viewed from above, as in the 2 of Swords, but now it is concentrated and enclosed within heavy barriers. Its lively colors suggest that it is held inside from choice, perhaps to protect itself in a kind of fortress. The single sword in the 9 of Swords looks weak relative to the heavy mesh that it has to penetrate, and its parts are not exactly aligned. Still, it shows its valor by giving a fight and passing through. Again we see that in relation to the opposition, the single sword is stronger in the five card, balanced in the seven card, and weaker in the nine card. Finally, in the 10 of Swords we can see two crossed swords, which normally would suggest a duel. But they are both entangled within the curved bundles in a way that limits their movement, as if it is a long and complex battle that leaves both sides exhausted.

2 OF COINS
DUALITY

The number two finds a concrete expression in the practical suit of coins as two tangible elements, projects, or options. The card shows two large and elaborate coins held together, but also separated, by a snaking banderole. Traditionally the name and details of the deck creator are inscribed on the banderole.

> **INTERPRETATION:** Two options or two elements. Collaborating with someone while keeping a safe distance. Different possibilities kept open for the moment. A winding road advancing in complex ways and not directly toward one's goal. Things related to recognition and acknowledgment.

3 OF COINS
PRODUCT

The productive and dynamic nature of the number three is expressed in the practical domain of coins as the first results of an effort or an investment. The illustration shows two coins above a plant decoration that looks gathered and enclosed. A similar decoration appears on top, more open and containing a third coin.

> **INTERPRETATION:** A productive outcome of an alliance or partnership. First results, modest but real. Potentials starting to realize. Interpersonal tensions eased by working together on a common project.

> **INVERSE:** Results too small compared to the effort. Collaboration ends in a disappointment.

4 of Coins

STABILITY

The conservative and practical nature of the number four fits well with the stable materiality of coins. The illustration shows a solid rectangle of coins decorated with large flowers and several dotted circles. At the center appears a shield with three fleurs-de-lys, the coat of arms of the French royal house of Bourbon.

INTERPRETATION: Material solidity, a secure base. Relations with respected and trustworthy institutions. Tradition, reputation, and honor. Reliability gained over time. Preserving the existing assets. Doing things in the old and time-tested ways.

inverse: A conservative attitude, rigidity, outdated perspectives.

5 OF COINS
DISRUPTION

The number five disrupts the solid stability of the four by adding a new element whose importance is magnified as it clashes with the conservative nature of the coins. The single coin at the center pushes the others to the margins and defines a big space for itself. But the pointed leaves in light blue above and below can signify a reaction from the existing structures that limits its movements.

> **INTERPRETATION:** Disruption of stable patterns. Success in something new. A new and exceptional element assumes a central place but also arouses resistance. Risk of finding oneself outdated and pushed to the side. Need to pay attention to the old habits and the traditional structures.

6 OF COINS
EXPANSION

The harmonic nature of the number six is expressed in the suit of coins as plenty of resources and possibilities. Rich plant decoration grows from the center point with a vortex pattern in the middle. The arrangement of the coins integrates stability in the middle square, dynamic expansion in the two triangles above and below, and harmonic roundness in the overall elongated hexagon.

> **INTERPRETATION:** Optimism; a positive outlook, especially in material and practical issues. A good balance between stability and flexibility. Advancement of projects without encountering a real challenge. Expansion in different directions without losing focus. Success.

7 OF COINS
ACCEPTANCE

The practical aspect of the coins subdues the dynamic three to the stability of the four, with the number seven depicted as an inverse triangle pointing down at a rectangle. The single coin finds its place between the three pairs, well positioned but not overly dominant. The plant decorations enclose it in a way that expresses protection and support.

> **INTERPRETATION:** A new or exceptional element is well-received in an existing framework. Help and support. Nourishment and protection. Balance between individualism and conformity.

> **INVERSE:** Excessive dependence on external support. Constant need to be accepted and approved by others.

8 of Coins
UNIFORMITY

The organized nature of the number eight is expressed in the practical domain of coins as a uniform and mechanistic structure. The card shows a regular pattern of four pairs of coins piled on each other. The plant decorations put each coin in its own separate box, but the developed flower at the center seems to combine them together into a working whole.

INTERPRETATION: Uniformity, regularity, conformity. Repetition of small tasks, a long and patient effort, routine. Profit achieved through hard work. Anonymity in a big system. Rational and pragmatic considerations. Machinery; something that works fine and achieves results but lacks a human touch.

9 of Coins

MOTIVATION

The number nine, looking forward to perfection, plants a seed for future practical advancement in the middle of a regular array of eight coins. The single coin at the center seems to be isolated in its limited space and pressured by the four pairs around it. But the big flowers above and below can indicate that its stamina and perseverance will bring positive results later on.

> **INTERPRETATION:** Ambition, motivation, a desire to advance. Carving a niche for oneself in an existing system. Courage, endurance, readiness to continue in spite of difficulties. A nonconformist person or an unconventional idea looks strange and useless but may hold the key for future advancement.

10 of Coins
ABUNDANCE

The number ten brings the material aspect of the coins into full realization. The card shows a large flower at the center with expanding tips. Around it are plenty of coins and plant decorations. The image suggests abundance in material things and a comfortable situation. The centers of the three coins at the top left are not colored red like the others.

> **INTERPRETATION:** Abundance and plenty; a lot of money. Preoccupation with financial and practical issues. Stability with a possibility for further gains. Success and achievements. Excessive materialism. Too little attention to the needs of others. An unequal or unfair distribution of resources.

2 OF CUPS
PARTNERSHIP

The duality of the number two is expressed in the emotional domain of the cups as a close relationship between two people. The middle plant grows from a stable base decorated with royal symbols. Its red shapes express passion and desire. The two legendary fish heads may be some kind of a garden fountain, but perhaps they are going to devour the flower between them.

> **INTERPRETATION:** A romantic union or a warm partnership. A personal alliance grounded in social norms. Collaboration and trust. The prospect of marriage. Passionate love, but emotions can turn around and extinguish themselves.

> **INVERSE:** A crisis in a couple relationship. A disappointment with someone you trusted.

3 OF CUPS
BIRTH

In the emotional cups, the creative nature of the number three generates the birth of something new from the affective alliance of two. The card shows a pair of cups with heart-shaped plant decorations growing from the red shape between them. A third cup appears in this protected and nourishing space, as if born from the union of the two.

> **INTERPRETATION:** Something new is born, bringing happiness and joy. Creating something out of love. Childbirth or caring for a child. Issues about the relations of the querent with their parents.

> **iNVERSE:** A problem in relationships with a child or with parental figures. Feeling neglected.

4 of Cups

FAMILY

In the suit of cups, the solid number four generates a stable framework for emotional relationships, such as a family or a community. The illustration shows four cups in a square arrangement. The plant decorations connect them while giving each one its own place, and they create a central axis of stability and continuity.

INTERPRETATION: A stable framework of close human relationships: the family, a group of friends, a community, or a tribe. Secure feeling of belonging. Issues of family relations, especially between parents and children. Emotional stability.

INVERSE: Family problems. Quarrels and discord in a group.

5 OF CUPS

LINKS

The number five adds a new element at the center of a stable structure. In the human relationships domain of the cups, it is expressed as an influential and well-connected personality. The single cup at the center is surrounded by rich and flowing plant decorations with a suggested fruit at the top. The plants connect all five cups into one group full of activity and movement.

> **INTERPRETATION:** Developed social skills; many connections and links with other people. Popularity, ability to establish and maintain friendships. Active and lively dynamics in a group.

> **INVERSE:** Excessive preoccupation with affairs of other people. Need to find a quiet place for oneself.

6 of Cups

CONTINUITY

The harmonious character of the number six is expressed in the emotional suit of cups as long-term and reliable relations. The repeating pattern of three pairs of cups on top of each other is organized around an axis of plant decorations with a clear focus on the central flower. The attention is more on the continuous process than on the individual cups.

> **INTERPRETATION:** A long-lasting marriage or a stable partnership. Continuity of different generations in a family. Feeling secure about a partner's feelings.

> **INVERSE:** Monotony, boredom, lack of novelty and interest in a relationship. A feeling of repetition without advancement. Recurrent emotional traps.

7 OF CUPS
INDIVIDUALITY

In the human relations domain of the cups, the number seven is interpreted as 1 + 6, an individual in a relation with a group. The card shows a single cup between two horizontal rows of three cups each. The plant decorations emphasize the central vertical axis, connecting the single cup with the two central ones above and below it.

> **INTERPRETATION:** An individual integrating into a group while keeping their own position and values. Close relations with influential people. Exceptional qualities or a unique personality are appreciated.

> **INVERSE:** Isolation and estrangement. Feeling lonely in the midst of a group.

8 of Cups
INVOLVEMENT

The emotional touch of the suit of cups constructs the number eight as 6 + 2, more flexible and rich in combinations than the mechanistic and uniform 4 x 2 of the coins. The card shows a pair of cups between two rows of three above and below it. The plant decorations show a focused center and emphasize both the pairing of the two and their integration with the other six.

> **INTERPRETATION:** Involvement of relatives and friends in a relationship or life of a couple. An extended family; many people interacting and interfering. A feast with friends or a family celebration.

> **INVERSE:** Lack of privacy. Pressures from family or a social environment.

9 of Cups
COORDINATION

The number nine presents itself in the human relations domain of the cups as the complex group dynamics of 3 x 3 rather than the individual factor of 8 + 1, as in the coins. The card shows nine cups in a square array. The plant decorations mark a separate space for each one but also express movement and interaction. The abundance of cups and leaves looks happy and radiating.

> **INTERPRETATION:** General harmony; every person or part is in its proper place. A complex but productive group dynamic. Feeling oneself part of a collective. Happiness in normal life and simple relationships.

> **INVERSE:** Difficulty in finding one's place in a group. Confusion in a complex social situation.

10 of Cups
LEADERSHIP

The number ten completes the social construction of the cups by putting one on top of the other nine, expressing the collective as a unity of a higher order. The card shows a large cup lying on its side over a group of nine smaller ones. Its mouth pattern resembles the coin icons, and it may be pouring nourishment on the others. There are no plant decorations, and the focus is only on the cups and their relations.

> **INTERPRETATION:** A leading figure. A position of responsibility and guidance for others. Caring for those dependent on you, but maybe this leaves you little space for yourself.

> **iNVERSE:** A leader toppled. Loss of popularity. Ingratitude from people that you helped.

2 OF WANDS
CROSSROADS

The duality of the number two is expressed in the forward-moving suit of wands as a junction of two ways. The card shows a crossing of two wands with rounded yellow bands that give the card an easy and optimistic feeling. Plant decorations flow from the center to all directions, perhaps indicating that in whatever way the querent chooses to go, they may find advantages and the potential for success.

INTERPRETATION: Two or more ways open before the querent, all of them promising. Stopping for a moment before taking a decision that will bear long-term consequences. Meeting someone going their own way as both paths cross each other.

IN A CONFLICT: Trying to block someone by cutting their line of advance.

3 OF WANDS
DIRECTION

The number three adds a third element to the junction of the two, thereby giving a clear direction to the dynamic wands suit. In the card a central wand passes under the intersection of two others, as if adding a new path to the junction in the previous card. The plant decorations are minimal, but their tips at the card edges are sharp and pushing outward.

> **INTERPRETATION:** Finding a way after a period of hesitation. A solution to a dilemma, perhaps combining elements from both sides. Time to go forward. Choices can still be reversed, but soon it will be impossible.

> **IN A CONFLICT:** A third party profits from keeping itself noncommitted between opposing sides.

4 of Wands
STALEMATE

The static number four freezes the movement of the dynamic wands. The four wands are interlocked so that none of them can easily move. The plant decorations are rich and flowing, but the spreading red shapes may hint at suppressed energy and tension. The top flower seems to be older than the bottom one, perhaps indicating that things continue to evolve under the surface immobility.

INTERPRETATION: A temporary rest. Preparing a base for future advancement. Time to enjoy previous achievements. Change will come, but not right now. Existing tensions are the source for new and creative future moves.

IN A CONFLICT: A stalemate. It may be dangerous or harmful to move now.

5 of Wands
OVERCOMING

The number five introduces a new element that breaks the stalemate of the four and enables the dynamic wands suit to advance. In the card a single wand passes under four interlaced ones. The plant tips recede from the card edges, focusing attention on the action at the center. Just above the crossing, the single wand covers the edges of the perpendicular yellow bands as if overcoming their opposition.

> **INTERPRETATION:** Breakdown of equilibrium. Opposition and difficulties, but not too hard to overcome. Focusing attention on a main effort.

> **IN A CONFLICT:** Seizing the moment to make a winning move.

> inverse: (with the covering part of the central wand below) Walking into a trap. Losing an advantage.

6 OF WANDS
COLLABORATION

The harmonious number six integrates as 3 + 3 two opposite movements of the wands suit. The card shows two bundles of three wands each, interwoven to form a strong and durable structure. The plants in three directions have long and narrow leaves with sharp tips undulating to the card edges. The top flower has a sort of a fancy collar.

> **INTERPRETATION:** An alliance between two parties with different goals but common interests. Pushing to advance in various directions. A taste for luxury made possible by favorable conditions, but misplaced if the decorated flower is below (inverse).

> **IN A CONFLICT:** Finding an ally. Breaking up the alliance of opponents.

7 OF WANDS
STRUGGLE

The conflictual aspect of the wands interprets seven as one standing against six. The card shows a single wand passing through a mesh of six interlaced ones. Different segments of the single wand are misaligned, as if passing through the mesh has its price. The plant leaves look like sharp blades with tips curving in. They can also resemble flames or sparks flying around from the central conflict area.

> **INTERPRETATION:** Present difficulties may be overcome, but at a price. A situation that pits one against many. Striving to keep one's own way even when it involves clashes with the environment. Persistence, endurance.

> **IN A CONFLICT:** A hard struggle with an uncertain outcome.

8 of Wands
REGULATION

The structured character of the number eight organizes the movements of the wands suit in a complex array of clearly marked paths. The card shows a symmetrical structure of eight interlaced wands. The center can resemble a woven mat, but also a maze of crossing paths in which one can get lost. There are no plant decorations on the sides. The upper flower has white petals at the top.

> **INTERPRETATION:** A controlled environment in which one can go only in certain predefined ways. Getting lost in rules and regulations. Putting one's thoughts and actions in order.

> **IF THE WHITE PETALS ARE ON TOP:** The existing rules can work in the querent's favor.

> **IN A CONFLICT:** A tight, complex situation. A roadblock.

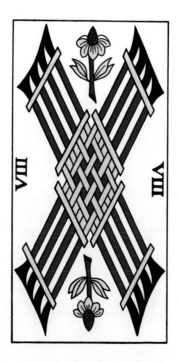

9 OF WANDS

INTERRUPTION

The intricate currents of the number nine derail the aspiration of the dynamic wands suit to go straight ahead. The cards show a single wand divided into two parts by the crossing bundles of four wands each. Unlike in previous odd cards, we cannot see the single wand continuing into the middle mesh. There are no plant decorations.

INTERPRETATION: Difficulties and oppositions force the querent to stop. It is possible to resume progress later, but from a new position. Spending energy in continuous efforts and struggles. No time to relax.

IN A CONFLICT: Avoiding a clash with superior forces by letting them have their way.

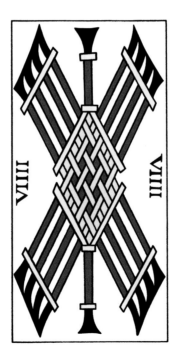

10 OF WANDS
LOYALTY

The number ten creates an alliance of two, thus making the dynamic wands overcome the heavy entanglement of eight. The card shows two connected wands passing beneath a crossing of eight and reemerging together. The lateral plant decorations that disappeared in previous cards appear again, growing from a small white circle on each side.

INTERPRETATION: A partnership or a couple's relationship goes through a difficult period but endures it without falling apart. Someone you can trust in times of trouble. Persistence and pure intentions pay off.

IN A CONFLICT: Success is achieved by remaining loyal to one's friends and principles.

2 of Swords
BOUNDARIES

The dividing swords suit expresses the duality of two as a first separation between inside and outside. Two arching swords mark the boundaries of an elongated space. A symmetrical flower with a central focusing symbol is shown inside in top view. It seems to be growing comfortably in its assigned space. The arching swords carry perpendicular yellow bands with rounded edges.

> **INTERPRETATION:** Boundaries and limits, not only blocking but also protecting and defining a space for growth. Taking full advantage of the existing conditions. Preparations for future advancement, but without crossing any borders yet. A clear perception of a situation, which is both focused and encompassing.

3 OF SWORDS
VICTORY

With the decisive and penetrating aspect of the swords, the dynamic number three overcomes the boundaries of the two. A single upright sword breaks through a crossing of two curved ones. It looks thicker and more solid, and it is decorated with two bay laurel branches, which are a traditional symbol of victory. One flower tip, the cross-guard, and the pommel button of the upright sword are white.

> **INTERPRETATION:** A victory or a breakthrough achieved without much difficulty. Pure intentions and righteous conduct win the day. Cutting through a dilemma or a quandary. A third party intervenes in a quarrel of two and wins over both.

> **INVERSE:** Defeat. Failure in an attempt to make a decisive move.

4 OF SWORDS
RESTRICTION

The static number four brings out the blocking and limiting aspect of the swords. Two pairs of curved swords create a solid border around the center. In the middle a branch in side view completely fills the enclosure. It looks constrained, with a narrow top flower and the tip of the right-hand leaf touching the swords. Emerging on the left of the branch is what seems like a tiny white berry on a stalk.

> **INTERPRETATION:** A stable but limited situation. Pushing against boundaries. Working under pressure and constraints. A potential for future growth that cannot fully express itself in the present conditions.

> **INVERSE:** Limitations and confinement. Giving up an attempt to break out of an oppressive situation.

5 of Swords
BREAKTHROUGH

The subversive nature of the number five is expressed in the active suit of swords as a forward push that breaks through the existing barriers. A single upright sword with a white pommel button, thicker than in all the other odd cards, pushes its way out of a space confined by four curved swords. We can see its continuation as it passes inside the upper interlacing of the arches.

INTERPRETATION: An initiative to push forward and go beyond the present limitations. Perseverance in a tight situation brings success. Going your own way regardless of disturbance by others. Imposing your will on adversaries who are weaker.

INVERSE: Failure to change things by brute force.

6 of Swords
ADAPTATION

The harmonic and easy-going character of the number six accepts the limits imposed by the blocking aspect of the swords. The branch in the middle of the enclosure formed by six curved swords adapts its form to the available space, keeping a neat distance from the borders on all sides.

INTERPRETATION: Accepting the limits of the situation and adapting oneself to them. Giving up personal ambitions in order not to disturb the present balance. Making the best of the present conditions.

INVERSE: Resignation, surrender, despair.

7 of Swords
SHARPNESS

Both hard suits interpret seven as one against six, but the swords give the single element sharpness and determination. In the card a single sword pierces its way through a mesh of six curved swords, grazing the tips of their side bands as it passes. It looks straight, narrow, and efficient, with a single line running the length of its blade.

> **INTERPRETATION:** Focus and determination. Fighting with a clear goal in mind. Concentrated will and a no-nonsense attitude, but keeping the original motivation pure. Winning over an opponent where the forces are roughly balanced.

> **INVERSE:** Sharp skills and determination expressed in a wrong direction.

8 OF SWORDS
DEFENSES

The structured number eight expresses the separating aspect of the swords as elaborate shields and defenses. The card shows a small symmetrical flower with a central focusing symbol heavily protected by two thick bundles of arched swords. But its colors integrate well with the middle sections of the swords, and the curved yellow bands provide a sense of a possible opening.

> **INTERPRETATION:** A defensive attitude, putting up shields and protecting walls. Psychological defense mechanisms and rationalizations. Feeling safe but isolated and blocked. Loss of motivation to change things. A hidden asset or treasure, well protected and difficult to reach.

9 OF SWORDS
COURAGE

The determination of the swords overcomes the inner confusion of nine. In this card a single sword pushes its way out of an enclosure formed by eight arching swords. In spite of the thick barrier and the limited space for maneuver, it boldly goes its way and passes through. Its different segments are not properly aligned.

INTERPRETATION: Winning a battle against superior forces through courage and determination. Keeping up hope in a difficult situation. Pushing forward with imperfect means.

INVERSE: Losing a fight against a stronger opponent. A battle lost in advance. Sloppiness and lack of necessary preparations lead to failure.

10 of Swords
EXHAUSTION

The number ten maximizes the combative aspect of the swords. But with so many weapons and clashes, they just neutralize each other. In the card two straight swords penetrate the space between the arches. They are crossed, as if in a duel, but their bases are stuck and cannot move. The left sword, with a plain pommel, has a gap in the middle, and its tip is covered by the other sword.

> **INTERPRETATION:** A period of battles and clashes leaves all the sides exhausted. A complex situation with many conflicting interests. A sophisticated approach will win over a simple one. Finding an ally to confront the situation from another angle.

> **INVERSE:** Immobility. Feeling attacked from various sides.

CHAPTER · 11

ADDITIONAL SPREADS

EXTENSIONS OF THE BASIC SPREAD

In chapter 3 we described the basic spread of the open reading: three cards from the major suit laid down side by side from left to right. Later, in chapter 7, we discussed the extension of this spread to include the minor suits, but the basic spread can be extended in other ways as well. For example, during the reading we may feel the need to add more cards to clarify an unfinished issue or to finish the reading on a more optimistic note if the querent appears to be in a difficult emotional state.

A card that we can see without opening additional cards is the "hint card." This is the card that sits at the bottom of the deck, so that we can see it just by turning the deck over. Sometimes I glance at this card before laying out the spread, but I don't say anything about it for the time being. Later on I might want to integrate the hint card into the reading without defining its role in advance. For example, I can interpret it as a general statement about the query, as an additional or side issue that is relevant for the reading, or as offering a useful perspective through which to look at things. If I feel this would serve the reading, I can also take the hint card out of the deck and lay it open to the querent's view beside the other cards.

It is also possible to obtain a single card that sums up the three-card spread by means of a numerological technique called theosophical addition. By this method, we add up the numbers of the cards that came out in the spread. If the total is less than 22, we pick out the card in the major suit with this number, and this becomes the summary card. If the sum is 22 or more, we add its digits together. For example, if the three cards in the spread are the Wheel (10), the Star (17), and the Sun (18), the sum of their values is 45. Adding these two figures together (4 + 5) gives the Hermit card (9) as the summary. Should the summary turn out to be one of the cards already in the spread, we can see it as a special emphasis to be put on this card.

Naturally, the most direct way to extend the basic spread is just to take out additional cards from the shuffled deck and lay them beside the first three. We do this according to our spontaneous feeling during the reading. For example, when we read the cards as a story with a time line, we can add one or more cards on the right to see how the story continues. We can also add a card on the left to see the origin of the situation. Another option is to form a cross shape by adding two cards to the basic spread, one above the middle card and one below it. Interpreting them in the spirit of the symbolic language of the vertical axis discussed in chapter 4, we can see the top card as related to spiritual aspects or a higher level of meaning. The bottom card can represent deep underlying patterns, subconscious feelings, or the emotional base motivating the query.

THE CHOICE SPREAD

The choice spread, which I learned from Jodorowsky, is suitable for a situation where the querent has to choose between two or more options. First, we should make it clear to the querent that the cards will not decide for them; the cards will only give the querent a new perspective that might help them make their own choice. Then we ask the querent to make a mental division of the surface of the table (or the spread mat) into two equal parts, one beside the other. The querent should decide which part represents each one of the options, but at this stage it is better that they keep this choice unknown to us. We can naturally expand this to more than two options. Now we hand them the deck and ask them to shuffle it and lay three cards facedown in each part.

Instead of exposing the cards right away, it's a good idea to begin by trying to figure out the querent's emotional attitude from the way in which they lay the cards down for each option. First of all, we may watch their movements. Do they lay the cards in a confident or hesitant manner? After laying them down, do they correct the cards' position or orientation in order to create a more orderly structure? We should also notice the order in which they lay the cards. For example, if they lay the first card on the left, the second card on the right, and only then a third card in the middle, this creates a movement of convergence and retreat after an initial advance.

Now we should look at the way the cards are arranged on the table. For example, if the querent laid the cards in the bottom edge of the available area, it means that they aren't taking advantage of the entire range of opportunities available to them. If they lay each card in a higher position than the previous card, this expresses rising and advancement. If the cards aren't parallel and their top parts are farther away from each other, it may mean expansion or divergence. If their top parts come closer to each other, this expresses convergence, or a process of focusing. In other words, we apply the rule "everything is a sign" to the way the querent lays the cards on the table.

Now is a good moment to stop and share our observations with the querent. This could also be a good time to ask them which option each part represents and refine our observations accordingly. Having done this, we can turn over the cards to expose them and then read them as a separate spread for each option. Of course, we should pay special attention to parallels or opposing features arising between the two sides.

The basic idea of the choice spread can be further extended to other situations, and we can improvise on it in different situations. The idea is to let the querent lay the cards facedown, and then turn them over and read normally. In general, we can interpret the first stage as expressing the querent's emotional preferences and the second one as the expected dynamics or outcome of the situation.

SPREADING ON A SHAPE

In the open reading method we usually do not use spread layouts with a fixed role for each card, but sometimes we may want to do something of the sort, either having decided about it beforehand or as an improvisation during the reading. We can use one of the many spreads that appear in various books and websites or we can create a spread of our own.

A common source of inspiration for creating spreads is geometrical shapes, which have a symbolic meaning. For example, several books present a spread based on a five-pointed star oriented with one tip at the crown. In my version of it the star corresponds to a human shape, with the star's points representing the head, two hands, and two feet. Imagining the star shape on the spread mat, I put a card on each of the five corners. The head card describes the querent's thoughts. The feet cards describe what the querent is standing on, meaning external factors. The hand cards describe the querent's actions in response to these factors. The hand and foot on the left describe internal influences, while the hand and foot on the right describe the external environment. In addition, at the center of the star I put a sixth card to represent what is in the person's heart.

Another source of inspiration for a spread may be shapes of physical objects: a house, a boat, a car, a tree, and so on. Jodorowsky once showed me such a spread when he asked me to think of some shape. I said "house" and he created the shape of a house using the cards. Then he started to interpret the meaning of the cards according to the function of the house parts. The roof is what protects me. The walls are what separate me from the surroundings. The windows are the way I look at reality. The door is what I let come into my life. The chimney is what I let out.

An interesting source of inspiration for a shape spread can be the arrangement of figures and objects in a tarot card. For example, we can get a perspective on the different aspects of the querent's life using a spread based on the World card. We lay four cards at the corners of a rectangle to represent the four animals of the card. We then lay a fifth card at the center to represent the dancing figure. We interpret the first four cards as a description of the four life domains according to the correspondence table in chapter 7: body, desire, emotion, and intellect. The fifth card represents the querent's unified being as an individual acting in the four domains.

We can do something similar with other cards as well. For example, with the Wheel card we can put a card for each of the three animals in order to describe influences that are on the rise, at their peak, and diminishing. A fourth card at the center of the wheel can represent the central factor driving the process. A fifth card under it may represent the wheel's base standing on the ground, meaning external conditions and unchangeable factors.

With the Lover card, the standing figures can be represented by three cards: the querent as they are now, the past that they are disengaging from, and the future that they are supposed to advance toward. A fourth card on top can also represent the angel, indicating a divine hint or message.

With the Magician we can devise a shape spread inspired by a well-known psychological model called the Johari window. A top card, corresponding to the magician's face, represents the querent's basic feeling of self-identity. A card at the center is "on the table," representing what is known both to self and others. A card on the left, where the magician is looking but outside the card frame that is our field of vision, represents what is known to self but not to others. A card on the right represents what is unknown both to self and others. Finally, a card at the bottom, "below the table," represents what we can see but the magician cannot, which is what is known to others but not to self.

THE WORDS SPREAD

The words spread is based on an original idea by the Israeli poet David Avidan. It is suitable for focused questions that can be formulated as a short and clear sentence. After shuffling the cards, we lay down one card for each word in the sentence, plus one additional card for the final answer. Prepositions and other connecting words don't count as separate units but are joined to the words following them. We can also group together several words and lay one card for the entire group instead of a single card for each word.

We lay the sentence cards in a horizontal row, moving from left to right, and under the row we lay the final answer card. In the reading we interpret each card according to the meaning of the corresponding word and its function in the sentence. An opening word of interrogation (such as what, when, or why) represents the status of the querent and their attitude toward the query. We can also combine this method of reading according to the word meaning with the usual way of interpreting the card images, as we do in the row spread. The single card below summarizes the complete spread and represents a final answer to the question.

For example, if the question is "What bothers me in my relationship with Mira?" we can draw five cards for the words and one more card for the final answer:

WHAT—the querent's attitude toward the question, from what position he's asking

BOTHERS—the bothering factors from the querent's point of view

ME—the querent's role in the relationship

IN MY RELATIONSHIP—the relationship itself, what it involves

WITH MIRA—the position of the partner and her role in the relationship and its problems

FINAL ANSWER—an overall view of the difficulties and perhaps a hint for a possible remedy

QUICK INTERPRETATIONS

The following list of interpretations may be helpful as a quick reference in reading. If nothing comes to mind when you look at the card, you can use this list as a starting point, but it should not limit you from finding your own meanings. If you don't use inverse cards in the reading, the "inverse" sections can be taken as negative aspects of the same card and integrated with the positive aspects.

THE MAJOR SUIT

CARD 1—THE MAGICIAN: The start of something.
Beginner's luck. Having various tools and means at our disposal.
Use of supernatural forces. Creating reality with mind power.
Training and acquisition of practical skills. Improvisation.
Display or show for other people.
MESSAGE: Create a new reality.
inverse: Trickery, sleight of hand, cheating. Showing off,
pretending. Lack of self-awareness about body, sexuality, or
basic motives. Near miss due to inexperience or inaccuracy.

CARD 2 – THE POPESS: Wisdom combining intellect and intuition. A spiritual mother. A woman hiding her strengths in a world of men. Modesty. Secrets, something hidden, mystery. Getting a hint of something that remains largely unknown. Impossible to give a definite answer now.

MESSAGE: Know how to set boundaries.

inverse: A need to hide our true nature behind the conventions of normal society. Conservative approach to sex and the body. Emotional blockage.

CARD 3 – THE EMPRESS: Abundance, growth, productivity. Natural or human touch within an artificial framework. Emotional intelligence. Protection and care. Motherhood. A powerful female figure. Strong feminine identity.

MESSAGE: Act from the gut.

inverse: Impulsive behavior. Someone difficult to reason with. Overprotectiveness. Excessive involvement in the lives of others. Problems with a strong mother figure.

CARD 4 – THE EMPEROR: Practical and material achievements. Matters relating to the workplace or source of income. Authority and control. A commanding position. A protective father figure, patron, or sponsor. Assertiveness. Military affairs.

MESSAGE: Show leadership and responsibility.

inverse: Belligerence, violence, trying to solve things by brute force. Dictatorship. Possibility of sexual abuse. Difficulty in coping with a dominant father figure. Denial and hiding of inner weaknesses.

CARD 5 – THE POPE: Teacher, instructor, or counselor. Education and knowledge. Academic expertise. Organized religion, conventional medicine, or psychology. Spiritual father. Consultation or treatment by a specialist. Marriage.

MESSAGE: Respect knowledge and education.

inverse: Excessive adhesion to conventions and outdated norms. Bureaucracy. An oppressive establishment. Hypocrisy, discrimination. Divorce.

CARD 6–THE LOVER: Love, amorous relationship. Emotional entanglement. Need to make a choice or disengage oneself from past influences. Inclinations of the heart correspond to the will of heaven. Small steps actually taken are the visible signs of inner desire.

MESSAGE: Follow the path of the heart.

inverse: Complex relationship between several people, e.g., a romantic triangle or a tension between mother and wife. Hesitation, quandary. Confusion as to one's own feeling and will.

CARD 7–THE CHARIOT: Victory or an achievement putting the querent in a strong and protected position. Ambition, energy, motivation to move forward. Public honor. Power and high status.

MESSAGE: Dare and win.

inverse: Inner weakness hidden behind external show-off. Arrogance, vanity. Overprotectiveness. Emotional closure. Confusion about one's goals. Losing the simple touch with people and reality.

CARD 8–JUSTICE: Law and order, legal and court issues. A fair and balanced judgment. A developed conscience. Rationality. Reasoning by clear rules and common norms. A touch of grace and humanity beyond objective considerations.

MESSAGE: Act with reason and by the accepted norms.

inverse: Petty accountability. A critical and judgmental attitude. Guilt feelings. Repressive control of self and others. Negative ideas blocking change and advance.

CARD 9–THE HERMIT: A quest for truth or spiritual understanding. Concentrating on a clear purpose. Caution, careful examination. Self-privation for the sake of a meaningful cause. Loyalty to principles. Strong faith.

MESSAGE: Look for the essence of things.

inverse: A closed and reclusive attitude. Isolation, loneliness. Fixed ideas. Excessive caution and suspicion. A critical approach, looking for defects. Hidden and denied desires.

CARD 10–THE WHEEL OF FORTUNE: Change in circumstances and position. A rise after a fall. Gambling, putting faith in capricious luck. Life cycles, closure of circles. Adapting to the routine of everyday life. A hint at previous incarnations.

MESSAGE: Accept life's ups and downs.

inverse: A decline after a period of rising. Danger lurks at the summit. Moving in a closed circle. Capricious mood changes. Feeling powerless to change one's situation.

CARD 11–FORCE: Power and courage to face challenges. Controlled expression of creative urges, drives, and desires. Mobilization of inner resources toward a common goal. Taking risks.

MESSAGE: Take control of yourself.

inverse: A need to keep things under control leads to constant tensions. A risk of losing one's grip. Internal conflict and unrealistic assessment of one's own forces may lead to failure.

CARD 12–THE HANGED MAN: Seeing things from a unique point of view. Enduring difficulties for a worthy cause. A period of deep self-examination. Passivity. Acceptance of reality even if it is the opposite of what one expects.

MESSAGE: Look at things from the opposite perspective.

inverse: Isolation. Emotional stance of a victim. Inability to act. Denying one's own unique qualities, striving to be "normal" at all costs. Living in one's private and imaginary reality.

CARD 13: The end of something whose time has come. Cutting off past influences or attachment to dominant figures. Giving up the superfluous and keeping only the essential. Disintegration of the old makes room for the new.

MESSAGE: Give up what is over.

inverse: Difficulty in coping with loss or change. Temporary difficulties, a trying challenge. Disintegration. Realization of a painful truth. Does not predict future death but may reflect anxiety about dying or mourning over a loss that has already happened.

CARD 14 – TEMPERANCE: Reconciliation, compromise, relaxation of tensions. Integration of opposites. Ability to do the seemingly impossible. A slow process of distillation and improvement. Patience, perseverance. Self-improvement.

MESSAGE: Find the golden mean.

inverse: Going back and forth without making real progress. Losing patience with a lengthy process. Emotional preoccupation with oneself, pushing away others who might come to help.

CARD 15 – THE DEVIL: A burst of creativity. Paradoxes and contradictions. Irony and mocking of common norms. Acting from desires, passions, and impulses. Moving on from a past family trauma.

MESSAGE: Express passion and desire.

inverse: Temptation, attraction to the dark and forbidden. Exploitation, egotism, domination. Compulsive self-gratification. Senseless behavior has its price. Difficulty in detaching oneself from an unhealthy bond.

CARD 16 – THE TOWER: Breaking up of solid structures. Getting free from confinement. Sudden breakthrough after long preparations. Sparkling sexual encounter. Success lies in simplicity and modesty.

MESSAGE: Return to the solid ground of reality.

inverse: Shock. Collapse of projects or trusted structures. A fall from an apparently solid and secure position. Chaos, confusion, difficulty in understanding what is going on. Vanity and pride lead to failure.

CARD 17 – THE STAR: Openness, simplicity, return to nature. Purity, honesty. Showing yourself "as you are," accepting one's body and desires. Generosity. Luck from heaven. Intuitive feeling of guidance or energy coming from a higher plane.

MESSAGE: Flow from a pure source.

inverse: Naive optimism and wishful thinking. Exposing oneself to danger or abuse. Difficulty in setting proper boundaries. Squandering, wastefulness.

CARD 18 – THE MOON: Deep emotions, perhaps related to a mother or feminine figure. A different experience of reality. Longing for the unreachable. Finding one's hidden strengths. Occupation with the remote past. A hidden treasure.

MESSAGE: Don't be afraid to go deep down.

inverse: Vague and disturbing feelings. Emotional difficulties. A period of depression. Danger lurking under the surface. Retreat. The road ahead is hard to find.

CARD 19 – THE SUN: Light and warmth, abundance, blessings. Pleasant feelings. Emotional or physical healing. Partnership, trust, sharing, brotherhood. Human touch. An ideal father figure. Matters relating to children. Setting limits in a moderate and nonoppressive way.

MESSAGE: Find suitable partners.

inverse: Living in a limited space. Difficulty facing reality "in the open." Immaturity, dependence on others. Someone or something too intense and energetic to feel comfortable with. An absent father.

CARD 20–JUDGMENT: Revelation, enlightenment, a new understanding. A turning point in a therapy process. Healing of a family relationship. Disclosure, secrets revealed, publicity. Birth of a baby or of a new thing.

MESSAGE: Awaken to spiritual reality.

inverse: Revelation of something that should have been kept hidden. Lack of privacy. Unpleasant realization. Problems related to child-parent relations. Too much noise and drama.

CARD 21–THE WORLD: Completion of a process. Balanced activity and achievements in various domains. Contact with far places. Harmony and correspondence between different planes. Pregnancy. Something new is about to be born. The dance of life.

MESSAGE: Everything is perfect as it is.

inverse: Life in a bubble. Difficulty sharing your world with others. Disconnection of inner feelings from external life. Preoccupation with oneself, idealized self-image, inability to move forward.

THE FOOL: Freedom from conventions and norms. Something or someone unique and exceptional. Options kept open. Giving up control. Spontaneity. Uncertainty. Attention to the here and now. Going on a trip.

MESSAGE: Keep on the move.

inverse: Difficulty in choosing and committing oneself to something stable. Restlessness. Lack of purpose. Getting lost. Foolish behavior. Eccentricity. Lack of acceptance by the social environment. Difficulty in planning ahead.

COINS

ACE OF COINS: A good start in material things. Financial and physical stability. A practical perspective. A significant sum of money. Utilitarian approach. Greed. Something basic and unsophisticated.

INVERSE: Similar.

2 OF COINS: Duality. Two options or two elements. Collaborating while keeping distance. A winding road advancing in complex ways. Recognition and acknowledgment.

INVERSE: Similar.

3 OF COINS: Product. A partnership or an alliance bears fruit. First results of a project. Good prospects.

INVERSE: Disappointment. A partnership or project does not bear the expected fruits.

4 OF COINS: Stability. Solid material assets. Time-tested reliability. Tradition, honor, and reputation. Established social institutions.

INVERSE: Conservatism.Clinging to old and outdated patterns.

5 OF COINS: Disruption. Something new appears and destabilizes existing structures. A new element gets attention but also awakens resistance.

INVERSE: Similar.

6 OF COINS: Expansion. Abundance of resources and possible ways to advance. A positive outlook, success. A good balance between stability and movement.

INVERSE: Similar.

7 OF COINS: Acceptance. Something new is well received. Help and protection. Integrating into a system without losing one's individuality.

INVERSE: Lack of independence, need to rely on help and acceptance from others.

8 OF COINS: Uniformity. A mechanical structure. Practical considerations prove efficient but lack a human touch. Routine work. A slow and patient advance.
INVERSE: Similar.

9 OF COINS: Motivation. Carving a niche for oneself in an existing system. Ambition. Endurance and independent thinking bear long-term fruits.
INVERSE: Similar.

10 OF COINS: Abundance. Intensive activity in practical affairs. Material success and achievements. Some may be getting more than others.
INVERSE: Similar.

PAGE OF COINS: A practical endeavor. Untapped potentials are within reach. Tangible success at the beginning. A solid material base for further advancement.
INVERSE: Hesitation, lack of clear purpose. Thinking in terms of past achievements misses present opportunities.

KNIGHT OF COINS: Advancement in a practical direction. A productive expression of creativity. A clear goal in sight.
INVERSE: Constant pursuit of money without reaching material stability. Passions and desires may interfere with practical plans.

QUEEN OF COINS: Tangible assets, material and personal stability, a sober and realistic vision. Looking at things from a practical and pragmatic perspective.
INVERSE: Conservatism, resistance to change, aiming only to preserve the existing assets. Looking at things only from the material perspective.

KING OF COINS: Confidence and security, a cautious but optimistic vision. Looking for new achievements while holding existing assets secure.

> INVERSE: Dissatisfaction with what one already has. Disregard of the good things in the present situation. A limited outlook.

CUPS

ACE OF CUPS: The beginning of a love relationship. Expression of warm feelings. Romantic longing for something extraordinary. Emotional and spiritual growth.

> INVERSE: Emotional dryness, feeling oneself empty. Avoidance of intimacy. Negative feelings. Heartbreak.

2 OF CUPS: Partnership. A romantic relationship or a close personal alliance. Interpersonal dynamics based on social norms. Passion in a love relationship, which may turn against itself.

> INVERSE: A crisis in a couple relationship. Disappointment with someone close to you.

3 OF CUPS: Birth. Something new brings joy and happiness. Caring for a child. Issues of child-parent relations. A common project motivated by feelings and not only by interests.

> INVERSE: Problems in relations with one's parents or child. A strong alliance of two persons leaves a third one outside.

4 OF CUPS: Family. A collective of people (family, community, etc.) with a history and a sense of belonging. Commitment to a group at the price of giving up personal interests.

> INVERSE: Problems and discord in the family or in a long-lasting community. A fixed social structure that doesn't allow for adaptation or flexibility.

5 OF CUPS: Links. Popularity, relations with many people. Becoming the center of attention in a group. Relying on connections with other people to advance oneself or overcome difficulties.

> INVERSE: Excessive preoccupation with social activity. Losing oneself in multiple superficial connections. Cultivating virtual instead of real contacts.

6 OF CUPS: Continuity. A long-term relationship. Repetition between different generations in the family. A stable personal alliance.

> INVERSE: Monotony, tedious repetition. Falling time and again into the same emotional traps.

7 OF CUPS: Individuality. A single person finding their place in a group. Contact with people in high positions. Exceptional qualities are appreciated.

> INVERSE: Problems of integration in a group or organization. Being part of a collective but feeling isolated and estranged.

8 OF CUPS: Involvement. Developing personal relationships within a group. A favorable human-relations environment. A feast or family event.

> INVERSE: Interference of the environment in a couple's relationship. Pressures from one's family in romantic or personal matters.

9 OF CUPS: Coordination. People or parts working together, each one in its proper place. Accepting one's role in a social or group environment. Happiness. Wishes coming true.

> INVERSE: A confusing social situation. Difficulty in situating oneself in a complex environment.

10 OF CUPS: Leadership. A person with special qualities receives appreciation and high status. Assuming responsibility for others. Maintaining a superior position.

INVERSE: A fallen leader. Loss of popularity. Disappointment because of ingratitude by people one has helped.

PAGE OF CUPS: First and unsure steps in a romantic endeavor. Shyness. Sincere intentions. Trying to figure out one's feelings.

INVERSE: Overabsorption in one's personal feelings. Losing contact with others. Sloppiness in practical affairs.

KNIGHT OF CUPS: A romantic gesture, offering one's heart, courting. Openness, sincerity, a simple heart. A potential lover may appear.

INVERSE: Superficial and unstable feelings. An overly optimistic but unrealistic attitude. An overt display of shallow or insincere feelings.

QUEEN OF CUPS: A rich inner world that is kept hidden. Guarding one's privacy or valuable assets. Strong feelings held under control.

INVERSE: Closure, defensiveness. Distrust of others due to negative past experiences. Hiding one's emotions under guise of rational criticism.

KING OF CUPS: Emotional maturity, optimism, ability to overcome past injuries and look ahead. Openness to new things but with prudence and caution. Closing one's ear to voices from the past.

INVERSE: Difficulty in overcoming an emotional blow. A pessimistic outlook caused by negative past experiences.

WANDS

ACE OF WANDS: Creative momentum. Active sexuality. Strong impulses. Energy and drive. Life force. Beginning of growth. Dispersing one's efforts in different directions.
INVERSE: Lack of energy, restriction, repressed sexuality, a creative block.

2 OF WANDS: Crossroads. Several options to choose from. Every course offers benefits. A brief encounter with someone going their own way. Blocking an opponent's line of advance.
INVERSE: Similar.

3 OF WANDS: Direction. Moving forward after a moment of hesitation. Finding a middle path between two courses of action. Gaining an advantage by keeping neutrality between two conflicting sides.
INVERSE: Similar.

4 OF WANDS: Stalemate. A temporary stop in order to prepare for future advancement. Tensions at present but good prospects in the long run. Making a move now is in nobody's interest.
INVERSE: Similar.

5 OF WANDS: Overcoming. Getting over a weak opposition. Breakdown of equilibrium. Focusing on the main objective. An initiative to make a winning move.
INVERSE: (with the covering part of the central wand below) Walking into a complex situation, losing one's edge.

6 OF WANDS: Collaboration. A strong alliance between two parties with different goals but common present interests. A taste for luxury made possible by favorable conditions.
INVERSE: (with the decorated flower at the bottom) Excessive pursuit of luxury. Need to break up an alliance of opponents.

7 OF WANDS: Struggle. Someone putting up a fight against many opponents. Obstinacy, endurance, keeping one's position in a conflict situation. A difficult combat with an uncertain outcome.
INVERSE: Similar.

8 OF WANDS: Regulation. It is possible to advance only by following the rules. Occupation with short-term goals while losing the long-term perspective. A roadblock.
INVERSE: Similar.

9 OF WANDS: Interruption. Difficulties and oppositions too hard to overcome. Giving up one's projects to avoid conflict. Starting anew after a challenging period.
INVERSE: Similar.

10 OF WANDS: Loyalty. A partnership or an alliance endures hardships and succeeds in getting over them. Pure intentions and perseverance lead to success. Honoring one's principles in spite of difficulties.
INVERSE: Similar.

PAGE OF WANDS: A creative potential that still needs processing. Keeping a safe distance from events and waiting for the right moment.
INVERSE: A task too heavy for the querent's strength. Difficulty in controlling desires and urges. Immature approach to sexuality.

KNIGHT OF WANDS: A change of direction, following one's urges and passions. A temporary stop, but there is still energy and a desire to advance.
INVERSE: Preoccupation with the satisfaction of one's own desires. Problem in defining long-term goals. Submitting to temptation.

QUEEN OF WANDS: A feminine figure with a strong personality. Things connected with food and eating. Speaking softly while holding a big stick. A secure, well-defended position.
INVERSE: Intimidation, menace. Using sexuality as a means of control. Problems with a strong mother figure. Fear of feminine power.

KING OF WANDS: A mature attitude to urges and desires. Controlled creativity. Prodding oneself to make a move forward. Investing present assets in future projects.
INVERSE: Plans to move forward are frustrated by self-defeating acts. Hesitation, conflicts. Tendency to make things too heavy and complex.

SWORDS

ACE OF SWORDS: A planned initiative. Rational and logical thinking, sharpness of mind. A conclusive decision. Readiness to fight. Ambition, competitiveness. A victory with stable achievements.
INVERSE: Negative and unproductive thoughts. Misconceptions, delusions. Self-defeat. Injury.

2 OF SWORDS: Boundaries. Limits that protect and define something that is in development. Making full use of the present situation. Preparations for future advancement. A clear view encompassing the overall situation.
INVERSE: Similar.

3 OF SWORDS: Victory. Overcoming a weak opposition. Cutting through a quandary and going forward in a clear direction. A third party intervenes and wins over two weakened opponents.
INVERSE: A failure. Defeat from a weaker opponent. An unsuccessful attempt to make a decisive move.

4 OF SWORDS: Restriction. A limited space for development and maneuver. Trying to push against constraints. Potentials to grow once the present limitations become less solid.

INVERSE: Confinement and blocking. Lack of motivation or energy to break out of a limited situation.

5 OF SWORDS: Breakthrough. A forward thrust overcoming the existing limits. Keeping up spirits in a tight situation. Doing things one's own way.

INVERSE: A failed initiative to change the situation. Stubbornness leading nowhere. Oppressing factors cannot be removed now.

6 OF SWORDS: Adaptation. Accepting limitations and adapting oneself to them. Respecting the present order. Compromising in order to make the best of the existing situation.

INVERSE: Resignation, surrender, giving up the ambition to change things for the better. Lack of fighting spirit.

7 OF SWORDS: Sharpness. A focused and determined attitude. Concentrating on a clear goal and doing what it takes to reach it. Winning a fight with the odds evenly balanced.

INVERSE: A narrow and overconcentrated vision. Investing one's efforts and resources in a lost cause.

8 OF SWORDS: Defenses. Putting up shields and blocks. Psychological defense mechanisms. A need to be in total control. A well-guarded treasure. Entering another's domain with permission.

INVERSE: Similar.

9 OF SWORDS: Courage. Winning a fight against a superior force. Pure intentions. Putting imperfect means to good use.

INVERSE: Losing against a stronger opponent. Sloppiness. Imperfect preparations for a challenge.

10 OF SWORDS: Exhaustion. A complex situation with many conflicting interests. A long battle without a clear outcome. Need to find an ally who will attack the problem from a different direction.

INVERSE: Immobility. Impossible to move now. Feeling attacked from different sides. A painful and humiliating defeat.

PAGE OF SWORDS: Preparation for a future challenge. Looking for a compromise between reason and strong desires. Hesitating to use one's power.

INVERSE: Confusion, negative and inhibiting thoughts, self-defeat. Sloppy use of one's own tools may cause damage.

KNIGHT OF SWORDS: Energy and resources to advance. Still looking for the right direction. Hovering above practical constraints. Determination and perseverance.

INVERSE: Trying to force one's misguided views. Insisting on a wrong direction. Losing touch with the ground.

QUEEN OF SWORDS: A secure and protected position. Defending one's territory. Preparation of something that shouldn't be exposed yet.

INVERSE: Defensiveness and rigidity. Suspicion and fixed ideas block advancement and preclude new connections.

KING OF SWORDS: A determination to break from the past. A strong will. Feeling equipped to deal with uncertainty. Wisdom and intellectual maturity.

INVERSE: A divided heart. A need to cut off from something to which one is still attached. Overcalculating in a vain attempt to overcome uncertainty.